Seasons of Santa

A Cookbook

by

Kitchen Angels

Kitchen Angels provides free, nutritious, and delicious hot meals to homebound Santa Feans with cancer, AIDS, and other life-challenging conditions.

The proceeds from the sale of this book will go to Kitchen Angels, for the continuation of our service to the community.

Kitchen Angels, Publishers
Santa Fe, New Mexico

KITCHEN ANGELS

Kitchen Angels
500 N. Guadalupe Street – Suite G-505
Santa Fe, New Mexico 87501
505/471-7780
www.kitchenangels.org

Additional copies may be obtained by contacting Kitchen Angels. For your convenience, order forms are included in the back of the book.

Cover Design: Jerry Harper
Cover Photographs © by Jack Parsons and Charles Mann (Sol y Sombra)
Kitchen Angels logo design (™): Tony D'Agostino
Printed by: The Wimmer Companies
Memphis, Tennessee

First printing: January 2000 – 5,000 copies
Second printing: July 2000 – 5,000 copies

ISBN 0-9671929-0-0

Library of Congress Catalog Card Number: 99-95475

Angel's Creed

KITCHEN

ANGELS

I am here to be helpful.
I take care of myself so that I can
take care of others.
Although the tasks I do may seem
small or unimportant, I contribute light
and healing by the very fact
that I show up and care.
I remember that the only correct way
to do anything is to do it with love.
I bless myself by helping others.
I am rich with the gifts of compassion,
understanding, joy and hope
that I freely give.
I believe that one person can
make a difference.

– Tony D'Agostino

KITCHEN

ANGELS

It's time to let you know how much I appreciate the food you send me so faithfully–and how much it means to my survival in this world and the quality of my life. The food always looks good, tastes good and is nutritious. And by saving me money, it allows me to pay for more medical care...but the most important part is the caring that goes into it. That is the true blessing you all send me: the message that I am cared for.

In love, Jesse

The History of Kitchen Angels

Kitchen Angels was founded in April 1992. It was the synchronistic vision of Tony D'Agostino, Leise Sargent, and Anna Huserik, who were soon joined by the Founding Circle. They created a volunteer organization to meet an urgent need in our community: to prepare and deliver appetizing, healthful hot meals to people unable to cook such meals for themselves. Since then we have provided over 100,000 free, delicious, "home-cooked" dinners to Santa Feans, Mondays through Fridays, every week of the year.

Each day our clients receive a meal consisting of soup, salad, bread, a main course, side dish, and dessert. (The portions are large, so that some food may be saved for lunch the next day.) People with specific diets – vegetarian, diabetic, or macrobiotic, for example – are provided with special meals. Those unable to tolerate wheat are given alternative grains; those who cannot eat dairy products, certain vegetables, salt, nuts, and such, are furnished with dishes geared to their individual needs. Some meals must be puréed; some clients request healthful, protein shakes. Whatever the need, our daily cooks fill it. Each meal is then delivered with warmth and compassion by our friendly drivers.

We believe that our food and visits alleviate the debilitating problems of malnourishment and social and emotional isolation. Our clients tell us regularly how much they appreciate this service. "There are never enough words to express my gratitude for the existence of this wonderful organization! I definitely attribute my continued health to the good, nutritional meals provided by your volunteer angels," a client wrote recently.

Kitchen Angels has a volunteer pool of 400 people, 150 of whom are active on an ongoing basis. Volunteers with specific assignments include client home visitors, meal deliverers and delivery coordinators, food sorters, preparers and head chefs, a consulting nutritionist, intake workers, board members, and office assistants. Kitchen Angels employs only two full-time staff people: a Program Director and administrative assistant who oversee all aspects of the day-to-day administration.

Some of the food we serve is provided by Santa Fe grocers, bakeries, and the Food Depot. The bulk of it, however, comes from individual donations, small grants from community organizations, and from our many fund-raisers. This cookbook has been compiled, written, edited, and designed by a volunteer staff. All of the proceeds will go to direct client services.

By buying this cookbook, giving copies as gifts, and telling your friends about it, you become a Kitchen Angel, too. We and our clients thank you and bless you.

Tony McCarty
Kitchen Angels Executive Director
Santa Fe, New Mexico

Table of Contents

This book is composed of favored family recipes, long held, enjoyed, and donated generously by the volunteers and friends of Kitchen Angels of Santa Fe. These recipes have been arranged in the menus that follow, scattered through the seasons, celebrating some of the occasions that make life special in our City Different.

The seasons of Santa Fe are punctuated by an ongoing series of events and festivities that bring the community together and add spice to life here. Living in Santa Fe, or visiting, becomes in itself a reason for gatherings of friends and family. And what better way to enjoy it all than feasting on Northern New Mexican cuisine? There are recipes from other regions also, as you would expect with as much diversity as there is in our city.

We hope this cookbook will remind you of what you love about Santa Fe, and bring its essence into your kitchen, your heart, and your soul.

Spring

Summer

Autumn

Winter

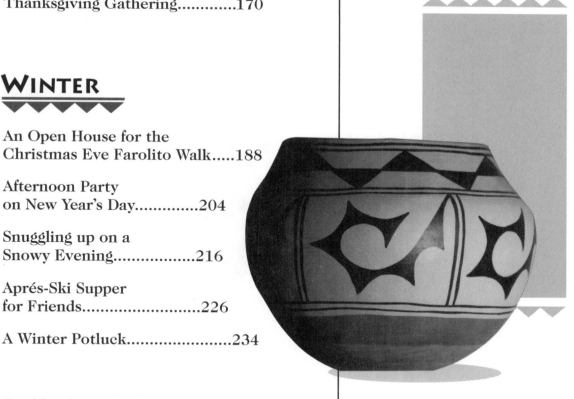

Spring

PHOTO BY JACK PARSONS

SPRING IN SANTA FE

THE SPRING SECTION IS
IN MEMORY OF FRIENDS LOST TO HIV/AIDS

PHOTO BY JACK PARSONS

FEAST FOR CINCO DE MAYO

SPONSORED BY:
MICHAEL MAHAFFEY & ASSOCIATES ARCHITECTS
ELISABETH WAGNER ARCHITECT

Feast for Cinco de Mayo

Our neighbor Mexico won its independence from Spain in 1821, then faced internal struggles and further invasions by the United States, Spain, and France. Cinco de Mayo commemorates the Mexican victory over French forces in the Battle of Puebla on May 5, 1862. Even though the French subsequently recaptured Puebla and ruled Mexico for five more years, Cinco de Mayo remains a potent symbol of Mexican unity and national pride. Nowadays, the holiday is observed by Hispanics north of the border even more than by the Mexicans themselves.

Santa Feans do not celebrate Cinco de Mayo in any official way, but usually on the Saturday closest to May fifth we will gather together a group of friends to eat spicy New Mexican foods, dance to mariachi music, thwack candy out of a piñata, and exult in the glorious spring weather. Some years, a maverick snowfall may drive us indoors, but there is nothing more beautiful than copper rose bushes or tulips covered with a dusting of sparkling white powder that we know will melt within a few hours.

No matter what the weather, Cinco de Mayo is a fine time for an all-out feast. Here is our festive menu, with optional selections, for six people.

Menu

Piña Coladas
or
Margaritas *(page 122)*

Guacamole and Chips

Tortilla Soup

Red Snapper Fillets
with Avocado Sauce

Nacho Potatoes
or
New Mexican
Dinner Cornbread

Rice and Green Chile

Assorted Greens
with Señora's Vinaigrette

Flan

Coffee

Piña Coladas

SERVES 4 OR 5

Refreshing with or without rum.

INGREDIENTS

6 ounces	**frozen pineapple juice concentrate**
1/2 cup	**rum**
3/4 cup	**piña colada mix**
Ice cubes	

Place all ingredients in a blender, and fill with ice. Blend until slushy and serve immediately.

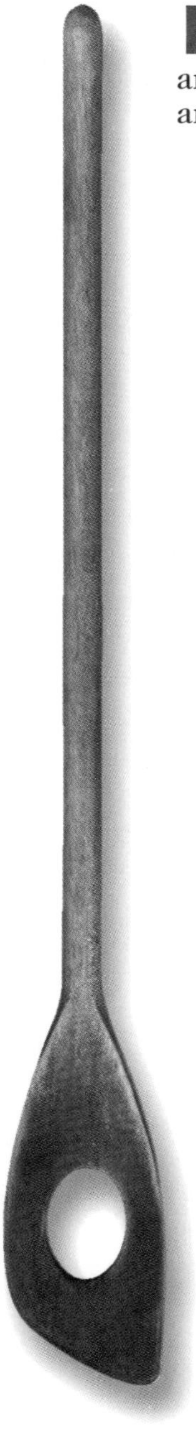

It's often said that Angels have no body...but there are people on this earth who use their bodies, skills, talents...to assist others who have a special need. We call them Kitchen Angels. H.H.

Guacamole

Makes 2 or 3 Cups

A Southwestern specialty that has kept avocado growers thriving.

Ingredients

1/4 small	**red onion – coarsely chopped**
1	**tomato – seeded and coarsely chopped**
2 large	**ripe avocados – peeled, pitted, and chopped**
1 or 2	**cloves of garlic – chopped**
1 tablespoon	**olive oil**
3 tablespoons	**fresh lime juice**

Salt and freshly ground pepper, to taste

1	**green chile or jalapeño pepper – seeded and chopped (optional)**
1/2 teaspoon	**cayenne pepper (optional)**
1/2 teaspoon	**ground cumin (optional)**
1/4 cup	**sour cream (optional)**
1/4 cup	**scallions – finely chopped (optional)**
1/4 cup	**cilantro leaves-minced (optional)**

Corn or flour tortilla chips, jicama sticks, *or* romaine lettuce leaves

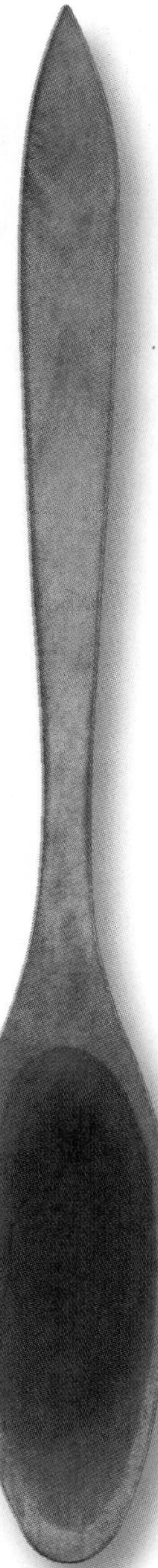

In a food processor, combine onion, tomato, avocado, garlic, oil, lime juice, salt, pepper, and whichever optional ingredients you choose – the more, the better. Using repeated pulses, blend until mixture is a very coarse purée, about 8 quick pulses. Serve immediately with chips, jicama sticks, or lettuce leaves. If not serving right away, place an avocado pit in the center of the mixture and chill with plastic wrap pressed directly onto surface of guacamole to keep from darkening.

Tortilla Soup

SERVES 4 TO 6

A New Mexican favorite! Best when made the day before.

INGREDIENTS

1/3 cup	olive or vegetable oil
1/4 cup	flour
1 small	green bell pepper – seeded and chopped
1 small	yellow onion – chopped
2	carrots – peeled and chopped
2	celery ribs – chopped
2 or 3	cloves of garlic – minced
1/3 cup	cilantro leaves – chopped
1 1/2 teaspoons	chili powder
1 1/2 teaspoons	ground cumin
1 can (15 ounce)	pinto beans, drained
5	corn tortillas – shredded
2 quarts	chicken stock
10 to 12 ounces	canned tomatoes – drained and chopped
1 teaspoon	pepper
2 large	chicken breast halves, boneless and skinless – poached or grilled, and shredded
1/2 cup (2 ounces)	Monterey Jack or Cheddar cheese – shredded (garnish)
1	ripe avocado – peeled and chopped (garnish)
2 additional	corn tortillas – cut into thin strips and fried until crisp (garnish)

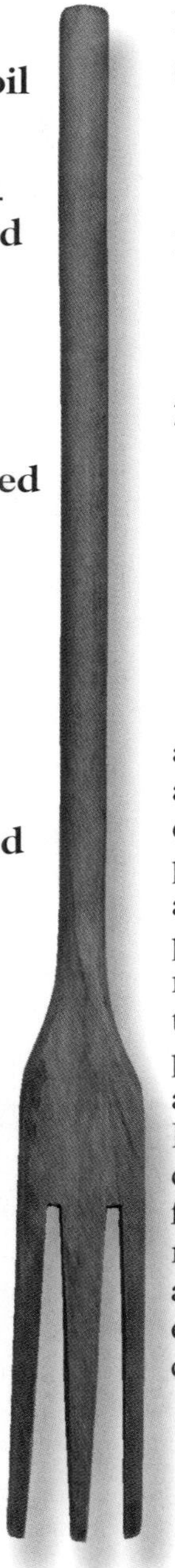

Heat oil in a large heavy saucepan and whisk in the flour. Lower heat and cook until browned, stirring constantly. Add the chopped pepper, onion, carrots, celery, garlic, and cilantro along with the chili powder and cumin. Cook 5 to 10 minutes. Add beans, shredded tortillas, chicken stock, tomatoes, pepper, and shredded chicken. Bring to a boil, and cook for 20 minutes. Remove from heat and refrigerate, covered, all day or overnight for the flavors to blend. Before serving, reheat the soup. Ladle into bowls and garnish each serving with grated cheese, chopped avocado, and crisp tortilla strips.

Red Snapper Fillets with Avocado Sauce

SERVES 6

The delicate sauce complements all varieties of fish as well as poached chicken.

INGREDIENTS

2	ripe avocados – peeled and seeded
2	limes – juiced
2 teaspoons	salt
1 teaspoon	white pepper
2	cloves of garlic – minced
2 tablespoons	mayonnaise
2 tablespoons	sour cream
1/2 teaspoon	hot pepper sauce, or to taste
3/4 cup	cornstarch *or* rice flour
1/2 teaspoon each:	tarragon, salt, and black pepper
6	red snapper fillets
3 tablespoons	olive or vegetable oil
2 additional	limes – sliced (garnish)

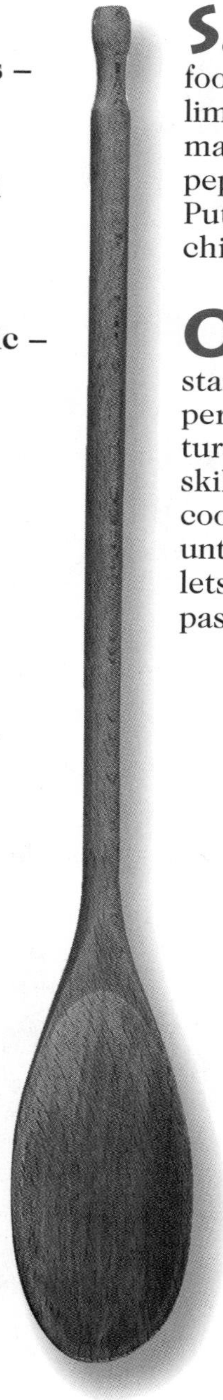

Scrape the avocado pulp into a food processor or blender. Add the lime juice, salt, white pepper, garlic, mayonnaise, sour cream, and hot pepper sauce. Purée until smooth. Put into a small serving bowl and chill, covered, until needed.

On a plate, combine the cornstarch with tarragon, salt, and pepper. Dredge fish fillets in this mixture, shaking off excess. In a heavy skillet, heat oil to hot. Add fish and cook about 3 minutes on each side, until golden brown. Drain. Serve fillets garnished with lime slices, and pass around the avocado sauce.

Nacho Potatoes

SERVES 6 TO 8

Very easy and deliciously New Mexican.

INGREDIENTS

5 large	**potatoes – scrubbed and sliced**
$1/2$ cup	**water**
2 tablespoons	**butter – cut into cubes**
$1/4$ teaspoon	**salt**
$1/4$ teaspoon	**pepper**
1 to 2 tablespoons	**olive or vegetable oil**
$1/2$ cup	**mushrooms – chopped**
$1/2$ cup	**scallions – chopped**
$1/2$ cup	**green bell pepper – seeded and chopped**
$1/2$ cup (2 ounces)	**Cheddar cheese – shredded**
$1/2$ cup (2 ounces)	**Monterey Jack – shredded**
$1/2$ to 1 cup	**sour cream (garnish)**
$1/2$ to 1 cup	**guacamole (garnish) ***

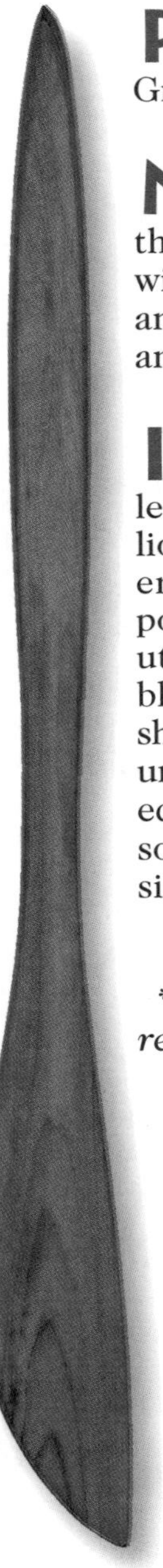

Preheat oven to 350 degrees. Grease a shallow baking dish.

Neatly arrange potato slices in the baking dish. Add water, dot with butter, and sprinkle with salt and pepper. Cover tightly with foil and bake for 20 minutes.

In the meantime, heat oil in a skillet and sauté the mushrooms, scallions, and green pepper until softened but not mushy. After the potatoes have baked for 20 minutes, sprinkle the cooked vegetables over them and top with the shredded cheeses. Continue baking, uncovered, until the cheese is melted, about 10 minutes. Serve with sour cream and guacamole on the side.

** Buy prepared guacamole or see recipe on page 11.*

New Mexican Dinner Cornbread

SERVES 6 TO 8

A hearty, savory main course and a favorite of our Kitchen Angels clients.

INGREDIENTS

2 tablespoons	**olive or vegetable oil**
1 pound	**lean ground beef**
1 medium	**onion – diced**
2 to 4	**cloves of garlic – minced**
2 cans (4 ounce)	**diced green chiles, drained**
1 teaspoon	**oregano**
1 teaspoon	**ground cumin**
Salt and freshly ground pepper, to taste	
1 cup	**cornmeal**
½ teaspoon	**baking soda**
2	**eggs – well beaten**
1 cup	**milk or buttermilk**
1 can (15 ounce)	**corn kernels, drained, or 1½ cups frozen corn**
⅓ cup	**olive or vegetable oil**
½ cup (2 ounces)	**Cheddar or Monterey Jack cheese – shredded**
1 cup	**sour cream (garnish)**
½ to 1 cup	**mild, medium, or hot salsa (garnish)**

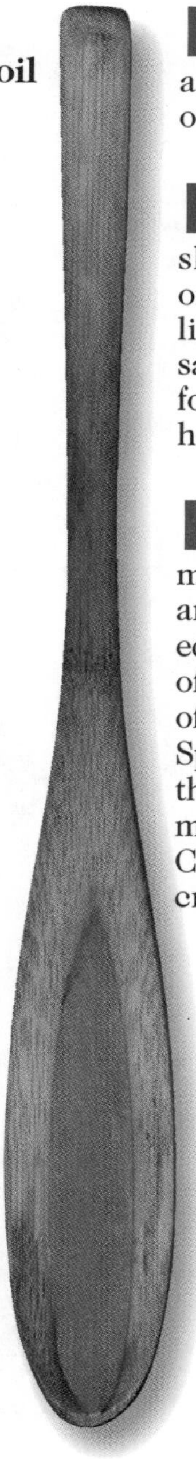

Preheat oven to 350 degrees. Oil a 10½-inch skillet and place in the oven to heat.

Heat 1 tablespoon oil in a large skillet, and brown the beef and onion until well done. Add the garlic, green chile, oregano, cumin, salt, and pepper, stirring well. Cook for 3 or 4 minutes and remove from heat.

In a medium bowl, mix the cornmeal, baking soda, eggs, milk, corn, and ⅓ cup oil. Remove the heated skillet from the oven. Pour in half of the cornmeal mixture. Spread all of the beef mixture evenly over this. Sprinkle with the shredded cheese, then cover with the remaining cornmeal batter. Bake for 50 minutes. Cut into wedges and serve with sour cream and salsa.

Rice and Green Chile

SERVES 6 TO 8

Instant rice is essential to this quick-and-easy dish.

INGREDIENTS

2 cups (16 ounces)	**sour cream**
2 cups	**raw instant rice**
2 cans (4 ounce)	**diced green chiles, undrained**
1 pound	**Monterey Jack cheese - grated or shredded**

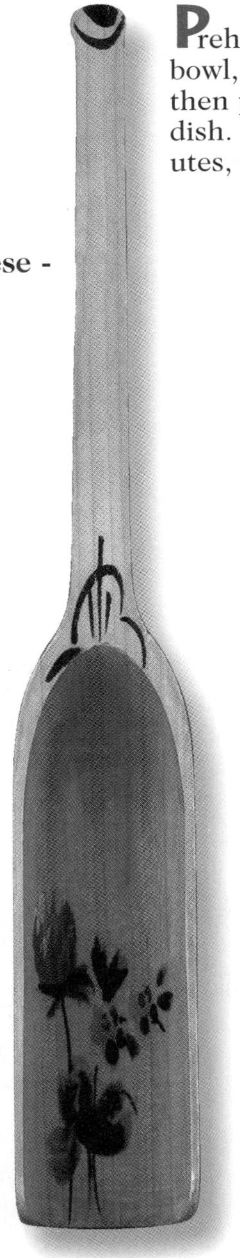

Preheat oven to 350 degrees. In a bowl, mix all ingredients together, then pour into a greased casserole dish. Bake, covered, for 30 minutes, until bubbly.

I have had multiple sclerosis for nearly 27 years and have been a recipient of the Kitchen Angels' service for four years. Kitchen Angels means that I can continue living independently, and I am extremely grateful for this. B.D.

Assorted Greens with Señora's Vinaigrette

SERVES 6 TO 8

This vinaigrette goes well with cooked chilled broccoli or cauliflower, or drizzled over slices of ripe summer tomatoes.

INGREDIENTS

3 to 5 cups	**assorted salad greens – washed and dried**

<u>Señora's Vinaigrette:</u>
(makes about 3/4 cup)

3 tablespoons	**red wine vinegar**
1 teaspoon	**Dijon mustard**
1/2 teaspoon	**salt**
1/4 to 1/2 teaspoon	**celery salt**
1/4 to 1/2 teaspoon	**garlic salt**
1/2 teaspoon	**freshly ground pepper**
1 teaspoon	**dried basil**
6 tablespoons	**olive oil**

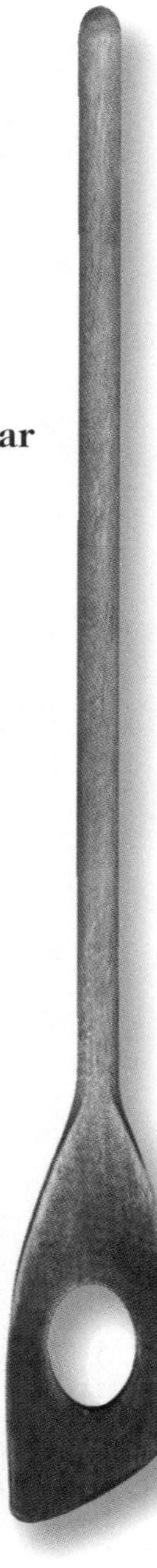

Place salad greens in a large bowl. Put all the vinaigrette ingredients, except the oil, in a pint jar. Cover and shake well. Add oil and shake again. Toss salad greens with enough dressing to coat the leaves lightly. Leftover vinaigrette may be stored in the refrigerator.

Flan

SERVES 10 TO 12

This caramelized custard is a Mexican specialty. Chilled leftover custards are delicious the next day.

INGREDIENTS

3/4 cup	**sugar**
2 cups	**whole milk**
2 cans (14 ounce)	**sweetened condensed milk**
3	**eggs**
1 teaspoon	**vanilla extract**

Preheat oven to 350 degrees.

Heat a heavy saucepan to very hot. Add the sugar and stir constantly until it has melted and turned a light caramel in color; do not overcook or the sugar will burn. Pour this syrup into 10 or 12 ovenproof custard cups. Put remaining ingredients into a blender or food processor and blend until thoroughly mixed. Pour into the custard cups. Set cups in a pan of hot water, and bake for 25 to 35 minutes, until the custard is set. Serve warm or chilled.

PHOTO BY TOM PARRISH

LUNCH ON THE PATIO
TO PONDER A LILAC YEAR

IN MEMORY OF:
MAMIE ATKINSON AND CLAUDE JESSUP

Santa Feans will tell you that some years are Lilac Years and some are not. They cannot be forecast. You have to wait until you are in one before you know. Most people do not even notice the years that are not, because the lilacs still bloom and delight. But when we get a real Lilac Year, we all know it.

Among the legacy of work documenting the beauty of our everyday life is a woodcut by Santa Fe's beloved printmaker, Gustave Bauman, entitled "A Lilac Year." It is dated 1949 – obviously a magnificent year for lilacs – and it shows how glorious the experience can be. Masses of blossoms, sudden and wonderful, crown a lane of coyote fences, calling forth overnight a presence of high purple against an endless sky.

Every May, all over town, there are stands of heirloom bushes – lavender or garnet or burgundy, orchid, russet, or pristine white. In a Lilac Year, they sing, "All things possible!" The shrubs are blanketed with blooms, no leaves seen, panicles reaching, amethyst fires arching and smokeless. "Is this enchantment?" they ask us. "Are we blessed?"

Why not host a party on your patio to celebrate the flowering of the genus *Syringa* that Santa Feans have come to love so much? Whether it is an exceptional Lilac Year or not, none of your guests will be disappointed by the abundance of color and the intoxicating fragrance. There is no better way to enjoy our luncheon menu for six to eight.

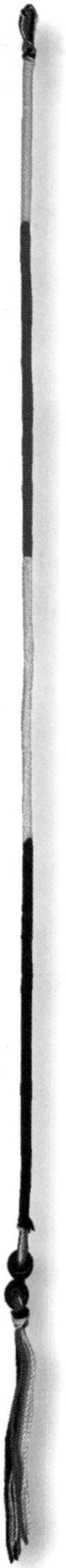

Lunch on the Patio to Ponder a Lilac Year

Menu

Asparagus with Sesame Mayonnaise

Hot Chicken Salad

Fava Beans and Apples

Mango or Papaya Slaw

French Bread *(page 139)*

Lemon Cheese Pie

Iced Tea

Asparagus with Sesame Mayonnaise

SERVES 6 TO 8

This mayonnaise with its Asian flavors makes a tasty dip for assorted *crudités*.

INGREDIENTS

1 to $1\frac{1}{2}$ pounds	**fresh asparagus – pared and steamed *al dente***

<u>Sesame Mayonnaise:</u>
(makes about 3 cups):

$2\frac{1}{2}$ cups	**mayonnaise**
3 or 4 tablespoons	**toasted sesame oil**
$2\frac{1}{2}$ tablespoons	**soy sauce**
1 tablespoon	**rice wine vinegar**
1 tablespoon	**Dijon mustard**
1 teaspoon	**oriental chili oil**
4 tablespoons	**grated orange zest (about 1 large orange)**

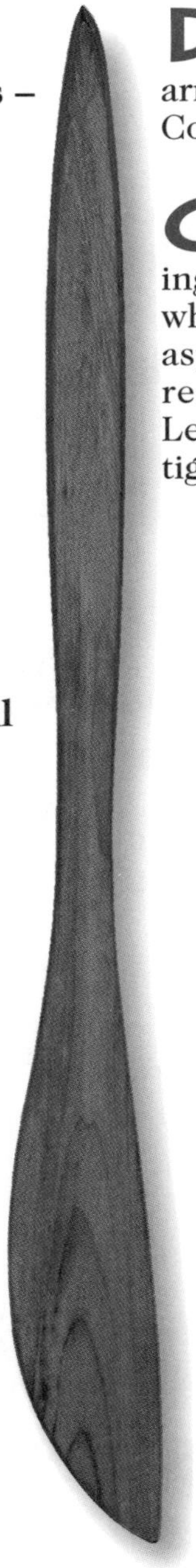

Drain the steamed asparagus and arrange among 6 to 8 serving plates. Cool.

Combine all of the mayonnaise ingredients in a medium bowl, and whisk well. Drizzle a bit over each asparagus serving, and place the rest in a bowl to pass around. Leftover mayonnaise keeps well, tightly covered, in the refrigerator.

Hot Chicken Salad

SERVES 8

This flavorful dish must be assembled a day before serving.

INGREDIENTS

3 cups	**cooked chicken – cut into 1/2-inch cubes**
2 cups	**celery – thinly sliced**
1 cup	**toasted bread cubes**
1/2 small	**onion – grated**
1 1/2 cups	**mayonnaise**
1/2 teaspoon	**salt**
2 tablespoons	**fresh lemon juice**
1/2 cup	**sliced almonds – lightly toasted**
1/2 cup (2 ounces)	**Cheddar or Parmesan cheese – grated, *or* 1 cup crushed potato chips**

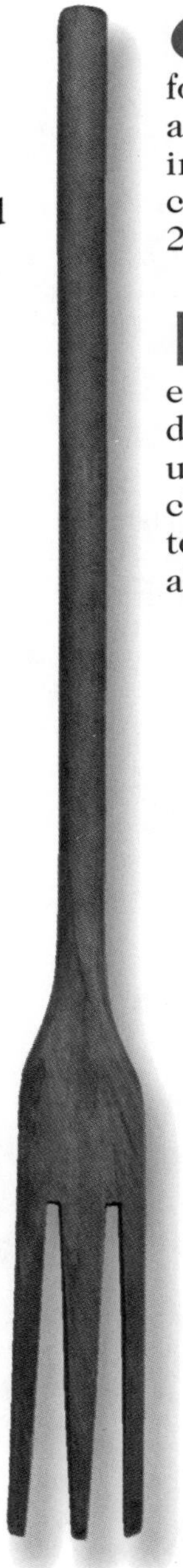

Combine all ingredients, except for the cheese or crushed chips, in a large bowl and mix well. Scrape into a lightly greased ovenproof casserole. Refrigerate, covered, for 24 hours.

Remove casserole from the refrigerator and preheat oven to 425 degrees. Bake for 10 minutes, uncovered. Top with the grated cheese or crushed chips. Return to the oven and cook until bubbly, about 10 minutes longer.

Fava Beans with Apples

SERVES 6 TO 8

Fresh steamed fava beans may be substituted for canned in this appealing side dish.

INGREDIENTS

4 tablespoons	**butter**
4 strips	**bacon (optional)**
6 large	**apples – cored, and chopped**
2 medium	**yellow onions – chopped**
2 cans (19 ounce)	**fava beans – drained and rinsed**
2 teaspoons	**fresh thyme, or 1 teaspoon dried thyme**

Salt and freshly ground pepper, to taste

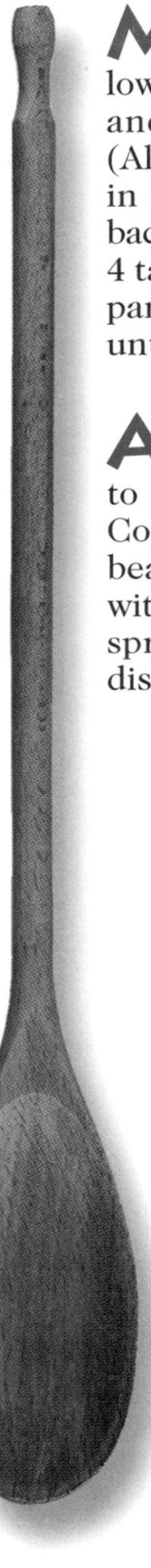

Melt butter in a large skillet over low heat. Add the apples and onion and sauté until nearly soft. (Alternatively, fry the bacon strips in a large skillet. Drain and chop bacon, and set aside. Remove all but 4 tablespoons of bacon fat from the pan and sauté the apples and onion until nearly soft.)

Add the fava beans and thyme to the softened apples and onion. Cook, stirring frequently, until the beans are heated through. Season with salt and pepper. If using bacon, sprinkle chopped bacon over the dish before serving.

Mango or Papaya Slaw

SERVES 6 TO 8

Excellent with grilled tuna or swordfish.

INGREDIENTS

3 large green (unripe)	mangoes *or* papayas
1 small	red bell pepper – seeded and cut into $1/8$-inch strips
$1/4$ to $1/3$ cup	mayonnaise
1 tablespoon	sugar
$1/4$ to $1/3$ cup	fresh lime juice
$1/4$ teaspoon	hot pepper sauce, or to taste
$1/2$ teaspoon	salt
$1/4$ teaspoon	freshly ground pepper

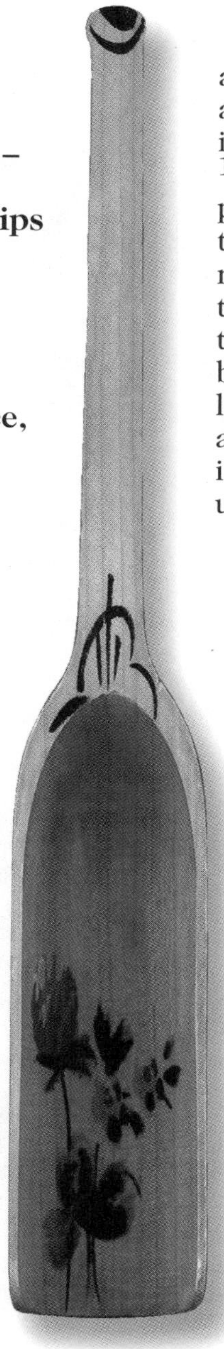

Peel the mangoes and cut the flesh away from the inner flat seed. Using a hand grater or mandolin, shred as if for coleslaw, or cut by hand into $1/8$-inch julienne strips. (If using papayas, peel, halve, and seed them, then shred or cut via the same method.) In a large bowl, combine the shredded mango or papaya with the red pepper strips. In a small bowl, mix the mayonnaise, sugar, lime juice, hot pepper sauce, salt, and pepper. Add to the salad, tossing well. Cover and refrigerate for up to 2 hours before serving.

Lemon Cheese Pie

SERVES 6 TO 8

This lemon treat needs no altitude adjustment.

INGREDIENTS

24	**vanilla wafer cookies**
1 stick (4 ounces)	**unsalted butter – at room temperature**
2 packages (8 ounce)	**cream cheese – at room temperature**
4	**eggs**
1/2 cup	**sugar**
1 jar (8 ounce)	**English lemon curd**

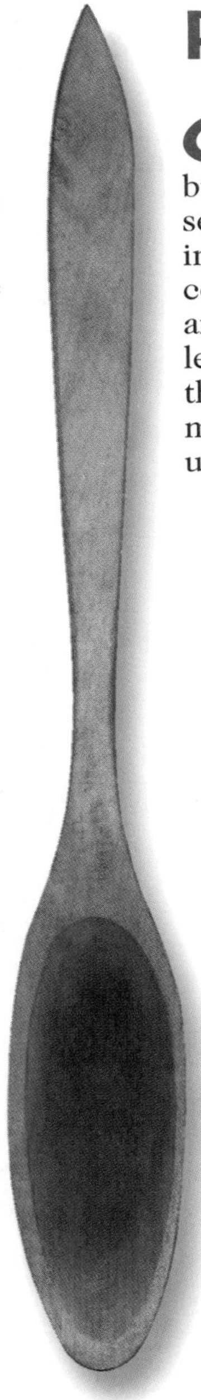

Preheat oven to 350 degrees.

Combine the vanilla wafers and butter in a food processor for 30 seconds. Press mixture into a 9-inch pie plate. In a food processor, combine the cream cheese, eggs, and sugar for 30 seconds. Spoon the lemon curd evenly over bottom of the pie crust, then the cream cheese mixture. Bake for 45 to 50 minutes. Serve at room temperature.

Thank you for all the gifts you gave me for my birthday and the holidays. The gifts were greatly appreciated. Thank you to everyone who made it happen.

O.A.

Photo courtesy of Randall Davey Audubon Center

Twilight Supper
After Watching Birds

In memory of:
Peggy Baker, a true gourmet

"I want to hear the music that birds make," a fairy tale character announces, dismissing her suitors. "The twittering of beaks...the flapping of wings." She leaves them abruptly, and climbs a tree.

Santa Feans do not have to climb trees or dismiss their suitors. They can transport themselves, as quickly as some spells take, to the Randall Davey Audubon Center on Upper Canyon Road, less than fifteen minutes from the heart of Old Santa Fe. The late artist's former residence opens out to a secluded woodland canyon that is home to a variety of resident species as well as a stopping point in the migration of many birds.

Spring is a great time to greet them as they are courting – the resident jays, for example, the noisy Scrub, Piñon, or crested Steller's. Watch them nest. And did you know that common raven chicks resemble baby dinosaurs? See the varieties of hummingbirds returning for the summer – the Black-chinned with their whirring wings, the green and red Broad-tailed, the bright red-brown Rufous, the occasional small Calliope. Search for those passing through, such as the astonishing sight of the fishing osprey in our dry high desert.

Then return home to a gracious dinner in the company of friends. Marvel over your own rare twilight sightings: a Bullock's Oriole, perhaps, a glory of orange in the darkening pines, or the heart-melting rosy head of a Western Tanager. Listen to the sweet robin's song, or the soulful Mourning Dove. Pass this supper for six off as your own. Preen a little; dazzle your suitors. Why not flap your own wings?

Twilight Supper after Watching Birds

Menu

Southwestern Clam Chowder

Herb-Roasted Chicken
or
Orange and Rosemary Poached Catfish

Panzanella

Avocado Cream Dessert

Chardonnay

Southwestern Clam Chowder

SERVES 6

A zippy variation on the traditional.

INGREDIENTS

4 tablespoons	**butter**
1 large	**onion – diced**
1	**green pepper – seeded and diced**
2	**leeks or scallions – diced**
$1/2$ cup	**celery – diced**
3 cups	**potatoes – peeled and diced**
Water	
1 can (14.5 ounce)	**diced tomatoes**
2 cans (4 ounce)	**diced mild or medium green chiles ***
4 tablespoons	**ketchup**
1 tablespoon	**fresh parsley leaves – minced**
Pinch each of:	**thyme, marjoram, and cayenne pepper**
2 cans (8 ounce)	**minced clams**

Salt and freshly ground pepper, to taste

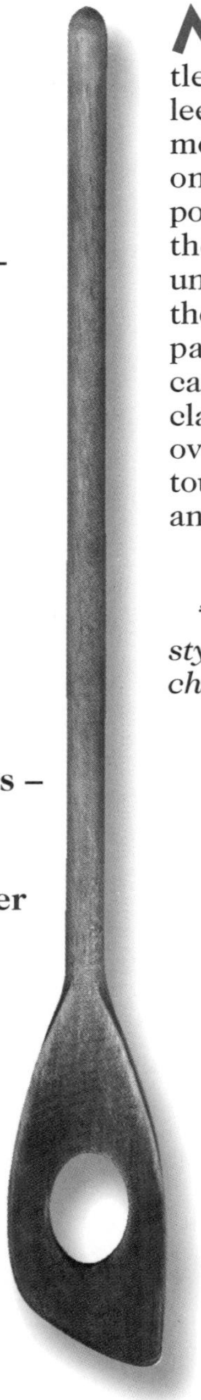

Melt butter in a large soup kettle, and sauté the onion, pepper, leeks or scallions, and celery over medium heat for 5 minutes, or until onions are translucent. Add the potatoes and enough water to cover them. Simmer for 20 minutes, or until potatoes are almost done. Add the tomatoes, green chiles, ketchup, parsley, thyme, marjoram, and cayenne. Bring to a boil. Add the clams and heat thoroughly. Do not overcook or the clams will become tough. Season with salt and pepper, and serve immediately.

**For a traditional Manhattan-style clam chowder, omit the green chiles.*

HERB-ROASTED CHICKEN

SERVES 6

This succulent chicken is roasted in a clay pot. The fresh herbs are essential.

INGREDIENTS

1 whole (7 pound)	roasting chicken
Salt or seasoned salt	
1 bunch	fresh sage
1 bunch	fresh tarragon
1	lemon – cut in half (optional)
6	cloves of garlic – peeled (optional)

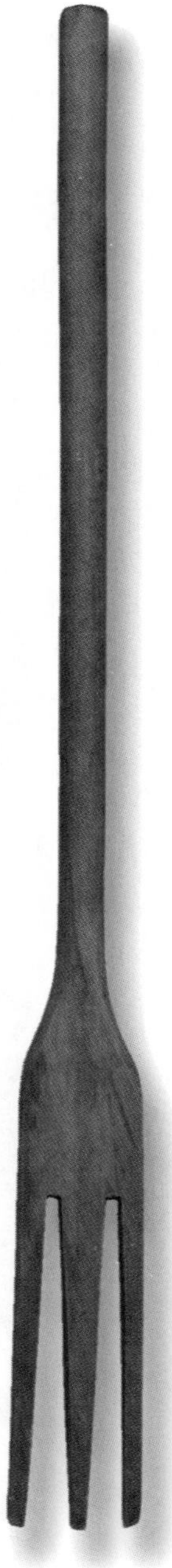

Soak top and bottom of a clay stoneware roaster in cold water for 15 minutes. In the meantime, rinse the chicken inside and out. Dry the chicken, and sprinkle the skin and cavity with salt. Slide sage and tarragon leaves under skin of the breast and as far down the thigh as your fingers can reach. Stuff remaining sage and tarragon into the cavity, along with lemon halves and garlic, if desired. Put chicken into the pre-soaked roaster. Place in a cold oven and set the heat to 400 degrees. Cook chicken until the skin is browned and the legs move easily, approximately 1 to $1^1/_2$ hours.

Orange and Rosemary Poached Catfish

SERVES 6

Other fish fillets may be substituted in this delicate and delicious dish.

INGREDIENTS

2 tablespoons	**olive or vegetable oil**
$^1/_2$ small	**red onion – diced**
$^1/_2$ teaspoon	**salt**
$^1/_8$ teaspoon	**freshly ground pepper**
$^1/_2$ to $^3/_4$ teaspoon	**dried rosemary leaves – crushed**
$^1/_3$ cup	**fresh orange juice**
$^1/_2$ teaspoon	**grated orange zest**
6	**catfish fillets**
1	**orange – thinly sliced (garnish)**

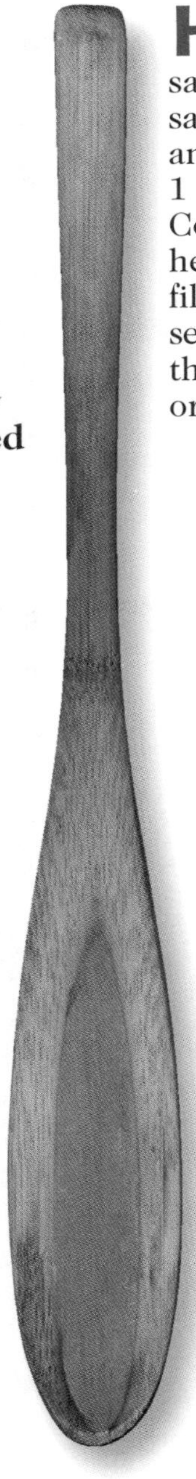

Heat oil in a large skillet and sauté the onion for 5 minutes. Add salt, pepper, rosemary, orange juice, and grated zest. Stir and cook for 1 minute, then add the fish fillets. Cover and cook over medium-low heat for 8 to 10 minutes, until the fillets are opaque. Place fillets on a serving platter and spoon sauce from the skillet over them. Garnish with orange slices.

Panzanella

SERVES 6

This popular salad from Italy is traditionally made with leftover bread. Make it at least an hour in advance.

INGREDIENTS

2 loaves	**chewy sourdough or peasant bread – cut into $^{3}/_{4}$-inch cubes**
$2^{1}/_{2}$ pounds	**ripe plum tomatoes**
4	**cloves of garlic – crushed**
$^{1}/_{2}$ teaspoon	**salt**
Freshly ground pepper, to taste	
1 cup	**extra virgin olive oil**
4 tablespoons	**red wine vinegar**
3	**red bell peppers**
3	**yellow bell peppers**
2	**fresh hot red chiles**
1 cup	**black Gaeta olives – pitted**
1 large bunch	**basil, leaves only – chopped**
$^{1}/_{2}$ cup	**capers**
2 cans (2 ounce)	**anchovies – drained and chopped**

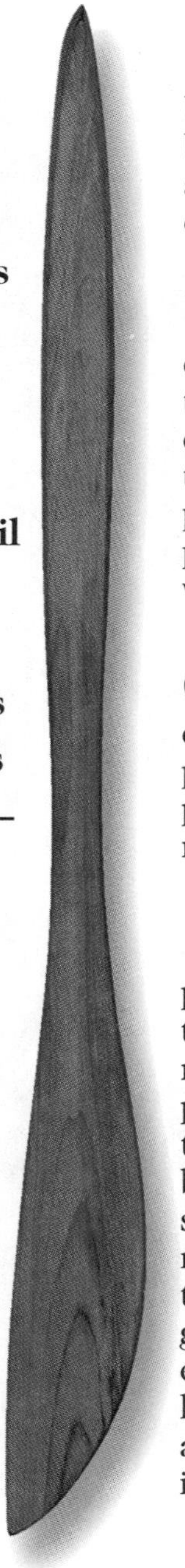

Preheat oven to 325 degrees. Place bread cubes on a baking sheet and bake until lightly toasted and crusty, approximately 20 minutes. Remove cubes to a large mixing bowl.

Peel the tomatoes. Cut into chunks, removing seeds and saving the juice in a medium bowl. Add crushed garlic and salt to the tomato juice, along with freshly ground pepper, oil, and vinegar. Mix and pour over the bread cubes, tossing well.

Grill or broil the bell peppers and chiles until blackened. Cool in a paper bag, then peel and seed. Cut peppers into $^{1}/_{4}$-inch strips, and mince the chiles.

In a small bowl, set aside enough peppers, tomatoes, olives, and basil to garnish the top of the salad. Then mix the remaining tomatoes, peppers, chiles, olives, and basil with the capers and anchovies in a large bowl. Cover the bottom of a deep serving dish with a layer of marinated bread, then a layer of the tomato mixture. Repeat layers, and garnish with the reserved ingredients. Allow to sit for at least one hour before serving. Serve with additional extra virgin olive oil, if desired.

Avocado Cream Dessert

SERVES 6

This delightfully rich and novel dessert must be made at least 4 hours before serving.

INGREDIENTS

3 large	**ripe avocados – peeled and pitted**
3/4 cup	**sugar**
1/3 cup	**heavy cream**
1/3 cup	**fresh lime juice**
1/3 teaspoon	**salt**

<u>Crème Chantilly:</u>

1 cup	**heavy cream**
1 tablespoon	**sugar**
1/2 teaspoon	**vanilla extract**

<u>Garnish:</u>

2 1/2 cups	**fresh raspberries *or* sliced strawberries**
1	**lime – thinly sliced**

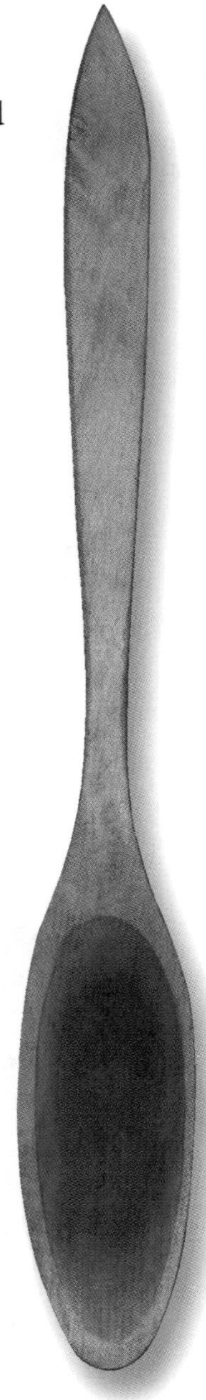

In blender or food processor, combine the avocado pulp, sugar, cream, lime juice, and salt. Purée until smooth. Divide among 6 serving bowls, and chill for at least 4 hours.

Just before serving, whip together all of the ingredients for the Crème Chantilly until soft peaks form. Spoon the whipped cream over the avocado desserts. Garnish with berries and lime slices.

Photo by Charles Mann

Brunch after "the Flea"

Sponsored by:
Jane O'Toole

Brunch after "The Flea"

One of the great ways to get some fresh air in Santa Fe – without strapping on a pair of hiking boots – is to hop in the car and head for the Tesuque Pueblo Flea Market, located north of town next to the Santa Fe Opera. Open from early March until after Thanksgiving, this is the place to spot everything from silver to skulls to celebrities and old friends. There are some smaller flea markets scattered around town that you are likely to come across in your wanderings, and they are lots of fun. The pièce de résistance, however, is the huge, bustling one on highway 285-north.

There are quite a number of permanent stalls where you can buy beautiful Indian jewelry, pots, and fetishes, furniture and home accessories, dried chiles and posole, handmade candles, beads and fine gemstones, even colorful, ethnic clothing. But there are also temporary booths where you can pick up inexpensive yard sale-ish items, such as books, costume jewelry, puppets, house plants, and little pieces of nostalgia. Early morning is when you are likely to unearth rare treasures. Sunday afternoon, when the vendors are packing up, is the time to ferret out real deals.

Now, if you have a craving for Frito pie, go no further than the food stalls at the entrance to "the flea." But if your feet hurt and the crowds are beginning to get to you, invite your bargain-hunting pals back home, where you can show off each other's treasures and enjoy this lovely brunch – which you have made ahead, by the way - for six to eight hungry shoppers.

Menu

Breakfast Apple Treat

Sausage Casserole
or
Baked Eggs

Venison Sausage

Bran Muffins

Freshly Squeezed Juices and Coffee

Breakfast Apple Treat

SERVES 6 TO 8

Cook this dish all night in a crockery pot and awaken to a house filled with the fragrance of cooked apples and cinnamon.

INGREDIENTS

6 to 8 firm	**Granny Smith apples – peeled, cored, and cut in $1/2$-inch slices**
$1\frac{1}{2}$ to 2 cups	**old-fashioned oats**
$3/4$ to 1 cup	**white sugar**
1 to 2 tablespoons	**cinnamon**
1 to 2 tablespoons	**butter**

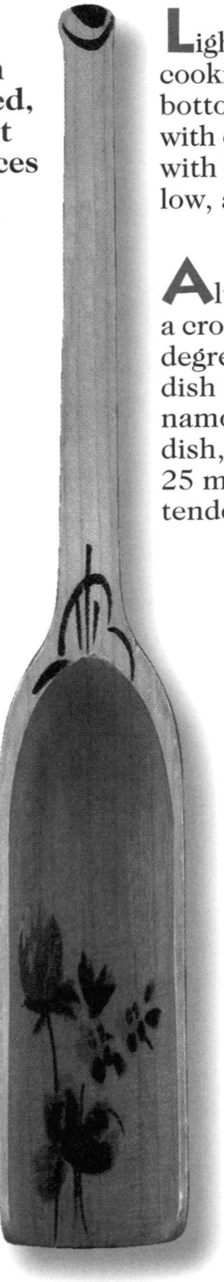

Lightly grease the inside of a slow-cooking crockery pot and cover the bottom with apple slices. Sprinkle with oats, sugar, and cinnamon. Dot with butter. Turn the pot setting to low, and cook all night.

Alternatively, if you do not own a crockery pot, preheat oven to 375 degrees. Mix apple slices in a large dish with the oats, sugar, and cinnamon. Pour into a greased baking dish, and dot with butter. Bake for 25 minutes, or until the apples are tender.

Sausage Casserole

SERVES 6 TO 8

This breakfast casserole can be assembled the night before and popped into the oven half an hour before serving. An easy recipe to double for a crowd.

INGREDIENTS

6 to 8 slices	whole wheat bread – crusts removed
6 to 8 tablespoons	yellow or Dijon mustard
$1\frac{1}{2}$ pounds	pork or turkey sausage, in bulk
$\frac{1}{2}$ teaspoon	crushed red pepper flakes
$\frac{1}{2}$ teaspoon	thyme
$\frac{1}{2}$ teaspoon	dried or fresh sage leaves – crumbled
1 cup (4 ounces)	Swiss or Monterey Jack cheese – shredded
4 or 5	eggs – beaten
$1\frac{1}{2}$ cups	milk
$\frac{3}{4}$ cup	light or heavy cream
1 teaspoon	Worcestershire sauce
$\frac{1}{2}$ teaspoon	nutmeg
$\frac{1}{2}$ teaspoon	salt
$\frac{1}{4}$ teaspoon	pepper

Preheat oven to 375 degrees. Grease a 9 x 13-inch or 10 x 16-inch baking dish.

Spread tops of bread slices with mustard. Arrange bread in a single layer along the bottom of the baking dish, mustard side up. In a heavy skillet, brown the sausage, breaking into small pieces while cooking. Drain sausage on paper towels, then spoon over the bread slices. Sprinkle with crushed red pepper, thyme, sage, and shredded cheese.

In a medium bowl, combine the beaten eggs, milk, cream, Worcestershire, nutmeg, salt, and pepper. Pour this mixture evenly over the sausage and cheese. *(The casserole may be prepared to this point, covered, and refrigerated before baking.)* Bake for 25 to 30 minutes, until golden and bubbly, or longer if the casserole has been chilled. Serve immediately.

Baked Eggs

SERVES 6 TO 8

A hearty and flavorful brunch dish.

INGREDIENTS

3 slices	**thin bread – crusts removed**
3	**scallions – coarsely chopped**
$^{1}/_{2}$ cup	**fresh parsley leaves**
1 cup	**milk**
$^{3}/_{4}$ cup	**water**
2 to 3 tablespoons	**butter**
12	**eggs – beaten**
1 cup (4 ounces)	**Swiss cheese – grated**
1 cup (4 ounces)	**Cheddar cheese – grated**
$^{1}/_{4}$ cup (1 ounce)	**Mozzarella cheese – grated**
8 to 10 slices	**bacon – cooked, drained, and crumbled (optional)**

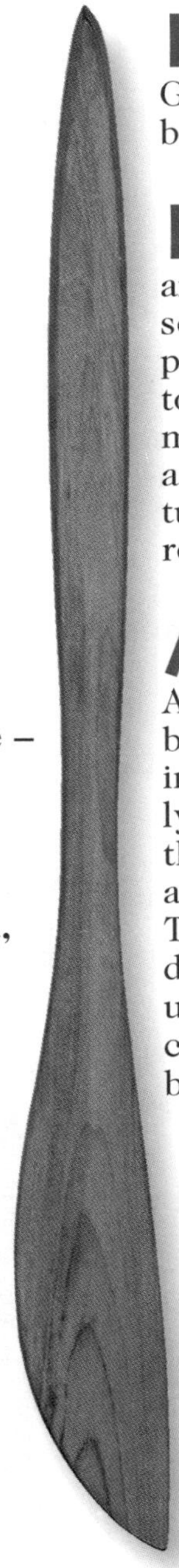

Preheat oven to 400 degrees. Grease a 9 x 13-inch or 10 x 16-inch baking dish.

Break the bread into large chunks and add to the bowl of a food processor, along with the scallions and parsley leaves. Pulse several times to coarsely chop the mixture. In a medium bowl, combine the milk and water, then add the bread mixture and soak for 5 minutes. Drain, reserving both bread and liquid.

Melt butter in a large skillet. Add the leftover milk liquid to the beaten eggs and mix well. Pour eggs into the skillet, and scramble loosely. Add the bread mixture and three-fourths of the grated cheeses, and combine gently with the eggs. Transfer to the prepared baking dish. Top with crumbled bacon, if using, and the remaining grated cheeses. Bake for $^{1}/_{2}$ hour, or until browned and puffy.

Venison Game Sausage

MAKES 12 LINKS OR 12 LARGE PATTIES

If you have access to fresh venison, make a large batch of this spicy, aromatic sausage. It freezes well and is also an excellent winter supper dish. Prepare a day ahead to allow flavors to blend.

INGREDIENTS

1 1/2 pounds	**boneless pork loin – cubed**
2 pounds	**boneless venison – cubed**
1/4 pound	**hard fatback *or* suet**
1/2 tablespoon	**coriander seeds**
1/2 tablespoon	**allspice berries**
1/2 to 1 teaspoon	**dried crushed hot red peppers**
1 tablespoon	**black peppercorns**
3	**cloves of garlic – crushed**
2 tablespoons	**salt**
3/4 cup	**red wine or port**

Sausage casings, if links are desired *

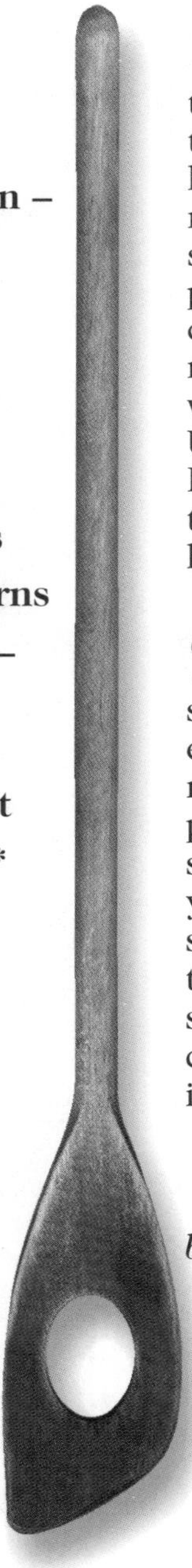

Put the cubed pork and venison through a meat grinder, and remove to a large bowl. Dice the fatback by hand, then mix into the ground meats. Crush the coriander, allspice, red pepper, and black peppercorns in a mortar (or grind coarsely in a coffee grinder) and mix into the meat mixture, along with the crushed garlic and salt. Using your hands, mix thoroughly. Pour the wine over the sausage mixture. Cover, and let stand for a few hours

Soak the casings in water. Mix the sausage again with your hands. Stuff enough sausage into each casing to make short fat links. Alternatively, pat sausage into large, hamburger-sized patties (or smaller patties, if you prefer). Cover and refrigerate sausage for 24 hours before cooking, to allow flavors to develop. The sausage is best when grilled over charcoal, but it may also be sautéed in a heavy skillet.

**These may be ordered from your butcher.*

Bran Muffins

MAKES 24 MUFFINS

An easy recipe for healthy, mouth-watering muffins. Leftover muffins, tightly wrapped, will keep in the refrigerator for days.

INGREDIENTS

$1/2$ cup	**brown sugar**
3 cups	**bran**
$1/2$ cup	**oil**
1 cup	**raisins or currants**
1 cup	**boiling water**
2	**eggs – lightly beaten**
2 cups	**buttermilk**
$1/2$ cup	**molasses**
$2\,1/4$ cups	**whole wheat flour**
4 teaspoons	**white sugar**
2 teaspoons	**baking soda**
Pinch of	**salt**

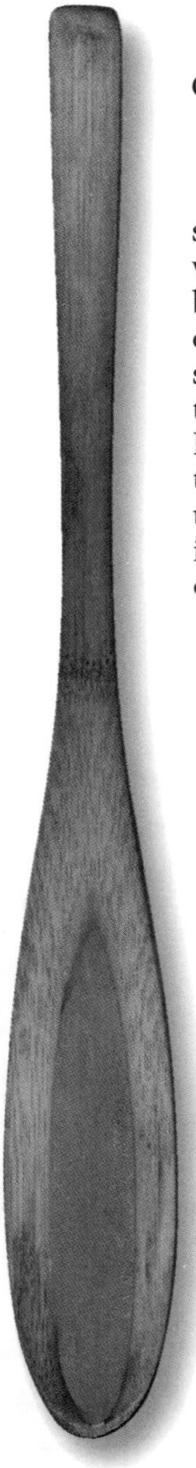

Preheat oven to 400 degrees. Grease 24 muffin tins.

In a large bowl, combine the brown sugar, bran, oil, raisins, and boiling water, mixing well. Stir in the eggs, buttermilk, and molasses. In another bowl, mix together the flour, white sugar, baking soda, and salt. Add to the bran mixture, and blend well. Distribute the batter evenly among the 24 muffin tins. Bake for 15 minutes, or until a toothpick inserted into the center of a muffin comes out clean.

Courtesy of Linda Durham Contemporary Art, photo by Robert Shaw

After an Evening of Gallery Hopping

Sponsored by:
Susan Munroe and Terry Smith

Santa Fe bursts with art for every budget and taste, from southwestern to cutting-edge contemporary. More than 250 galleries, six museums, Site Santa Fe, Plan B Evolving Arts, and other art-related businesses give our city its well-deserved reputation as an arts Mecca. To become familiar with the local scene, why not devote several hours some Friday evening to a leisurely art trek?

Begin with the downtown museums, which offer free admission from 5 to 8 p.m. The Fine Arts, Georgia O'Keeffe, and historic Palace of the Governors all provide changing exhibitions that never fail to fascinate. Mosey over to the art galleries along the Plaza and surrounding streets, then up to Canyon Road where – throughout the year – you are likely to find dozens of opening receptions for either solo or group shows. Check the newspaper listings for galleries that are hosting openings. The public is always welcome, and you can enjoy wine, cheese, and a variety of visual experiences while mingling with patrons, connoisseurs, and the artists themselves. You may even find a special piece of art that you will want to buy and treasure forever.

On any given Friday there will be more events than you can attend without turning your walk into a marathon. So, after you and your friends have reached the saturation point, saunter back home for a stimulating discussion of your favorite exhibits. And while you're at it, enjoy our colorful dinner for eight.

After an Evening of Gallery Hopping

Menu

Roasted Zucchini Spread
with Pita Toasts

Santa Fe Shrimp Salad
in Avocado Halves

Chili Ravioli

Two Shades of Red Salad

Nanaimo Bars

Sparkling Water
and Chardonnay

Roasted Zucchini Spread with Pita Toasts

SERVES 6 TO 8

A light, healthy spread that may be prepared up to a week in advance. The pita toasts make a tasty substitute for crackers.

INGREDIENTS

6 or 7 medium	**zucchini – halved lengthwise and cut crosswise into $^1/_8$-inch slices**
2 to 3 tablespoons	**olive oil**
2 teaspoons	**salt**
$^1/_2$ cup	**plain yogurt**
4	**scallions – minced**
$^1/_2$ teaspoon	**curry powder (optional)**

Salt and freshly ground pepper, to taste

Pita Toasts:
(makes 64 pita toasts)

4	**6-inch pita breads**
2 to 3 tablespoons	**olive oil**

Salt or seasoned salt, to taste

2 to 3 teaspoons	**dried rosemary leaves – crushed**

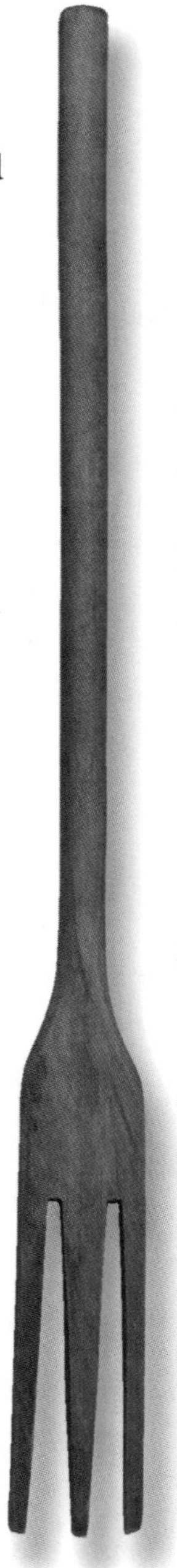

Preheat oven to 500 degrees.

In a large, shallow roasting pan, toss the zucchini with oil and salt, then spread into a single layer. Roast in the middle of the oven, stirring once, for about 25 minutes, or until browned. Cool and purée coarsely in a food processor. Remove to a bowl and mix in the yogurt, scallions, and curry powder, if using. Season with salt and pepper. Cover tightly and chill. Before serving, bring to room temperature.

For pita toasts, preheat oven to 350 degrees.

Split pita breads horizontally to form 8 rounds. Brush the rough surfaces with oil and season with salt and crushed rosemary. Cut each round into 8 wedges. Bake in two batches on a baking sheet placed on the middle rack of the oven until golden, about 10 minutes. Cool before serving. Toasts may be made up to 1 week ahead. Keep tightly sealed in plastic bags at room temperature.

Santa Fe Shrimp Salad in Avocado Halves

SERVES 8

Delicious either as an appetizer or luncheon dish.

INGREDIENTS

$2\frac{1}{2}$ cups	**small shrimp – cleaned and deveined (use fresh, frozen or canned)**
$1\frac{1}{4}$ cups	**celery – thinly sliced**
$\frac{3}{4}$ cup	**cucumber – seeded and diced**
$\frac{1}{4}$ cup	**red onion *or* scallion – diced**
1	**jalapeño pepper – seeded and minced (optional)**
3 tablespoons	**cilantro leaves – minced (optional)**
3 tablespoons	**lemon juice**
7 tablespoons	**mayonnaise**
Salt and freshly ground pepper, to taste	
4 large	**ripe avocados – peeled, pitted, and cut in half lengthwise**
2 to 3 cups	**assorted crisp greens**
2	**lemons – seeded and cut into wedges (garnish)**

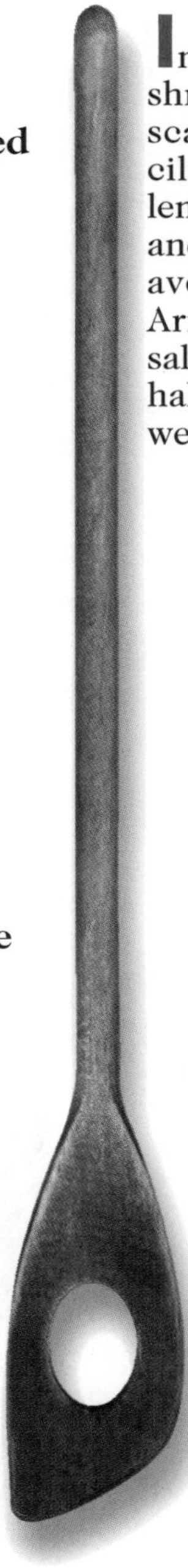

In a medium bowl, combine the shrimp, celery, cucumber, onion or scallion, and the jalapeño and cilantro, if using. Sprinkle with lemon juice. Add mayonnaise, salt, and pepper. Toss well. Fill each avocado half with shrimp salad. Arrange the greens on individual salad plates and place an avocado half on top. Garnish with lemon wedges.

Chili Ravioli

SERVES 8

A vegetarian main dish that is well worth the effort!

INGREDIENTS

Pasta:

1/2 cup	unbleached flour
1 1/2 cups	semolina flour
4	eggs
1 tablespoon	water
1/4 cup	chili powder
1 teaspoon	olive oil

Filling:

2 cups	whole milk ricotta cheese
1/4 cup	tomato – chopped
1/4 cup	onions – grilled and chopped
1/4 cup (1 ounce)	Parmesan cheese – freshly grated
1 to 2	cloves of garlic – minced to yield 1 teaspoon
2 tablespoons	green chile – roasted, peeled, and chopped

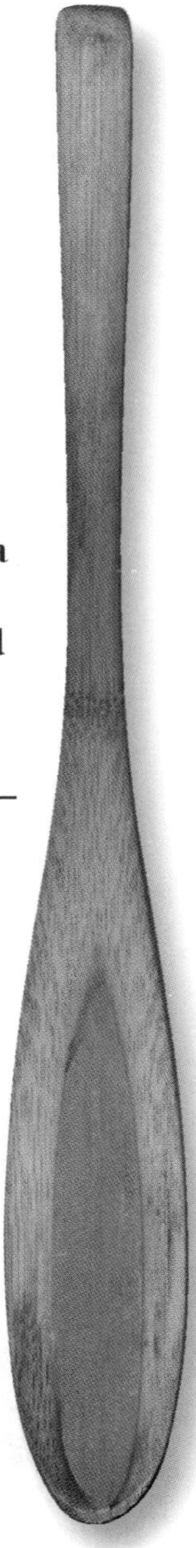

Sauce:

1/4 cup	olive oil
1 or 2	cloves of garlic – minced to yield 1 teaspoon
2 cups	Swiss chard leaves – chopped
1 cup	arugula – chopped
1/2 to 1 cup	chicken broth

Salt and freshly ground pepper, to taste

Garnish:

1/2 cup (2 ounces)	Parmesan cheese – freshly grated
8	parsley sprigs

Chili Ravioli – continued

Mix pasta ingredients together. Knead for 5 to 10 minutes to form a medium-soft dough. Roll thin or use the # 6 setting of a pasta machine to make thin sheets of dough. Set aside, covered with a towel.

Place all filling ingredients in a bowl, and mix well. Season to taste with salt and pepper; set aside.

For the sauce, heat oil in a large skillet or saucepan. Sauté garlic for 30 seconds, then add chard and arugula. Cook until very soft, adding chicken broth as desired for a thicker or thinner sauce. Season to taste with salt and pepper.

Cut pasta into squares, triangles, or any shape or size ravioli desired. Place a bit of filling in center of each. Dampen pasta edges with water and seal with a ravioli cutter or the tines of a fork. *(May be frozen up to a month – no need to defrost before cooking.)*

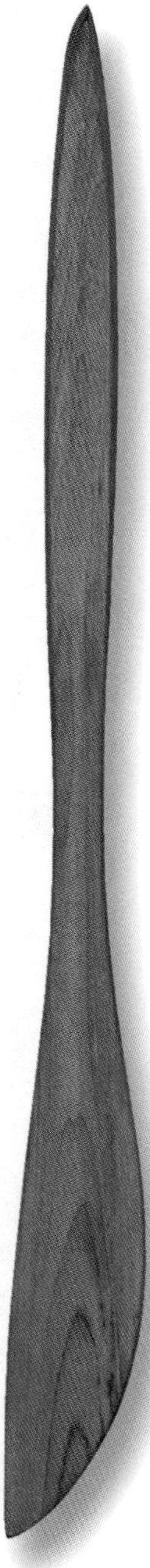

Bring 4 quarts of water to a boil. Add 1 tablespoon salt, then ravioli. Cook until *al dente*. Drain quickly in a colander: do not allow to stand or they will stick together. Divide warm sauce between 8 shallow bowls, and place ravioli on top. Garnish with grated Parmesan and parsley sprigs.

Your help was a Godsend, not only to us in terms of physical relief, but so important for Mom, too, for her self-esteem. She has a fierce attachment to her independence. Mom raves about the quality of her meals – so well-balanced nutritionally, deliciously prepared. And so kindly delivered. Thanks to each and every one of you who so generously and lovingly serve our community with such compassion.
T.G.

Two Shades of Red Salad

SERVES 6 TO 8

A delicious and aesthetically pleasing salad.

INGREDIENTS

1 pound	beets – washed and trimmed
1 pound	tomatoes – seeded and cut into 1/4-inch cubes
1/2 medium	red onion – diced
1	clove of garlic – minced
1/4 cup	Italian parsley leaves – chopped
1/4 cup	cilantro leaves – chopped
2 tablespoons	extra virgin olive oil
1/2 cup	fresh lemon juice
1/2 teaspoon	salt
Freshly ground pepper, to taste	
1/2 cup (2 ounces)	Feta cheese – crumbled

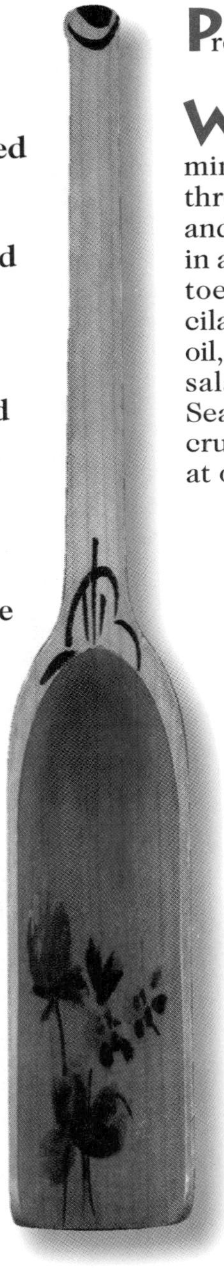

Preheat oven to 400 degrees.

Wrap the beets tightly in aluminum foil and bake until cooked through, about 1 hour. Cool, peel, and cut into 1/4-inch cubes. Place in a serving bowl and add the tomatoes, onion, garlic, parsley, and cilantro. In a small bowl, mix the oil, lemon juice, and salt. Add to the salad ingredients, tossing well. Season with pepper and sprinkle crumbled Feta over the top. Serve at once.

Nanaimo Bars

Makes 9 to 12 Bars

These decadently rich, tri-layered bars are pronounced "Nan-eye-mo," after a town in British Columbia. Enjoy!

Ingredients

<u>Layer # 1:</u>

1 stick (4 ounces)	**butter**
$1/4$ cup	**sugar**
5 tablespoons	**cocoa powder**
1 teaspoon	**vanilla extract**
1	**egg – beaten**
2 cups	**graham cracker crumbs**
1 cup	**shredded coconut**
$1/2$ cup	**walnuts – chopped**

<u>Layer # 2:</u>

$1/4$ cup (4 tablespoons)	**butter – at room temperature**
3 tablespoons	**milk**
2 tablespoons	**vanilla custard powder, *or* vanilla pudding mix**
2 cups	**powdered sugar**

<u>Layer # 3:</u>

4 squares (4 ounces)	**semi-sweet chocolate**
1 tablespoon	**butter**

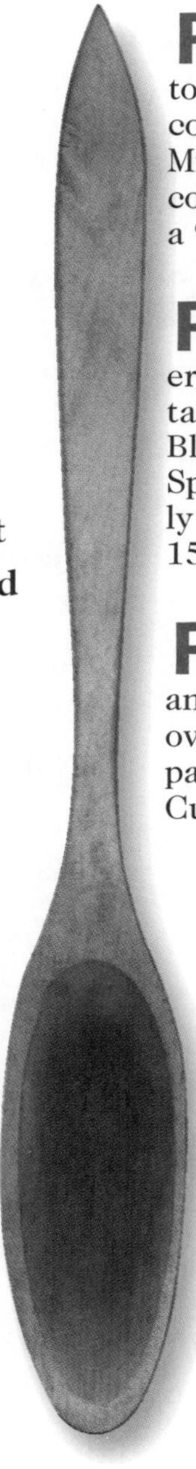

For the first layer, melt butter in top of a double boiler. Add sugar, cocoa, vanilla, and egg, stirring well. Mix in the graham cracker crumbs, coconut, and nuts. Pour evenly into a 9 x 9-inch pan.

For the second layer, mix together the butter, milk, and vanilla custard powder in a medium bowl. Blend in the powdered sugar. Spread this custard mixture evenly over the first layer. Let stand for 15 minutes, to harden.

For the top layer, melt chocolate and butter, stirring. Spread evenly over the custard layer. Cover the pan and chill for at least an hour. Cut into bars before serving.

Summer

PHOTO OF DINEH BY ALLAN HOUSER, 1981, AT SOL Y SOMBRA, BY CHARLES MANN

SUMMER IN SANTA FE

THE SUMMER SECTION IS SPONSORED BY BETH AND CHARLES MILLER, SOL Y SOMBRA

Photo by Ken Robbins

Afternoon Barbecue
Before the Rodeo

Sponsored by:
Linda and Mike Waterman
Caroline and Dick Carlson

The Rodeo de Santa Fe has been a traditional summer family attraction for many years, with good reason. Participants from all over the Southwest demonstrate true courage and wrangling skill, and for a few nail-biting hours spectators are transported back to the early days of the Wild West. Cowboys compete in saddle and bareback bronco riding, calf roping, and other death-defying events. Cowgirls, sequins sparkling and long hair whipping in the wind, push their ponies to the limit in the barrel-racing event. Young cowboys-to-be attempt, and mostly fail, to stay on the backs of itty-bitty calves.

Bull riding caps the evening's attractions as cowboys try valiantly to stay on the backs of bucking bulls until the time-limit buzzer blares. Frequently, the brave riders are thrown through the air before time is up, while the rodeo clowns do their best to distract the big bullies from goring our almost-heroes as they crash land.

All in all, this early summer event provides unique and exciting entertainment for all ages. It is a great occasion to enjoy with friends, and we suggest a festive barbecue for six to eight before your annual excursion to the rodeo grounds on Rodeo Road. Of course, if it's too hot to cook, you can take advantage of the rodeo's concession stands and feast on tacos, hot dogs, roasted corn on the cob, cotton candy, and much more. (One year we even saw lobster rolls!)

Afternoon Barbecue before the Rodeo

Menu

Southern Pineapple Cooler

Green Chile Salsa with Corn Chips

Barbecued Ribs
or
Aunt Susie's BBQ Brisket Poor Boys
or
Maria's Grilled Chicken

Rodeo Coleslaw
or
Corn and Bean Salad
or
Petey's Broiled Curried Beefsteak Tomato Slices

Best Brownies

Butterscotch Brownies

Old-Fashioned Lemonade

Southern Pineapple Cooler

SERVES 1

This is also known as a "pineapple bomb," so imbibe with caution!

INGREDIENTS

Ice cubes

1 shot ($1^1/_2$ ounces)	**Southern Comfort or bourbon**
1 shot ($1^1/_2$ ounces)	**Amaretto or almond liqueur**
$^1/_2$ cup	**pineapple juice, or to taste**
1 slice	**lemon or orange – garnish**

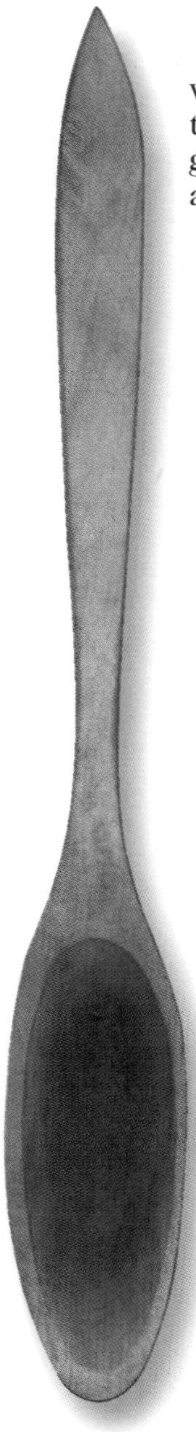

Fill a tall glass three-quarters full with ice cubes. Add liquors, and fill to the top with pineapple juice. Stir gently. Garnish with a citrus wedge, and serve with a straw.

Green Chile Salsa

MAKES 2 CUPS

A piquant dip for corn chips, this salsa also perks up grilled chicken or fish.

INGREDIENTS

4	**ripe tomatoes – peeled, seeded, and diced**
4	**scallions – chopped, including green parts**
2	**cloves of garlic – minced**
1/2 cup	**fresh parsley *or* cilantro leaves – chopped**
1 can (4 ounce)	**diced green chiles**
2 tablespoons	**pickled jalapeños – diced**
1 teaspoon	**ground coriander**
1/4 teaspoon	**sugar**
1/2 teaspoon	**salt**
1/4 teaspoon	**pepper**

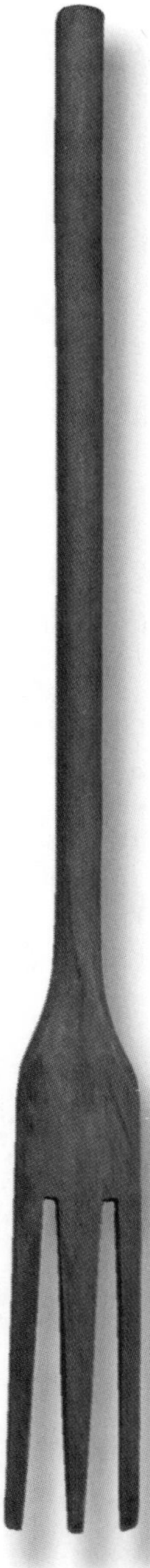

Combine all ingredients in a medium bowl, and mix well. Chill for at least an hour before serving. Tightly covered, the salsa keeps for several days in the refrigerator.

I can't thank Kitchen Angels enough for coming to my rescue when I was homebound, unable to drive and with no one to look after me. I don't know how I could have existed without the meals you provided. My thanks go to whomever planned the meals, the cooks and, not least, the people who made the deliveries. R.T.

Barbecued Ribs

SERVES 6 TO 8

Ribs, messy and delicious, are unbeatable at a summer barbecue. You can substitute baby back ribs for the spareribs.

INGREDIENTS

3 or 4 slabs	**spareribs (12 ribs to a slab) ***
1 large pot	**boiling water**
$1/2$ to $3/4$ cup	**Barbecue Rub *(page 60)*****

Barbecue Sauce:

2 cans (8 ounce)	**tomato sauce**
$1/4$ cup	**Worcestershire sauce**
$1/4$ cup	**apple cider vinegar**
$1/2$ cup	**brown sugar**
1 teaspoon	**thyme**
$1/2$ to 1 teaspoon	**medium-hot red chile powder**
1 teaspoon	**ground cumin**
$1/2$ teaspoon	**ground allspice**
$1/2$ teaspoon	**garlic salt**

Salt and freshly ground pepper, to taste

**A good rule of thumb is to allow 1 pound of spareribs per person.*

***A quick-and-easy rub may be made by mixing $1/3$ cup brown sugar with $1/4$ cup chili powder, 2 teaspoons ground cumin, and 1 teaspoon garlic salt.*

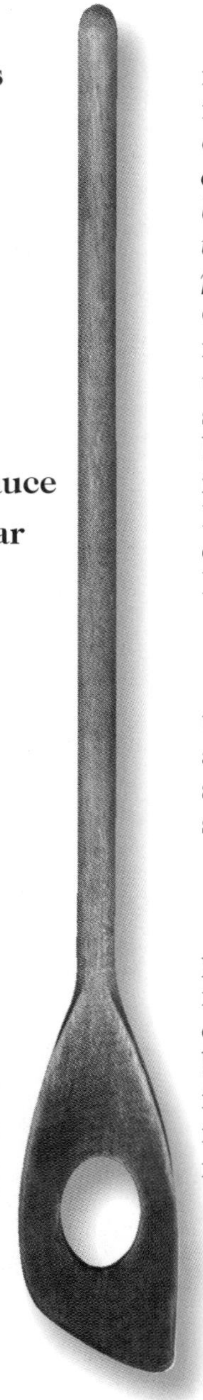

Prepare the grill as you would normally, using a mixture of good-quality charcoal and mesquite, apple, or other hardwood chips. *(Let the chips soak in water about 2 hours before using; add a few at a time to the charcoal during the cooking period.)* Prepare ribs by trimming off excess fat and removing the membrane that runs the length of the bone side of the rack. Lower ribs slowly into the boiling water and boil for 5 minutes to remove extra fat and reduce the barbecuing time. Drain. When cool enough to handle, rub both sides of ribs with Barbecue Rub.

In a large saucepan combine all of the sauce ingredients and bring to a boil, stirring. Reduce heat and simmer, uncovered, for 30 minutes, stirring occasionally. Set aside.

Place a pan of hot water next to the prepared hot coals, to make the ribs more tender. Grill the ribs slowly, covered, for 1 hour. Brush with barbecue sauce, and continue cooking about 30 minutes longer, turning occasionally and basting with more sauce.

Aunt Susie's BBQ Brisket Poor Boys

SERVES 6 TO 8

Traditionally, the brisket is served on hamburger buns, but it can be eaten as is, wrapped in flour tortillas, or ladled open-face onto cornbread.

INGREDIENTS

5 pounds	**first-cut beef brisket**
$^1/_2$ cup	**Barbecue Rub –** ***recipe follows***
3 cups	**Barbecue Mop –** ***recipe follows***
6 to 8	**hamburger buns**

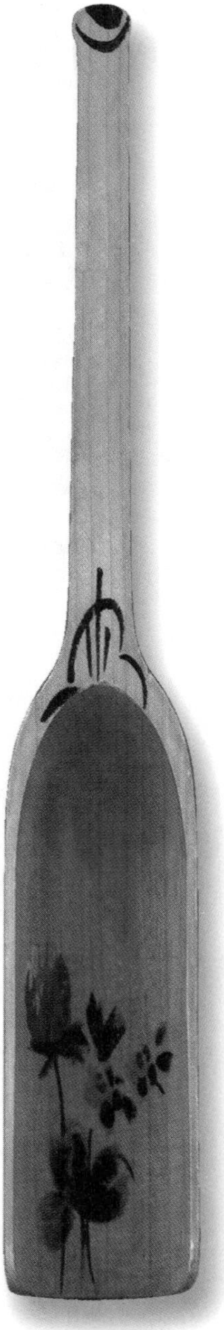

The day before serving, rub both sides of the brisket with Barbecue Rub. Wrap tightly in plastic, and refrigerate overnight.

About four hours before serving, preheat oven to 250 degrees.

Place the brisket in a large oven-proof pan, and pour the Barbecue Mop over the meat. Cover with foil and cook for 2 to $2^1/_2$ hours, or until tender. Remove from the oven and cool slightly. Place on a cutting board and slice about $^1/_4$-inch thick. Re-form the sliced brisket back into the cooking pan. Spoon the pan's sauce over the top. Cover and cook 1 hour longer, basting occasionally with the sauce. Serve the sliced brisket in its sauce on hamburger buns.

Barbecue Rub

This spice mixture is also good for pork, lamb, or chicken.

INGREDIENTS

3 tablespoons	**dark brown sugar**
2 tablespoons	**paprika**
2 teaspoons each:	**dry mustard, onion powder, and garlic powder**
1 teaspoon each:	**oregano, basil, ground bay leaves, and salt**
$^3/_4$ teaspoon each:	**thyme, ground coriander, ground cumin, white pepper, and freshly ground pepper**

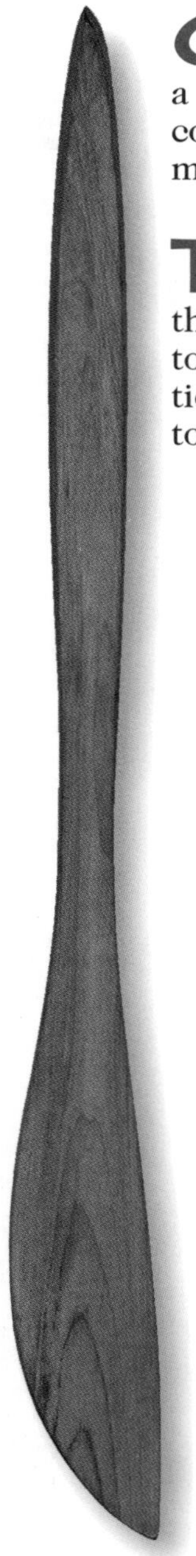

Combine all of the ingredients in a small bowl. Store in an airtight container. The mixture will keep for months.

To use the Rub, massage into meat thoroughly the day before you plan to cook it. Cover tightly with plastic wrap and refrigerate until ready to cook.

Barbecue Mop

MAKES ABOUT 5 CUPS

A savory barbecue sauce for any kind of meat.

INGREDIENTS

3 cans (14.5 ounce)	**beef broth**
3	**bay leaves**
1 teaspoon	**oregano**
2 tablespoons	**unsalted butter**
1/2 cup	**onions – diced**
1/4 cup	**celery – diced**
8	**cloves of garlic – minced**
3 tablespoons	**Barbecue Rub *(see previous page)***
1/4 teaspoon	**cayenne pepper**
1 pound	**bacon**
2	**lemons – zest finely grated, and juiced**
3 tablespoons	**soy sauce**
3 tablespoons	**vinegar**
2 tablespoons	**olive oil**
2 tablespoons	**toasted sesame oil**
3 tablespoons	**bourbon (optional)**

Bring the broth, bay leaves, and oregano to a boil in a large kettle. Reduce heat to a simmer. Melt butter in a skillet, and add the onions, celery, garlic, Barbecue Rub, and cayenne. Cook until browned, about 7 minutes. In another pan, fry the bacon, in batches, until crisp. Drain and crumble. Add to the simmering broth, along with the cooked onion mixture, the lemon zest and juice, soy sauce, vinegar, olive and sesame oils, and bourbon, if using. Mix well. Simmer until the sauce is reduced by a quarter, about an hour.

Maria's Grilled Chicken

SERVES 6 TO 8

Spicy and low in fat, the marinade is also great for steak or chops. The chicken can be marinated up to a day in advance.

INGREDIENTS

<u>Marinade:</u>

1/2 cup	**white wine, *or* lowfat chicken broth**
1/2 cup	**orange juice**
3	**cloves of garlic – minced**
2	**shallots – chopped (optional)**
1/4 cup	**cilantro leaves – chopped**
1 or 2 whole	**chipotle chiles – mashed and minced ***
6 to 8	**chicken breast halves, boneless and skinless**

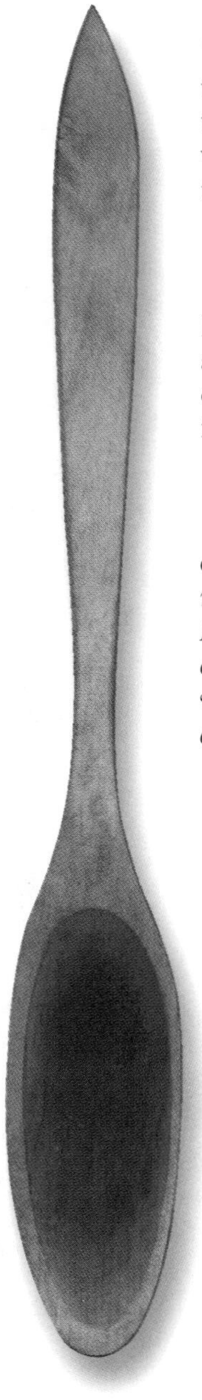

Combine all of the ingredients for the marinade in a large bowl. Add the chicken breasts, coating them well, and marinate in the refrigerator for several hours or overnight.

Preheat a gas or charcoal grill. Remove chicken from the marinade, and grill for about 5 minutes on each side, basting with the remaining marinade. Serve immediately.

**Spicy, smoky-tasting chipotle chiles can be found in most supermarkets, either dried or canned. For this recipe, canned chipotles are preferable. Leftover chipotles will keep for weeks in the refrigerator, covered tightly.*

Rodeo Coleslaw

SERVES 6 TO 8

Perfect for a hot summer day, this coleslaw contains no mayonnaise. It is best when made a day ahead, so the flavors will meld.

INGREDIENTS

Dressing:

1/2 cup	**olive oil**
1/2 cup	**apple cider vinegar**
1/2 cup	**sugar**
1 tablespoon	**celery seeds**
1 teaspoon	**ground cumin**
1 small	**white cabbage – shredded**
1 small	**red cabbage – shredded**
2 large	**carrots – peeled and shredded**
1 medium	**green bell pepper – seeded and chopped**
1 medium	**red bell pepper – seeded and chopped**
1 small	**onion – chopped (optional)**

Salt and freshly ground pepper, to taste

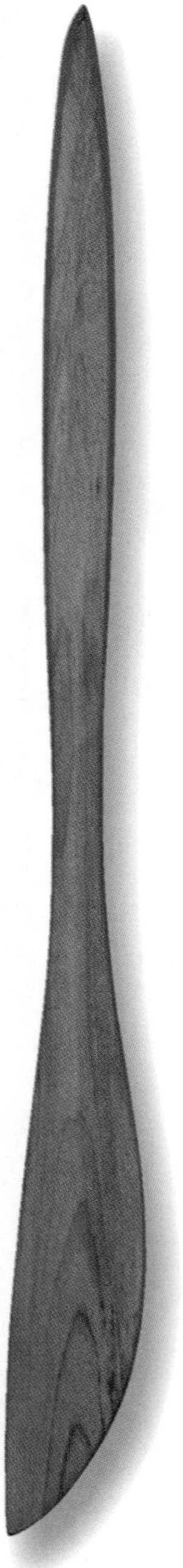

Put all of the dressing ingredients into a small saucepan. Heat until boiling, stirring until the sugar is dissolved. Remove from heat, and set aside.

Combine the shredded cabbages and other vegetables in a large serving bowl. Add the warm dressing and mix well. Season with salt and pepper. Chill for at least 2 hours or overnight. Toss again before serving.

Corn and Bean Salad

SERVES 6 TO 8

This delicious picnic salad may be assembled well ahead of time.

INGREDIENTS

2 cans (15 ounce)	**black beans – drained and rinsed**
1 can (15 ounce)	**corn kernels – drained**
1 medium	**red onion – chopped**
$^1/_4$ cup	**cilantro leaves – chopped**

Dressing:

3 tablespoons	**olive or vegetable oil**
1	**lime – juiced**
1 teaspoon	**ground cumin**
1	**jalapeño pepper – seeded and minced**

Salt and freshly ground pepper, to taste

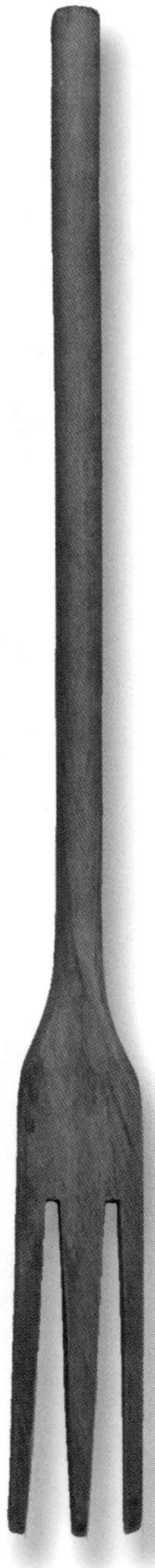

Mix the beans, corn, onion, and cilantro in a salad bowl. Add the oil, lime juice, cumin, and jalapeño. Toss well. Season with salt and pepper, and serve. *(If making ahead of time, cover and refrigerate. Allow salad to return to room temperature before serving.)*

Thanks for the wonderful meals. Since I'm not able to cook, I really appreciate the meals you provide. I look forward to them every day....they keep me alive.

R.M.

Petey's Broiled Curried Beefsteak Tomato Slices

SERVES 6 TO 8

This is an easy, flavorful way to showcase fresh-from-the-garden tomatoes.

INGREDIENTS

4 to 6	ripe beefsteak tomatoes – thickly sliced
$1^1/_2$ cups	mayonnaise or light mayonnaise
2 teaspoons	curry powder
$^1/_2$ teaspoon	white pepper
2 tablespoons	fresh parsley leaves – chopped

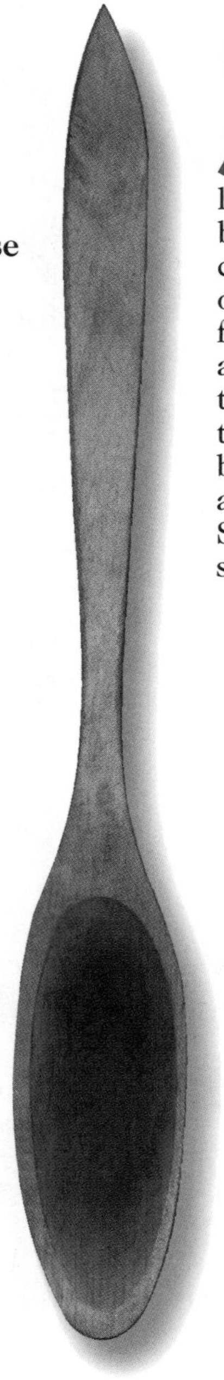

Preheat broiler.

Arrange tomato slices on a lightly-oiled baking sheet. In a small bowl, combine the mayonnaise, curry powder, and pepper. Spread onto the tops of the tomato slices, fairly thickly and evenly. Broil for approximately 4 minutes, until the tomatoes are heated through and the tops are golden brown and bubbly. Remove from the oven and arrange on a serving platter. Sprinkle with chopped parsley, and serve immediately.

Best Brownies

MAKES 24

These rich brownies need no high-altitude adjustment.

INGREDIENTS

1 cup	**butter – melted**
$1\frac{3}{4}$ cups	**sugar**
$\frac{3}{4}$ cup	**cocoa powder**
$1\frac{1}{2}$ teaspoons	**vanilla extract**
3	**eggs**
1 cup	**flour**
$\frac{1}{2}$ to $\frac{3}{4}$ cups	**pecans or walnuts – chopped (optional)**

Frostinġ:

$\frac{1}{2}$ cup	**cocoa powder**
3 tablespoons	**butter – at room temperature**
2 cups	**powdered sugar**
2 to 3 tablespoons	**milk**
1 teaspoon	**vanilla extract**

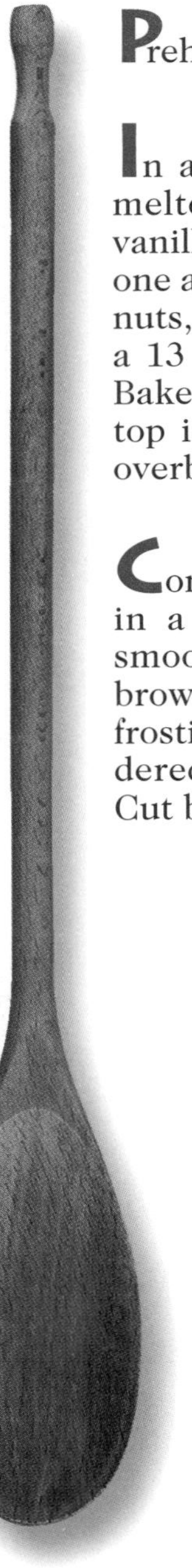

Preheat oven to 350 degrees.

In a medium bowl, combine the melted butter, sugar, cocoa, and vanilla. Mix well. Beat in the eggs, one at a time. Stir in the flour, and nuts, if using. Pour the batter into a 13 x 9 x 2-inch ungreased pan. Bake for 30 minutes or until the top is set and looks dry. Do not overbake. Let the brownies cool.

Combine the frosting ingredients in a small bowl, and mix until smooth. Spread evenly over the brownies. Alternatively, omit the frosting and sprinkle $\frac{1}{2}$ cup powdered sugar evenly over the top. Cut brownies into squares.

Butterscotch Brownies

MAKES 12

Although chocoholics will not be interested, these butterscotch brownies are sinfully delicious.

INGREDIENTS

$^1/_4$ cup	**butter – melted**
1 cup	**brown sugar ***
1	**egg – beaten**
$^1/_2$ cup	**flour ***
1 teaspoon	**baking powder ***
$^1/_2$ teaspoon	**salt**
$^1/_2$ cup	**pecans, almonds, or walnuts – chopped**
1 teaspoon	**vanilla extract**
$^1/_4$ cup	**powdered sugar**

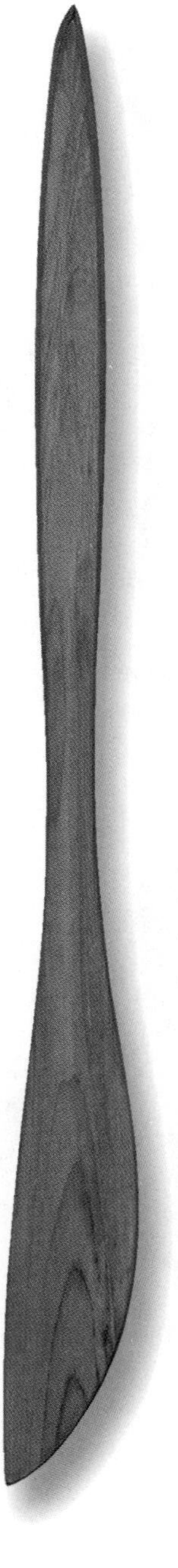

Preheat oven to 350 degrees. Lightly grease a 13 x 9 x 2-inch baking dish.

In a medium bowl, combine the melted butter and brown sugar. Cool for at least 10 minutes, then stir in the beaten egg. In a small bowl, sift together the flour, baking powder, and salt. Add to the egg mixture, and mix well. Stir in the vanilla extract and nuts. Pour the batter into the prepared baking dish, and bake for 20 to 25 minutes. Remove from the oven and sift powdered sugar over the top. Cut into squares.

**For 7000 feet and above, decrease the baking powder by $^1/_4$ teaspoon, decrease sugar by 3 tablespoons, increase flour by 1 tablespoon, and increase baking temperature by 25 degrees.*

Old Fashioned Lemonade

MAKES 1 QUART

The secret to making the best lemonade is to extract the aromatic oils from the rinds. Freeze an extra batch in ice cube trays, and defrost as needed.

INGREDIENTS

4	**lemons**
1 cup	**sugar**
1 quart	**boiling water**

It is so wonderful to know that there are still people in this world who care enough to give freely of their time and talents. *B.W.*

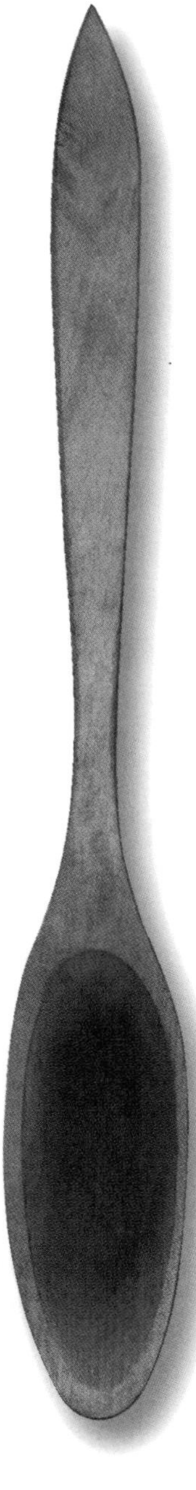

Roll lemons with your palm on a hard surface to soften, then peel. Put the rinds in a large bowl and cover them with sugar. Let stand for 30 minutes, to allow the sugar to absorb the lemon oils. Meanwhile, squeeze the peeled lemons, removing the seeds but keeping the pulp; set aside.

After 30 minutes, pour the boiling water over the sugar and lemon rinds. Steep until the water is cool, then discard the rinds. Add the reserved lemon juice and stir well. Pour into a pitcher and refrigerate until cold.

PHOTO BY MARK NOHL

OPERA TAILGATE PICNIC

SPONSORED BY:
THE SANTA FE OPERA

Opera Tailgate Picnic

Travelers arrive from around the globe to enjoy the myriad performing arts that flourish in our City Different throughout the year. During summer, however, there are performances to choose from virtually every night, and for every cultural taste: the Santa Fe Chamber Music Festival, the Desert Chorale, Santa Fe Stages, the Maria Benitez Teatro Flamenco, Shakespeare in Santa Fe, the Santa Fe Playhouse, Santa Fe Performing Arts Company, Santa Fe Festival Ballet, Santa Fe Symphony, the Santa Fe Opera, and contemporary music concerts at the Paolo Soleri amphitheater at the Indian School.

Any event becomes more festive with the addition of a thoughtful meal, before or after. Gathering with friends to enjoy a tailgate picnic before the Opera, however, has become a Santa Fe tradition. Although it may not seem an elegant place to dine, the Opera parking lot becomes a popular eating spot an hour or so before curtain time. Some groups snack out of the backs of their cars, but many people set up chairs and tables adorned with tablecloths, crystal, china, and vases of flowers.

You cannot get a better view in all of Santa Fe, and this is a terrific place to catch the sunset as you dine. The soft, velvety green Sangre de Cristo Mountains are to the east and the setting sun casts a golden red upon them, giving them their name: the Blood of Christ. Across the valley to the west, with the sun already behind them, the Jemez Mountains turn a shadowy blue. Above, the dancing clouds are tinged with pink and purple and orange.

Study the clouds through the bubbles in your glass of champagne, and hum *Libiam!*, for soon the music will soar. Oh, the glory of art! For now though, the air is soft, and our dinner is lovely. It serves six to eight.

Menu

Chilled Cucumber Soup

Baba the Turk's Ganoush

Picnic Salmon Loaf

Chinese Chicken Salad

Zozobouli

Lemon Bars

Iced Tea

Champagne

Chilled Cucumber Soup

SERVES 6 TO 8

This recipe earned its Kitchen Angel donor first prize at a contest given by a top restaurant on Captiva Island, Florida. It can be made a day ahead and chilled.

INGREDIENTS

2 tablespoons	**butter**
1 cup	**onions – chopped**
4 cups	**cucumber – peeled, seeded, and chopped**
2 tablespoons	**flour (optional)**
6 cups	**lowfat chicken broth**

Salt and white pepper, to taste

1/4 cup	**fresh chopped dill weed or mint (garnish)**

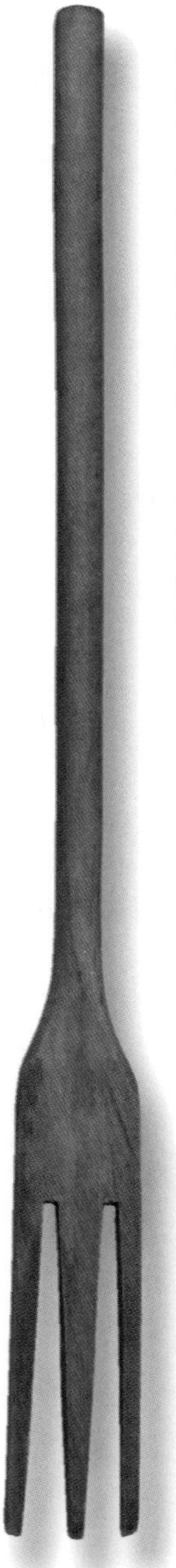

Melt butter in a large saucepan, and sauté the onions and cucumbers until tender. Add the flour, if using, and cook long enough to make a roux, stirring constantly. Gradually add the broth, stirring. Cover and simmer for 10 minutes. Season with salt and white pepper. Pour into a blender or food processor, and purée.

Chill thoroughly for at least 4 hours. At serving time, ladle the soup into mugs or bowls. Garnish with chopped dill or mint.

Baba the Turk's Ganoush

SERVES 6 TO 8

In Stravinsky's *The Rake's Progress*, Baba the Turk is the infamous bearded lady who is married briefly and disastrously to Tom Rakewell. She is known for throwing things, and this recipe can be thrown together more quickly than traditional *baba ganoush*, because the eggplant is roasted over the stove top rather than baked.

INGREDIENTS

1 large	**eggplant**
1/2 cup	**sesame tahini**
1	**lemon – juiced**
3	**scallions – coarsely chopped, including green parts**
3 or 4	**cloves of garlic – coarsely chopped**
1/4 cup	**fresh parsley leaves**
1/4 cup	**fresh cilantro leaves (optional)**

Pita bread, crackers, or assorted raw vegetables

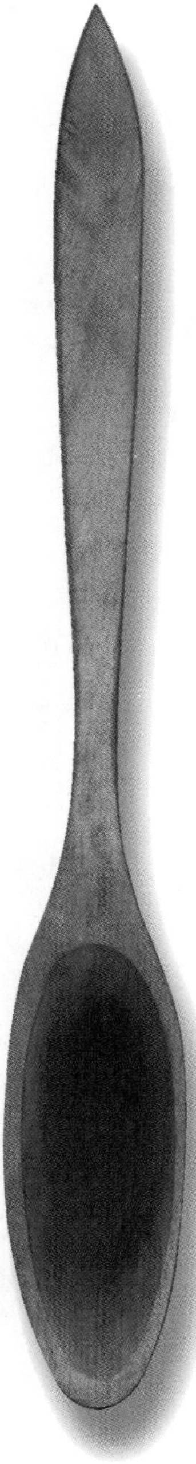

Roast the unpeeled eggplant on top of a gas or electric burner, turning often with tongs, until the skin is completely blackened and the eggplant has collapsed. Plunge into cold water, then peel. Rinse again, and put the eggplant and remaining ingredients in a food processor. Purée until smooth. Use as a delicious dip for *crudités* or serve with wedges of pita bread, pita chips, or sesame crackers.

In addition to bringing delicious food to the door – warm and ready to eat – Kitchen Angels makes a shut-in feel cared for and wanted in the community. I feel this organization is outstanding in its ability to provide an exceptional service to the community. S.D.

Picnic Salmon Loaf

SERVES 6 TO 8

This hors d'oeuvre may be made a day or two ahead and is great for a cocktail party.

INGREDIENTS

1 can (14.75 ounce)	red salmon, drained – skin and bones removed
1 package (8 ounce)	cream cheese – at room temperature
1 tablespoon	lemon juice
2 teaspoons	onion – grated
1 teaspoon	white horseradish

Salt and freshly ground pepper, to taste

1/2 cup	pecans – coarsely chopped
3 tablespoons	fresh parsley leaves – minced

Stoned wheat crackers

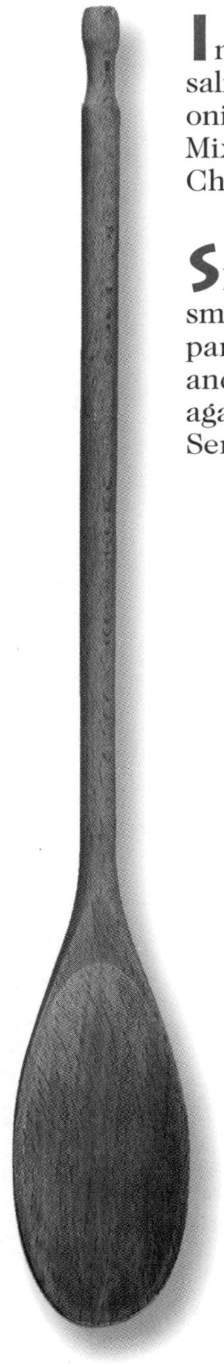

In a mixing bowl, combine the salmon, cream cheese, lemon juice, onion, horseradish, salt, and pepper. Mix well by mashing with a fork. Chill, covered, for several hours.

Shape the salmon mixture into a small loaf. Combine the pecans and parsley on a sheet of waxed paper, and roll loaf in this mixture. Chill again, wrapped tightly in plastic. Serve with stoned wheat crackers.

Chinese Chicken Salad

SERVES 6 TO 8

This salad also makes an excellent sandwich filling for pita bread.

INGREDIENTS

6 cups	water
4 to 6	chicken breast halves
5 slices	fresh ginger root
5 whole	scallions
2 or 3 large	European hothouse cucumbers – peeled and julienned *
1/2 cup	scallions – chopped
3 or 4 tablespoons	sesame seeds – toasted (garnish)

<u>Dressing:</u>

2 tablespoons	soy sauce
2 tablespoons	Japanese rice vinegar
2 tablespoons	toasted sesame oil
1 tablespoon	sugar
2 teaspoons	sake or dry sherry
1/2 teaspoon	salt
2 to 4 drops	hot pepper sauce

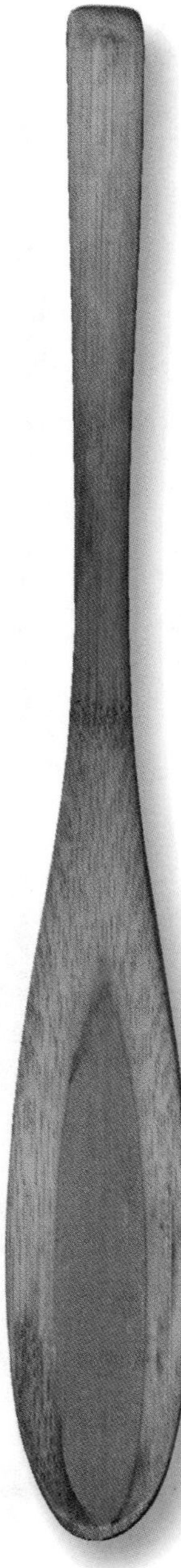

Bring water to a boil in a large pot. Add the chicken, ginger slices, and whole scallions, and return to a boil. Lower heat and simmer for 15 minutes. Remove pot from heat and let the chicken sit, uncovered, for 20 minutes. When cool enough to handle, remove skin and bones, and cut the chicken into julienne strips. Add the cucumber and chopped scallions and toss well.

Combine the dressing ingredients in a jar and shake to mix. Pour over the salad and toss well. Garnish with toasted sesame seeds.

**Can substitute 3 or 4 regular cucumbers, peeled, seeded, and julienned.*

Zozobouli

SERVES 6 TO 8

Make this salad at least two hours ahead so the flavors will harmonize.

INGREDIENTS

3 cups	cooked pearl barley *(al dente)*
1/2 cup	cilantro leaves – chopped
1/2 cup	parsley leaves – chopped
2 or 3 large	ripe tomatoes – seeded and chopped
8	cloves of garlic – minced
1	carrot – grated
2 tablespoons	uncooked quinoa
1 tablespoon	black sesame seeds

Dressing:

3 or 4	lemons – juiced *
1/4 cup	olive oil
1/2 teaspoon	salt
Freshly ground black pepper, to taste	
3 tablespoons	balsamic vinegar
2 tablespoons	Dijon mustard

Garnish:

1	lemon – thinly sliced
1/2 cup	parsley sprigs

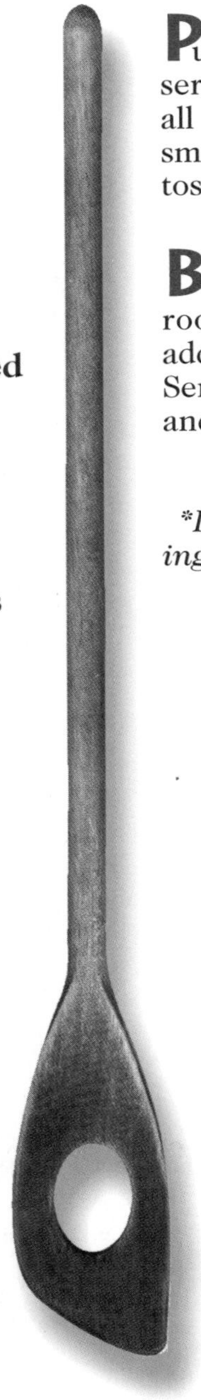

Put the salad ingredients into a serving bowl and mix well. Whisk all of the dressing ingredients in a small bowl. Pour over the salad and toss well. Refrigerate for 2 hours.

Before serving, bring the salad to room temperature. Toss again, adding more olive oil, if necessary. Serve garnished with lemon slices and parsley.

**Depends upon how tart a dressing you like.*

Lemon Bars

MAKES 24 BARS

These delicate treats need no adjustment for high altitude.

INGREDIENTS

1 cup	**butter – at room temperature**
1 cup	**powdered sugar – sifted**
2 cups	**flour**
4	**eggs**
2 cups	**sugar**
3 tablespoons	**flour**
6 tablespoons	**fresh lemon juice**
1 or 2 tablespoons	**grated lemon zest**

Icing:

1 cup	**powdered sugar**
1 to 3 tablespoons	**fresh lemon juice**

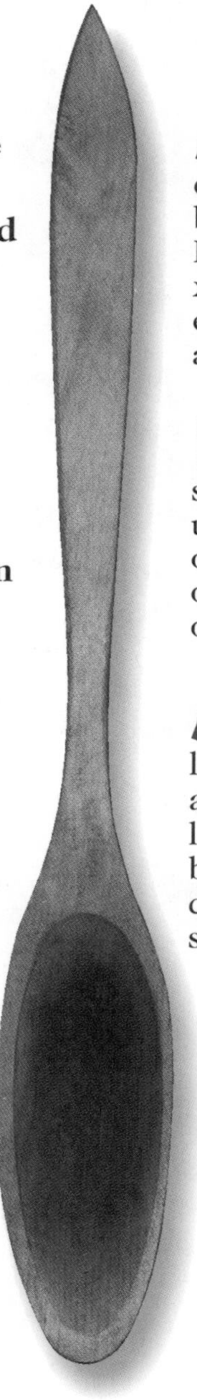

Preheat oven to 350 degrees.

Mix together the butter, powdered sugar, and flour in a medium bowl, as if you are making pie crust. Pat the dough into an ungreased 13 x 9 x 2-inch pan, and make "pizza-edges." Bake for 20 to 25 minutes and cool slightly. Leave the oven on.

In a medium bowl, mix the eggs, sugar, flour, lemon juice, and zest until well blended. Pour evenly over the baked crust. Return to the oven, and bake for 20 minutes more, or until set.

Mix the powdered sugar and lemon juice to a thin consistency and spread evenly over the top of the lemon bars. Alternatively, sprinkle bars lightly with $1/4$ cup sifted powdered sugar. Cool and cut into squares.

Photo by Gene Peach

Buffet after Spanish Market

Special Thanks to:
Kaune's Food Town

Buffet after Spanish Market

On the last weekend of July, New Mexico's rich Hispanic culture – past and present – is celebrated at a community festival on the Plaza. Brimming with art, music, dance, pageantry, and food, the Traditional Spanish Market is the oldest and largest exhibition of Spanish colonial art in the United States. Over 300 Hispanic artisans from all over New Mexico exhibit and sell their artwork at this event, which is popular with locals and tourists alike.

Spanish Market abounds with furniture, tinware, ironwork, hand-woven textiles, jewelry, pottery, and many other crafts, ranging in style from traditional to contemporary. While strolling around and munching a burrito, one can find everything from *santos* – depictions of religious figures in the form of *bultos*, or carvings in the round – to embroidery employing the *colcha* stitch, unique to this region. There are also tools carved from bone, paper garlands known as *ramilletes*, straw appliqué, and *reatas*, which are braided rawhide lariats

Spanish Market is a visual feast, and so is our buffet dinner to celebrate the occasion. Each recipe for this menu serves twelve, but the smaller portions people take to sample the variety at a buffet will make them go much farther. There should be plenty of food for a good-sized crowd.

Menu

Pico de Gallo with Corn Chips

Sun-dried Tomato and Chile Spread with Crackers

Chile Relleno Casserole

Sliced Chicken with Lime and Basil

Black Bean Torta

Confetti Salad with Champagne Vinaigrette

Tossed Green Salad with Creamy Lime Dressing

Picnic Cornbread

Fresh Fruit with Orange-Rum Sauce

Biscochitos

Sangria Blanca

Pico de Gallo

MAKES 2 CUPS

A spicy *salsa fresca*, it is delicious with corn chips or as an accompaniment to grilled chicken or fish. It is also spectacular in the Black Bean Torta *(page 84)*.

INGREDIENTS

3 medium	**ripe tomatoes – finely chopped**
2 medium	**yellow onions – finely chopped**
1 to 3	**Serrano chiles – seeded and minced ***
1	**Anaheim chile – seeded and minced**
$^1/_2$ cup	**cilantro leaves – coarsely chopped**
1 teaspoon	**sugar**
1 tablespoon	**fresh lime juice**

Salt and freshly ground pepper, to taste

Corn chips or flour tortillas

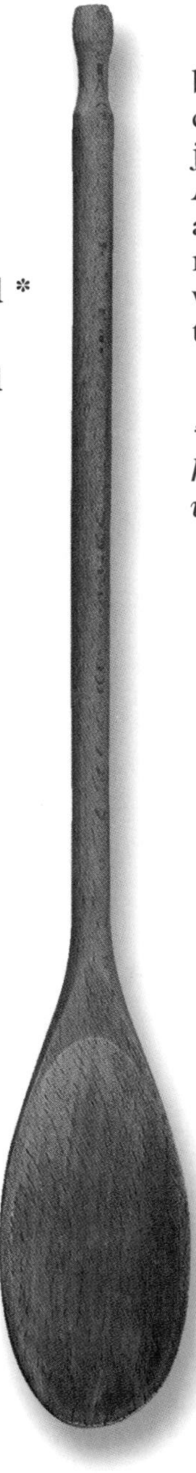

In a medium-sized non-reactive-bowl, mix the tomatoes, onions, chiles, cilantro, sugar, and lime juice. Season with salt and pepper. Allow the flavors to blend for at least an hour before serving with blue, red, or yellow corn chips. The salsa will keep, refrigerated, for up to two weeks.

**Salsa will be mild, medium, or hot depending on number of chiles used.*

Sun-dried Tomato and Chile Spread

MAKES 2 CUPS

This savory spread is great on crackers, as a topping for crostini, and as a chutney for grilled chicken, fish, or steak.

INGREDIENTS

6 large	**dried Ancho chiles**
6 to 8	**sun-dried tomatoes**
3 cups	**boiling water**
1 small	**red onion – coarsely chopped**
5	**cloves of garlic – peeled**
1 bunch	**fresh cilantro – leaves only**
1	**lemon – juiced**
1 can (8 ounce)	**tomato sauce**
$^1/_2$ teaspoon	**salt**

Water biscuits or other crackers

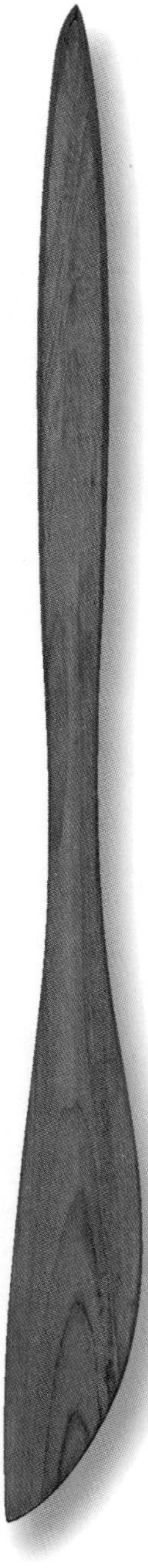

Remove the stems and seeds of the Ancho chiles, reserving seeds from two of the chiles. Put the chiles and sun-dried tomatoes in a medium bowl. Pour boiling water over them and allow to soften for 20 minutes.

Transfer the softened chiles and tomatoes, reserving the water, to a food processor or blender. Add the onion, garlic, cilantro, lemon juice, tomato sauce, salt, reserved chile seeds to taste (two pinches for a medium-hot sauce), and $^1/_4$ cup of the reserved chile water. Process into a thick paste. Add more chile seeds for a hotter sauce, or additional chile water to thin the paste, if necessary. Chill until ready to use. Bring spread to room temperature before serving with crackers.

Chile Relleno Casserole

SERVES 12

This casserole should be assembled a day ahead. It also makes an excellent brunch dish.

INGREDIENTS

1 baguette	**French bread, ends removed**
4 tablespoons	**butter – at room temperature**
4 cups (16 ounces)	**Monterey Jack cheese – shredded**
2 or 3 cans (4 ounce)	**diced green chiles, drained ***
12	**eggs**
3 cups	**milk**
1 teaspoon	**salt**
3 teaspoons	**paprika**
$1^1/_2$ to 2 teaspoons	**oregano**
$^1/_2$ to 1 teaspoon	**black pepper**
$^1/_2$ teaspoon	**garlic powder**
$^1/_2$ teaspoon	**dry mustard**

Cut the bread into $^3/_4$-inch slices and butter one side of each slice. Arrange bread, buttered side down, in a large baking dish. Sprinkle with cheese and top with the diced chiles.

In a medium bowl, whisk the eggs until frothy. Add the remaining ingredients and mix well. Pour evenly over the top of the casserole. Cover and refrigerate overnight.

Preheat oven to 375 degrees. Bake the casserole, uncovered, for 50 minutes, or until golden and bubbly. Serve immediately.

**For a spicier casserole, substitute one can (4 ounce) diced jalapeños.*

Sliced Chicken with Lime and Basil

SERVES 12

A terrific dish for a picnic. It must be made a day ahead, and its success depends upon fresh lime juice and fresh basil.

INGREDIENTS

1 medium	**onion**
8 to 10	**whole cloves**
3 quarts	**water**
8 large	**chicken breast halves**

Marinade:

2 cups	**fresh lime juice (about 16 limes)**
1/2 cup	**fresh basil leaves – chopped**
2 tablespoons	**fresh tarragon, or 1 teaspoon dried**
7 to 10	**cloves of garlic – minced**
4 large	**shallots – minced**
2 1/2 cups	**olive oil**
1 tablespoon	**sugar**
1/2 teaspoon	**salt**

Freshly ground pepper, to taste

Garnish:

6	**ripe tomatoes – cut into wedges**
1/4 cup	**fresh basil leaves**

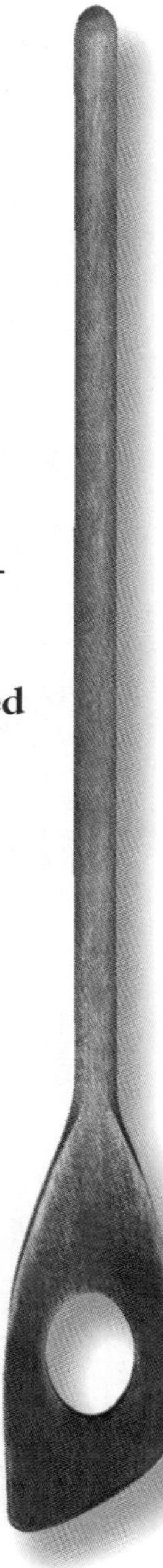

Stud the onion with cloves, and add to water in a large pot. Bring to a boil and carefully add the chicken breasts. Lower heat and simmer for 15 minutes. Remove from the stove and let the chicken cool in the cooking liquid for half an hour. Drain the cooled chicken, reserving the broth for another use. Remove skin and bones, and slice the chicken into strips about 1/2 -inch wide. Place in a large bowl.

Put all of the marinade ingredients in a medium bowl and whisk until well blended. Pour over the chicken and toss well. Cover and refrigerate for 24 hours.

At serving time, drain the chicken and arrange on a platter. Surround with tomato wedges and garnish the top with basil leaves.

Black Bean Torta

SERVES 6 TO 8

For a vegetarian entrée, substitute vegetable broth and omit the pork. This recipe doubles easily for a crowd.

INGREDIENTS

3 cups	**cooked black beans, or canned beans, drained**
$1/4$ cup	**chicken or vegetable broth**
1 tablespoon	**corn oil**
2 or 3 medium	**red onions – finely chopped**
2 medium	**red bell peppers – seeded and julienned**
2 medium	**zucchini – halved lengthwise and thinly sliced**
2	**cloves of garlic – minced**
1 cup	**yellow corn kernels (fresh, frozen, or canned)**
1 teaspoon	**ground cumin**
$1/4$ teaspoon	**cayenne pepper**
Salt, to taste	
12	**corn tortillas**
3 cups	**shredded roasted pork (optional)**
2 cups	**tomato salsa, or *salsa fresca* (page 80)**
2 cups (8 ounces)	**Asadero or Monterey Jack cheese – shredded**
1 bunch	**fresh cilantro leaves – chopped (garnish)**

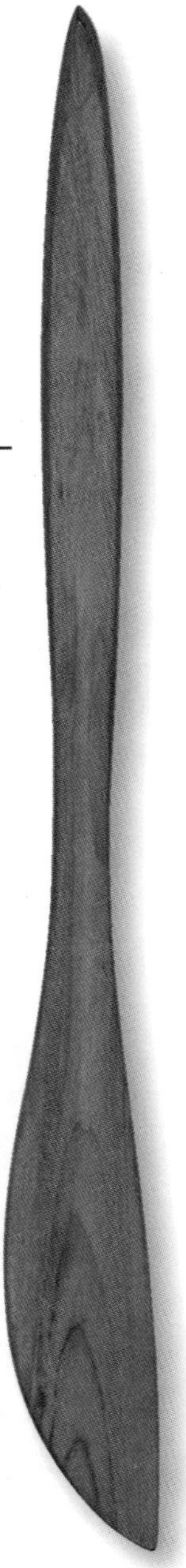

Preheat oven to 375 degrees. Lightly oil the bottom of a 6 x 12 x 3-inch baking dish.

Purée the black beans and broth in a food processor. Set aside. In a large skillet, heat the oil over medium heat. Sauté the onion, peppers, zucchini, and garlic, stirring until soft, about 10 minutes. Add the corn, cumin, cayenne, and salt. Cook for another 3 minutes.

Cut the tortillas to fit the bottom of the prepared baking dish, using 2 tortillas as a first layer. Spread with $1/2$ cup of the bean purée, then sprinkle with $1/2$ cup of the shredded pork, 1 cup of the vegetables, $1/3$ cup salsa, and $1/3$ cup of the shredded cheese. Repeat the layering until 6 layers deep, ending with the cheese. Bake for 45 minutes, until hot and bubbly. Let stand for 5 minutes before serving. Garnish with chopped cilantro, if desired.

Confetti Salad with Champagne Vinaigrette

SERVES 12

An excellent choice for a picnic, this colorful salad will not wilt.

INGREDIENTS

2 heads	**cauliflower – florets and stems finely diced**
2	**green bell peppers – seeded and diced**
2 bunches	**scallions – diced**
1 jar (6 ounce)	**pimientos – drained and diced**
1 can (6 ounce)	**pitted black olives – drained and diced**

<u>Champagne Vinaigrette:</u>

1 or 2	**cloves of garlic – minced**
1/2 cup	**champagne vinegar**
1 1/2 teaspoons	**Dijon mustard**
1 cup	**olive oil**
1/2 teaspoon	**salt**
1/4 teaspoon	**freshly ground black pepper**

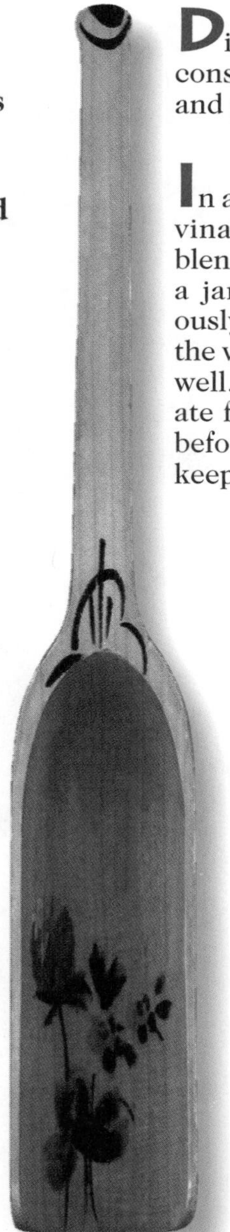

Dice all of the salad vegetables consistently, to resemble confetti, and place in a serving bowl.

In a small bowl, whisk together the vinaigrette ingredients until well blended, or place the ingredients in a jar and cover and shake vigorously. Pour enough dressing over the vegetables to coat them and toss well. Cover the salad and refrigerate for up to 24 hours. Toss again before serving. Leftover dressing keeps well in the refrigerator.

Tossed Green Salad with Creamy Lime Dressing

SERVES 12

The dressing can be made ahead; it keeps for a week in the refrigerator.

INGREDIENTS

2 heads	romaine lettuce
1 head	red-tipped lettuce
1 bunch	arugula

Creamy Lime Dressing:

1/2 cup	fresh lime juice (about 4 limes)
1/2 cup	mayonnaise
1/2 cup	sour cream
1 or 2	cloves of garlic – crushed
1 teaspoon	salt
1/2 to 1 teaspoon	ground cinnamon
1/2 teaspoon	oregano

Freshly ground black pepper, to taste

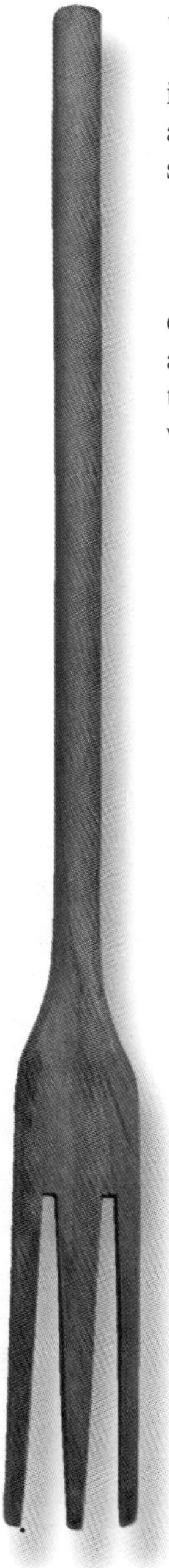

Wash and dry the greens and tear into bite-sized pieces, discarding any tough stalks. Place in a large salad bowl.

In a medium bowl, mix all of the dressing ingredients together, using a wire whisk. Pour dressing, to taste, onto the salad greens and toss well. Serve immediately.

Picnic Cornbread

SERVES 12 TO 16

This cornbread is moist and crunchy. Baking a day ahead is not recommended, as it will dry out.

INGREDIENTS

1 jar (16 ounce)	**roasted sweet red peppers**
2 tablespoons	**fresh lemon juice**
2 small	**red bell peppers – seeded and finely diced**
1 cup	**buttermilk**
$1/4$ cup	**corn oil**
2 medium	**eggs**
1 can (4 ounce)	**diced mild or hot green chiles, to taste**
3 teaspoons	**ground cumin**
$1/2$ cup	**unbleached white flour**
$2\,1/2$ cups	**stone ground yellow cornmeal**
1 teaspoon	**baking soda**
1 teaspoon	**baking powder**
$1\,1/2$ cups (6 ounces)	**sharp Cheddar cheese – shredded**

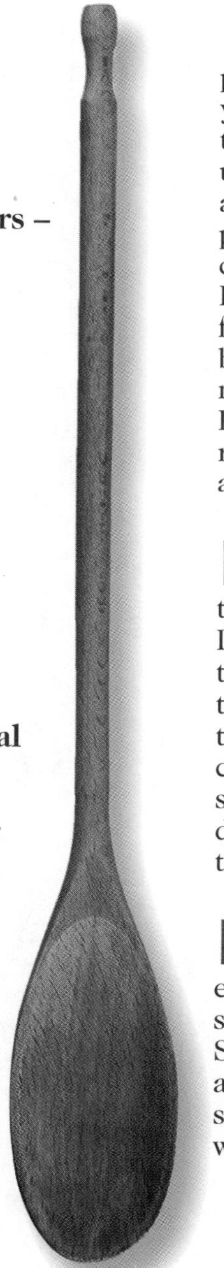

Place two 9-inch skillets in the oven and preheat to 425 degrees.

In a blender or food processor, purée enough roasted peppers to yield 1 cup, about half a jar. Save the remaining peppers for another use. Put purée in a large bowl and add the lemon juice, diced red peppers, buttermilk, corn oil, eggs, chiles, and cumin. Mix thoroughly. In another bowl, mix together the flour, cornmeal, baking soda, and baking powder. Add to the liquid mixture, beating until well blended. Pour approximately a third of the resulting batter into the second bowl and mix in the cheese.

Remove the heated skillets from the oven and lightly oil each. Distribute the cheese batter between the two, spreading evenly across the bottom. Divide remaining batter between the pans, spreading carefully over the cheese batter, and smoothing the top. Tap each pan down on a hard surface, and return to the oven.

Bake until the cornbread is golden and has pulled away from the sides of the pans, about 25 minutes. Slip each cornbread out of its pan and cool to room temperature. At serving time, cut into pie-shaped wedges.

Fresh Fruit with Orange-Rum Sauce

SERVES 12

A refreshing summer dessert. In winter, substitute canned Freestone peaches and canned apricot halves.

INGREDIENTS

4 to 6 large	**firm ripe peaches – peeled, pitted, and sliced**
12 to 16	**ripe apricots – pitted and cut into quarters**
2 cups	**seedless green grapes**
1 cup	**sugar**
1 cup	**water**
2 teaspoons	**grated orange zest**
$^{1}/_{4}$ teaspoon	**nutmeg**
1 to 2 tablespoons	**dark rum**

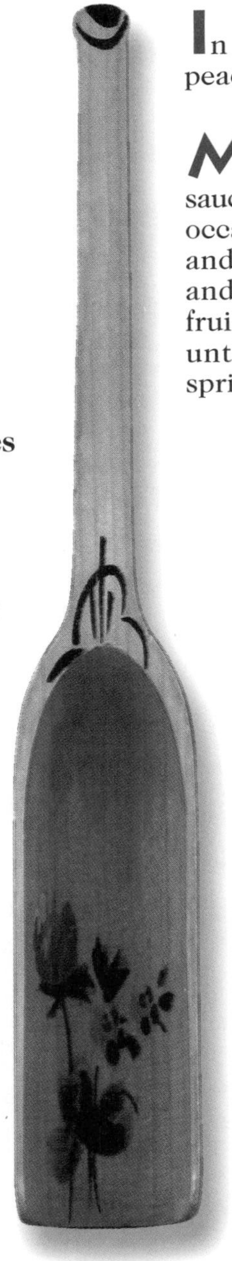

In a serving bowl, combine the peaches, apricots, and grapes.

Mix the sugar and water in a saucepan and bring to a boil, stirring occasionally. Add the orange peel and nutmeg. Remove from heat and cool slightly. Pour over the fruit and toss gently. Refrigerate until very cold. Before serving, sprinkle with rum.

Biscochitos

MAKES 6 TO 7 DOZEN

These traditional New Mexican cookies are crunchy and anise-scented with a texture similar to shortbread. In winter, they are wonderful with steaming mugs of cocoa.

INGREDIENTS

6 cups	all-purpose flour
3 teaspoons	baking powder
1 teaspoon	salt
$1^1/_2$ cups	sugar
2 cups	vegetable shortening or lard
1 tablespoon	anise seeds
2	eggs
$^1/_2$ cup	dry white wine

<u>For Dusting Cookies:</u>

$^1/_2$ cup	sugar
1 teaspoon	ground cinnamon

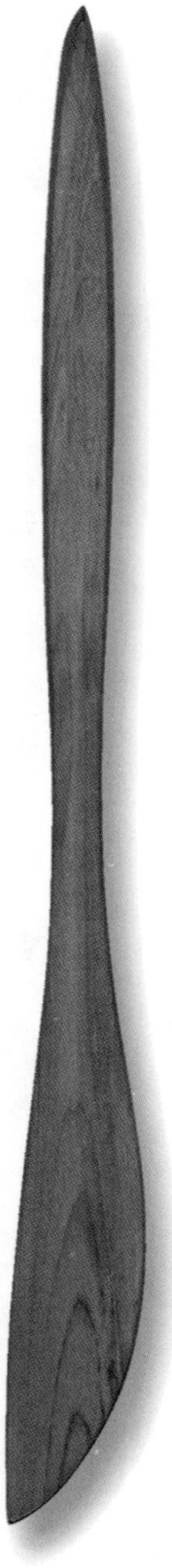

Preheat oven to 400 degrees.

Sift the flour, baking powder, and salt together onto a piece of waxed paper; set aside. In a large bowl, cream the sugar and shortening until fluffy. Add the anise seeds and eggs, and beat again until fluffy. Mix in the sifted dry ingredients and then the wine, to make a stiff dough. Divide the dough into quarters. On a floured surface or pastry cloth, using a lightly-floured rolling pin, roll each quarter to a thickness of $^1/_4$-inch. Cut into rounds with a floured $2^1/_2$-inch cookie cutter. Place on ungreased baking sheets, spaced an inch apart. Bake for about 10 minutes, or until pale tan.

Remove the cookies to a wire rack immediately. Mix the sugar and cinnamon together in a small bowl and dip both sides of each cookie into this mixture. Cool before serving.

Sangria Blanca

MAKES 1 QUART

This recipe by a Kitchen Angels volunteer appeared in *Bon Appetit* magazine. Begin preparations at least an hour before serving.

INGREDIENTS

1	**lemon – sliced**
2	**limes – sliced**
1	**orange – sliced (optional)**
1	**green apple – cored and cut into wedges**
1	**ripe pineapple – peeled, cored, and cut into vertical wedges**
1 bunch	**seedless green grapes – cut into small clusters**
1 fifth bottle ($3^1/_2$ cups)	**dry white wine – chilled**
$^1/_2$ cup	**Cointreau or orange liqueur**
$^1/_4$ cup	**sugar**
1 tray	**ice cubes**
1 bottle (10 ounce)	**club soda – chilled**

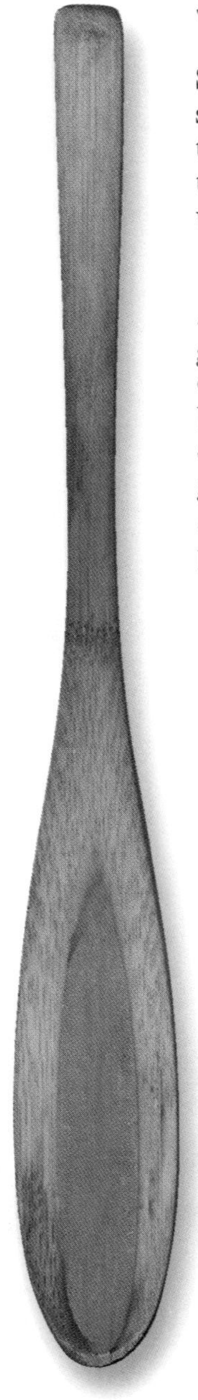

Wash and prepare all the fruit. Squeeze the juice from one lemon slice over the apple wedges to keep them from discoloring. Refrigerate the fruit in a bowl until ready to use.

At serving time, in a large, clear glass pitcher, combine the wine, Cointreau, and sugar until well blended. Stir in the ice cubes and club soda. Add the fruit and mix gently, reserving some citrus slices and grape clusters to garnish the pitcher.

PHOTO BY JACK PARSONS

SUNSET AND STARGAZING DESSERT PARTY

SPONSORED BY:
SARAH AND MIKE TYSON

The Land of Enchantment. That is what it says on our license plates and Santa Fe is just that, enchanting. Whether you are wandering downtown on the Plaza or following a path through the mountains, the City Different is a spectacle to behold. On afternoons in early July, the beginning of our monsoon season, clouds take over the sky faster than you can say "roadrunner." The rains are a blessing for us here in the desert. The dark clouds unleash tremendous bolts of thunder and lightning for a light show that rivals the fireworks on Independence Day.

But as quickly as this tempest vanishes, the clouds part and the real show begins. The magnificent colors in a Santa Fe sunset can only be matched in a box of crayons. Reds, oranges, purples, pinks, and golds swirl across the expansive sky and settle into the silvery horizon. Then the stars start to push through, slowly at first, but blink! and the sky is coated. There is always a chance to catch a falling star, but you may want to save up your wishes for the meteor showers that rain down in mid-August.

There is no better way to enjoy the majesty of a summer night in Santa Fe than to gather some friends for a glass of champagne, a mug of hot coffee, and a spread of sweets to rival the spectacle in the sky above.

Sunset and Stargazing Dessert Party

Menu

Fresh Mixed Berries

Cliff's Favorite Cake

Apricot Soufflé with Grand Marnier

Chocolate Mousse

Mable's Caramel Squares

Peach Pie

White Wine Spritzers or Champagne

Coffee

Cliff's Favorite Cake

SERVES 8 TO 12

Cliff Simon – cake artist *extraordinaire* – donates indescribably beautiful and delectable birthday cakes to our Kitchen Angels clients. He has also designed edible art masterpieces for many celebrities, including three-dimensional versions of Fabergé eggs and the New York skyline. He can even paint, in icing, an exact replica of a Matisse canvas. Cliff says, "This cake is based on an old recipe I found in a German book years ago."

INGREDIENTS

6 ounces	**unsalted butter – at room temperature**
10 ounces (exactly)	**sugar**
7	**eggs**
1 ounce	**fresh orange juice, *plus* grated rind of 1 orange**
2 teaspoons	**baking powder**
1 2/3 cups (7 ounces)	**sifted flour**
A few sprinkles of	**salt**
1/2 cup (or more)	**raspberry jam**

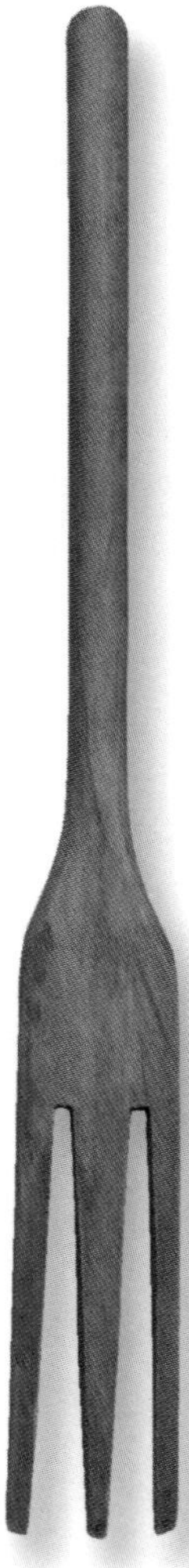

<u>Ganache Frosting:</u>

12 ounces	**best-quality semisweet chocolate – chopped**
6 ounces	**heavy cream – scalded**
1 tablespoon	**instant coffee**
1/2 ounce	**hot water**

Preheat oven to 325 degrees. Tear off a sheet of waxed paper larger than the bottom of a 9-inch springform pan. Open the springform and lay the waxed paper over the bottom layer. Enclose the top piece around the bottom and trim off the excess waxed paper. Oil or butter the pan.

Measure all the ingredients. Separate the eggs, placing the whites into a large stainless steel mixing bowl. In another bowl or Kitchen Aid mixer, beat the butter with about three-quarters of the sugar. Add the egg yolks, one by one, to the batter and beat well. Mix in the orange juice and rind, then the flour and baking powder, until well blended.

Place the bowl of egg whites over a very low flame on the stove and swirl them around with your hand. Remove from the heat when they have reached room temperature. Add a few sprinkles of salt to the egg whites. Begin beating them on low speed, gradually getting faster. When the foam starts to get very white, turn the speed to high. Add the remaining sugar and beat until stiff peaks form. Take a spatula full of the beaten whites and stir them into the cake batter, to lighten it. Then pour the remaining whites into the batter, folding until you have a homogenized mixture, being careful not to either under- or over-fold.

Pour the batter into the prepared springform pan and place it in the oven. The cake will bake in a little under 30 minutes, and will be ready when you are able to smell it and a toothpick inserted into the center comes out clean. Remove the cake from the oven and place it in the refrigerator or freezer for a few minutes, if you wish. When cool, slide a sharp knife around the sides of the cake. Then un-spring the pan, flip it over, and remove the bottom, including the waxed paper. There is a chance that the cake will sink in the center. If this happens, Cliff suggests, "Slice off the high side edges, crumble them, and mix them with some raspberry jam. Then, just before frosting the cake, shove the tasty mass into the valley in the center. No one will ever know."

Split the cake into two layers. Spread raspberry jam evenly over the bottom layer and replace with the lid.

For the Ganache Frosting, place the chopped chocolate into a bowl and add the scalded cream. Mix with a wire whisk until the chocolate is smooth and creamy. In a small bowl, dissolve the instant coffee in the hot water, then whisk it into the chocolate. Let the frosting stand until it is at room temperature and spreadable.

Pour the frosting over the cake and spread with a metal spatula. Let some fall over the sides and spread until smooth. Cliff advises, "As a rule of thumb, if most of the frosting slides down the side of the cake, it's too warm. On the other hand, if the cake disintegrates from the pressure of spreading the frosting, it's probably too cool. Refrigerate before serving. Diet after."

I was so astounded by the thoughtfulness of your sending a cake. It was not until I looked inside the box that I was totally blown away by its beauty. I even entertained the thought of how I could permanently preserve the cake and hang it on my wall as a piece of art. *N.T.*

Apricot Soufflé with Grand Marnier

SERVES 6

An airy dessert that can be served at room temperature.

INGREDIENTS

4	**egg whites**
1 jar (18 ounce)	**apricot jam**
3 to 6 ounces	**Grand Marnier or orange liqueur**

Let me first praise the food's variety, imaginative preparation, quantity, and quality. The delivery volunteers were true blessings on days when I could only walk with difficulty, and true nurturers of heart and spirit on the down and lonely days of slow healing. B. P.

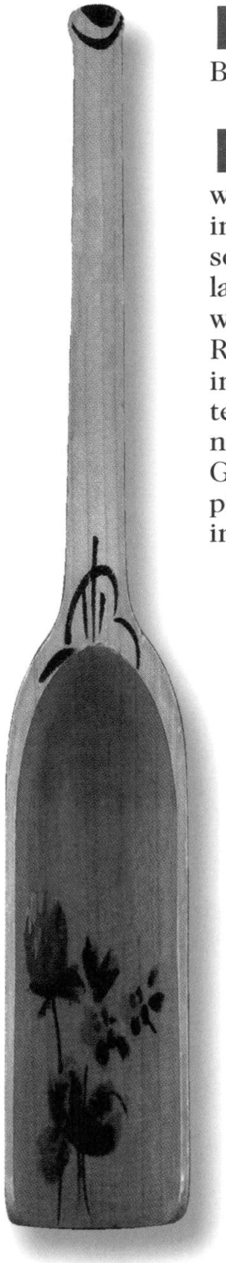

Preheat oven to 350 degrees. Butter a soufflé dish.

In a medium bowl, beat the egg whites until stiff but not dry. Fold in the jam. Pour into the prepared soufflé dish. Place in the oven in a larger pan containing one inch of hot water. Bake for 45 minutes. Remove from the oven. Serve immediately, or let stand at room temperature until ready to serve, no longer than half an hour. Pass the Grand Marnier separately in a small pitcher, for pouring over each serving.

Chocolate Mousse

MAKES 2 CUPS

Coffee or dark rum adds an unexpected nuance to this chocolate classic. The skim milk makes this rich dessert lighter than usual.

INGREDIENTS

2 tablespoons	**coffee liqueur, dark rum, *or* strong-brewed coffee**
1 envelope ($2^1/_2$ teaspoons)	**unflavored gelatin**
5 large	**egg whites**
1 large	**egg**
$^1/_2$ cup	**corn syrup**
$^3/_4$ cup	**unsweetened cocoa powder**
$1^1/_2$ cups	**skim milk**
3 ounces	**semisweet chocolate – chopped**
1 teaspoon	**vanilla extract**
Pinch of	**salt**

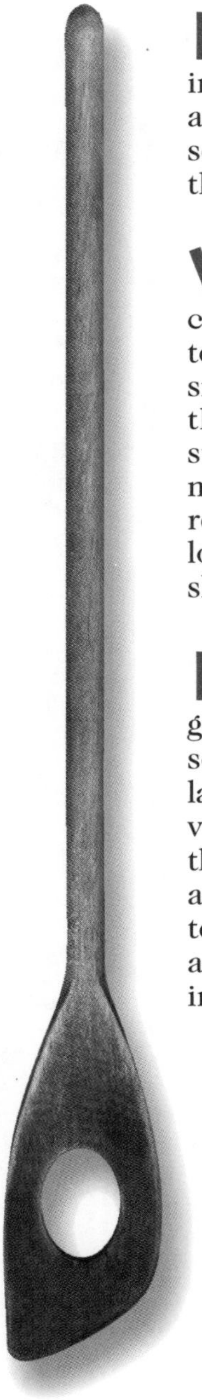

Pour the liqueur, rum, or coffee into a small bowl and sprinkle gelatin over the surface. Let stand to soften. In a medium bowl, whip the egg whites to form stiff peaks.

Whisk the whole egg, corn syrup, cocoa, and $^1/_2$ cup of the milk together, in a medium bowl, until smooth. In a heavy saucepan, heat the remaining cup of milk until steaming. Gradually whisk the hot milk into the egg mixture, and return to the saucepan. Cook over low heat, stirring constantly until slightly thickened.

Remove from heat and add the gelatin mixture, stirring until dissolved. Add the chopped chocolate and stir until melted. Mix in the vanilla and salt, and gently fold in the whipped egg whites. Transfer to a serving bowl and cool to room temperature. Chill in the refrigerator for at least 2 hours before serving.

Mable's Caramel Squares

MAKES 12

Sinfully delicious!

INGREDIENTS

$1^1/_2$ cups	**flour ***
$^1/_4$ teaspoon	**salt**
2 teaspoons	**baking powder ***
1 stick (4 ounces)	**butter**
1 cup	**white sugar ***
2 teaspoons	**vanilla or rum extract**
2	**eggs – separated**
1 cup (well packed)	**brown sugar ***

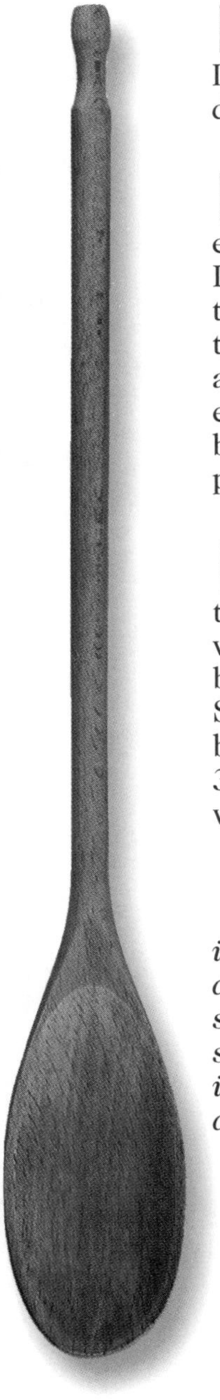

Preheat oven to 325 degrees. Lightly grease a 9 x 13-inch baking dish.

In a small mixing bowl, sift together the flour, salt, and baking powder. In a medium bowl, cream together the butter and white sugar. Beat in the egg yolks, reserving the whites, and 1 teaspoon vanilla or rum extract. Add the flour mixture, and blend well. Spread into the prepared baking dish.

Beat the egg whites until stiff. Add the brown sugar and 1 teaspoon vanilla or rum extract. Continue beating until the sugar is blended. Spread evenly over the top of the batter in the baking dish. Bake for 30 minutes. Cut into squares while warm.

**For 7,000 feet and above, increase the flour by 2 tablespoons, decrease baking powder by 1 teaspoon, decrease white and brown sugars each by 2 tablespoons, and increase oven temperature by 25 degrees.*

Peach Pie

SERVES 6 TO 8

Fresh summer peaches are essential in this luscious pie.

INGREDIENTS

$1\frac{1}{2}$ cups	**water**
1 cup	**sugar**
3 tablespoons	**cornstarch**
2 tablespoons	**peach or unflavored gelatin**
8	**ripe peaches – peeled, pitted, and thinly sliced**
$\frac{1}{2}$ cup	**blueberries (optional)**
1	**9-inch pie shell – baked and cooled**
1 cup	**heavy cream – whipped (optional garnish)**

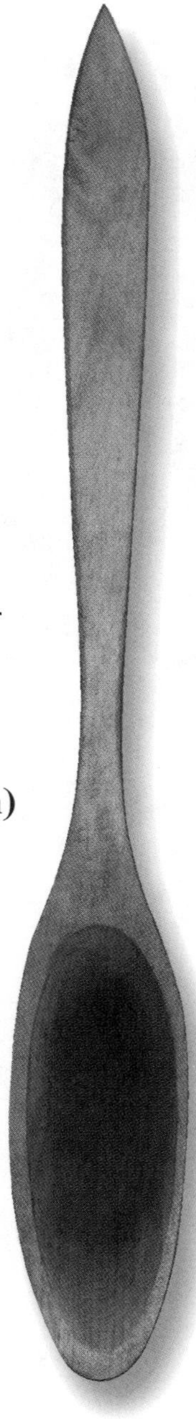

Combine the water, sugar, and cornstarch in a heavy saucepan. Cook over medium heat until thick. Remove from the heat and stir in the gelatin. Mix well. Stir in the peaches (and blueberries, if using). Pour into the baked, cooled pie crust. Chill for several hours before serving. At serving time, top with whipped cream, if desired.

PHOTO BY JACK PARSONS

Breakfast for Indian Market Weekend

Sponsored by:
Simons Cuddy & Friedman, LLP

Breakfast for Indian Market Weekend

A small gathering stands in front of the portale of the Palace of the Governors at six a.m. on a hot August Saturday. Suddenly the crowd parts, and this year's Best of Show winner approaches with her pottery. She settles into her booth and slowly unwraps each piece to reverent, "Ooohs" and "Ahhhs." The artist has spent all year making her pots, and the workmanship is astonishing.

For more than three-quarters of a century, Santa Fe Indian Market has been the largest exhibition and sale of American Indian art in the world. It is the culmination of a series of events sponsored by the Southwestern Association for Indian Arts (SWAIA), which includes the annual Wheelwright Museum's benefit auction.

Over 1200 artists representing eighty tribes fill booths on and around the Plaza during Indian Market weekend. The event draws up to 100,000 visitors annually, who come to admire – and buy – the extraordinary selection of jewelry, pottery, painting, sculpture, weaving, storyteller dolls, baskets, beadwork, drums, and more. It is possible to spend many thousands on a one-of-a-kind silver concha belt inlaid with semi-precious stones. You can also pick up a loveable treasure for only a few dollars.

The real experience lies in chatting with the artists about their work. The people-watching is tops, too: many shoppers arrive adorned with jewelry gleaned from previous years. When the sun grows too strong, take time out for a Navajo taco – fried bread topped with pinto beans, cheese, lettuce, tomatoes, and salsa. Or bring some friends home for a late breakfast, to discuss all of the beautiful things you have seen.

Menu

Fruit Medley with Lemon-Mint Dressing

Huevos Rancheros Brunch Casserole

Sopaipillas

Iced New Mexican Coffee

Fruit Medley with Lemon-Mint Dressing

SERVES 16 TO 20

For a festive presentation, serve the fruit in a basket carved from a scooped-out watermelon.

INGREDIENTS

1	**honeydew melon – cut into balls***
1	**cantaloupe – cut into balls ***
4	**ripe peaches – peeled, pitted, and sliced**
4	**Granny Smith apples – peeled, cored, and sliced**
3	**bananas – cut in 1/4-inch slices**
1	**pineapple – peeled, cored, and cut into chunks**
1 pint	**raspberries**
1 pint	**blueberries**
1 small bunch	**green seedless grapes – sliced in half**
2	**lemons – juiced**

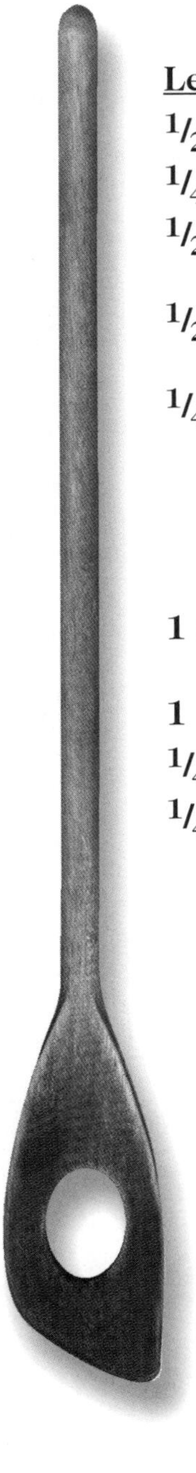

Lemon-Mint Dressing:

1/2 cup	**honey**
1/4 cup	**water**
1/2 teaspoon	**ground cardamom**
1/2 teaspoon	**ground coriander**
1/4 cup	**fresh mint leaves – minced or 1 tablespoon dried**
1 teaspoon	**grated lemon zest**
1	**lemon – juiced**
1/4 teaspoon	**salt**
1/4 cup	**olive oil**

Put all of the prepared fruit into a large bowl. Toss gently with the lemon juice. Chill.

Combine the honey, water, cardamom, and coriander in a small saucepan and bring to a boil. Reduce heat and simmer for 2 minutes. Remove from the stove and add the remaining ingredients. Mix well and chill. At serving time, mix the dressing and pour it over the fruit. Toss gently.

**If presenting the fruit salad in a hollowed-out watermelon, use the watermelon pulp, cut in chunks, in place of either the honeydew or cantaloupe.*

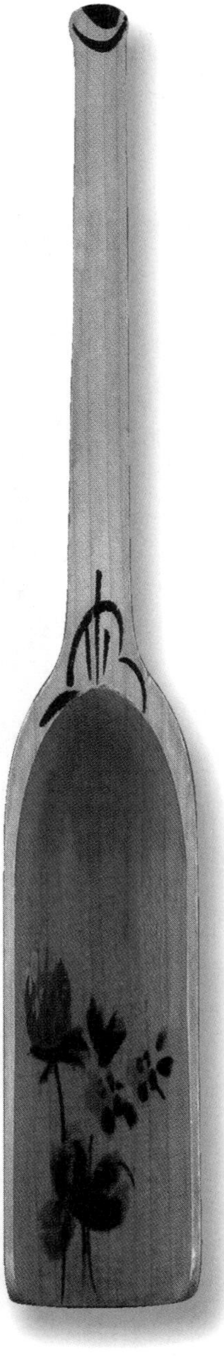

As a single mother of a small child, and also a patient suffering from a life-threatening illness, Kitchen Angels' service has been invaluable to my family. The cheery drivers bring a happy moment to our home. They have also brightened our holidays with special baskets and gifts. You cannot grasp the benefit this service brings unless you are a homebound person, like myself. V.D.

Huevos Rancheros Brunch Casserole

SERVES 16 TO 20

Can be prepared a day ahead, then baked before serving.

INGREDIENTS

2 tablespoons	olive oil
3 medium	onions – chopped
6 to 8	cloves of garlic – minced
2 to 4	jalapeño peppers – seeded and minced
$1\frac{1}{2}$ teaspoons	ground cumin
1 teaspoon	oregano
3 cans (14 ounce)	Italian tomatoes, with juice
2	bay leaves
1 teaspoon	salt
$\frac{1}{2}$ teaspoon	pepper
2 cans (16 ounce)	black beans
18 (6-inch round)	corn tortillas
3 tablespoons	canola oil
16 medium	eggs – hard-boiled and sliced

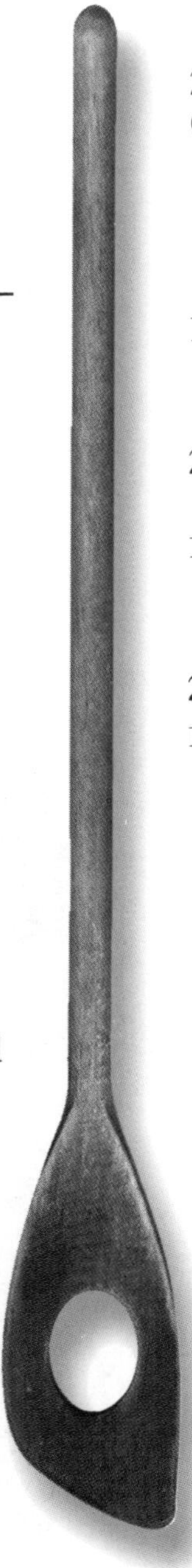

2 cans (4 ounce)	diced green chiles, or 8 ounces frozen mild green chiles, thawed
$1\frac{1}{4}$ pounds	Monterey Jack cheese – shredded
2 medium	red onions – finely chopped
$\frac{1}{2}$ cup	fresh cilantro leaves – chopped
2 cups	sour cream
$\frac{1}{4}$ cup	fresh cilantro leaves – chopped (garnish)

Huevos Rancheros Brunch Casserole - continued

Heat oil in a large skillet or Dutch oven, and sauté the onions until golden. Add the garlic, jalapeños, cumin, and oregano. Cook for 1 minute. Add the tomatoes, bay leaves, salt, and pepper. Bring to a boil. Reduce heat and simmer for 1 hour, stirring occasionally, until the sauce is reduced to about 4 cups. In a separate saucepan, bring the black beans to a boil and remove from the heat.

Preheat oven to 375 degrees. Brush the tortillas lightly on both sides with canola oil, and bake in batches until softened, about 2 minutes. Reduce heat to 350 degrees. *(If preparing casserole to bake later, turn off heat.)*

In a large baking dish, spread 1 cup of the tomato sauce over the bottom. Arrange 6 tortillas on top of the sauce. Place half of the black beans over the tortillas, followed by half of the sliced eggs and green chiles. Sprinkle with a third of the cheese, and top with $1\frac{1}{2}$ cups of the sauce. Sprinkle with half of the chopped red onion and chopped cilantro. Press down lightly with a large spoon to compress the casserole.

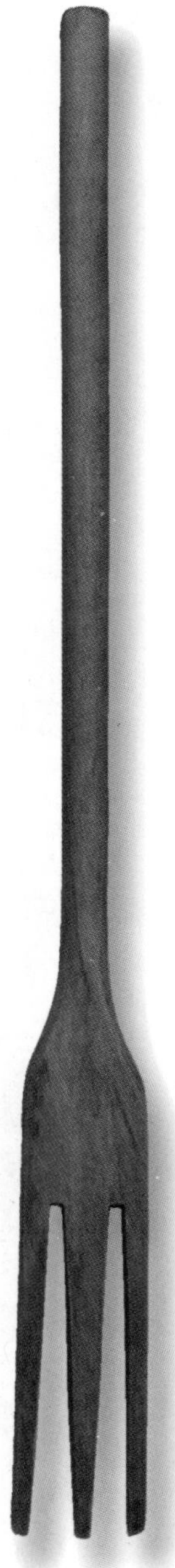

Arrange a second layer of 6 tortillas, covered with the remaining beans, egg slices, green chiles, tomato sauce, red onions, and cilantro, and half of the remaining cheese. Press down lightly. Top with the remaining tortillas, and spread sour cream over them. Sprinkle the remaining cheese on top. *(The recipe can be prepared to this point one day in advance.)*

Bake the casserole in a preheated 350-degree oven until bubbly and golden on top, about 50 to 60 minutes. Serve warm, garnished with chopped cilantro leaves.

Sopaipillas

MAKES 32

There are many variations of this bread, deep-fried to form hollow "sofa pillows," but this Kitchen Angel's recipe appeared in *Bon Appetit*. Sopaipillas are served traditionally with honey, but may also be stuffed with assorted fillings, such as beans, guacamole, chile, onions, cheese, grilled beef or chicken, and shredded lettuce.

INGREDIENTS

4 cups	**all-purpose flour**
1 tablespoon	**shortening**
1 tablespoon	**sugar**
1 teaspoon	**baking powder**
3 teaspoons	**salt**
2 tablespoons	**evaporated milk**
$1\frac{1}{4}$ cups	**warm water**

Lard or shortening, for deep-frying

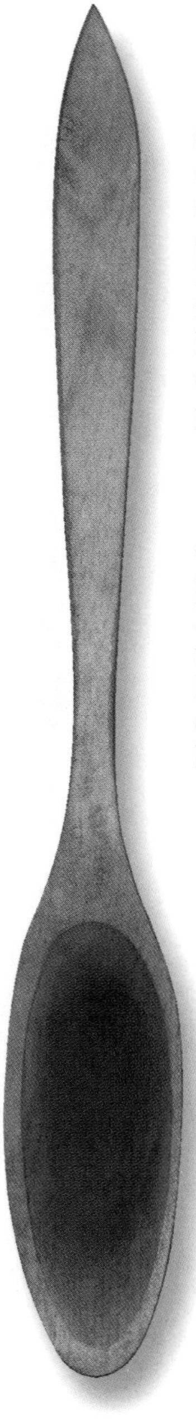

Combine the flour, shortening, sugar, baking powder, salt, and evaporated milk. Work into dough, adding water slowly. Divide the dough into eight equal portions. Roll each into a 12-inch circle, making certain the dough is rolled thinly, less than $\frac{1}{4}$-inch thick. Cut each circle into four triangular pieces.

In a deep fryer, heat about 3 inches of shortening (lard is preferable) to a temperature of 420 degrees. Fry one or two sopaipillas at a time, until puffy and brown on both sides. Drain on paper towels. Serve immediately with honey or a mixture of honey and butter.

Iced New Mexican Coffee

SERVES 6 TO 8

This can be made in an electric coffee maker. It is also delicious hot.

INGREDIENTS

1	**orange**
$1/2$ cup	**ground strong coffee, such as Italian espresso**
1 teaspoon	**cinnamon**
$1/4$ teaspoon	**ground cloves**
6 cups	**cold water**
2 tablespoons (or more)	**brown sugar (optional)**
Ice cubes	
1 cup	**milk or half-and-half (garnish)**

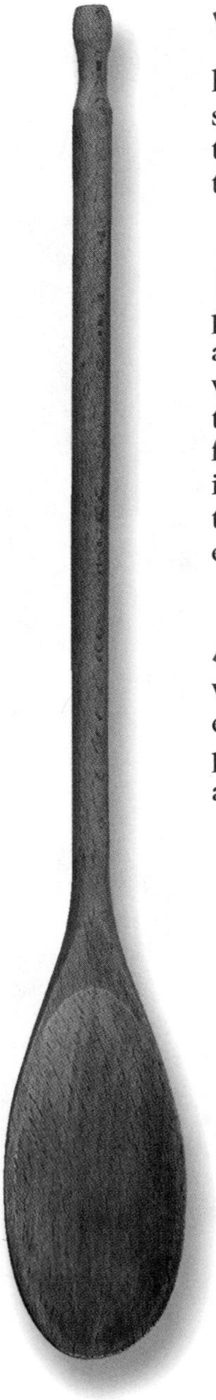

Wash the orange. With a sharp knife, slice the peel into long, thin strips, being careful not to include the white pith. Set aside 6 to 8 of the strips for garnish.

Into the filter of a drip coffee maker, place the coffee, cinnamon, cloves, and orange peel. Pour water into the water compartment, and let it drip through the basket into the coffeepot. When coffee is brewed, stir in the sugar, if using. Cool to room temperature or chill in the refrigerator.

At serving time, fill tall glasses with ice cubes and coffee. Garnish each glass with a strip of orange peel. Pass a pitcher of milk or half-and-half.

Photo by Jack Parsons

Celebrating the Chile Harvest

Special Thanks to:
Gregory S. Green

Celebrating the Chile Harvest

August's chile harvest is an anticipated local event. It begins with the trucking in of just-picked chiles – the piquant green vegetables of the *capiscum annum* family – mainly from the Hatch Valley in the southern part of the state. Roasting equipment is set up in parking lots all around town, and soon Santa Fe's air is permeated by the heady scent of roasting chiles. Propane-fired cylinders tumble the peppers until their skins are scorched. Then the chiles are put directly into paper or plastic bags to steam. This heightens their flavor and allows the skins to be peeled easily. The chiles are then either frozen or canned for use throughout the year.

By October, green chiles ripen to a bright red. Once picked, they are left to dry in the sun and are then ground into powder. Often, they are threaded into the beautiful long ropes or *ristras* that hang in our kitchens or outside our front doors. Good red chile pods grow in the south, but many contend that the best and most flavorful grow around Chimayo, north of Santa Fe. The mountainous terrain and short growing season yield much smaller crops, so Chimayo's red chile is prized.

"Chile" has many definitions. A green chile is a vegetable; a red chile...a spice. The state question, "Red or Green?" means, "What kind of chile do you want on those enchiladas?" The cognoscenti may answer, "Christmas," which means, "Both, and I know what I'm talking about."

Which is hotter? Red, *but not always.* And green chiles vary from mild to extra hot. So when ordering a quesadilla or breakfast burrito, ask which type of chile is hotter on that particular day. Your server will know the answer.

Our menu for six to eight features both. Enjoy!

Menu

Green Chile Chutney
Quesadillas
or
Chipotle Aiöli with
Raw Vegetables

Verde Elote Soup

Blue Enchiladas with
Red Chile
or
Green Chile Chicken

Tossed Green Salad
with Buttermilk-Parsley
Dressing

Jalapeño Cornmeal
Muffins

Burnt Margarita Sorbet

Green Chile Chutney Quesadillas

SERVES 6 TO 8

The green chile chutney is superb with grilled meats or poultry.

INGREDIENTS

6 large	**flour tortillas**
1 cup	**Green Chile Chutney – *recipe follows***
1$\frac{1}{2}$ cups (6 ounces)	**Monterey Jack or Cheddar cheese – grated**
Salt and pepper, to taste	
1 cup	**sour cream (garnish)**
1 cup	**salsa (garnish)**

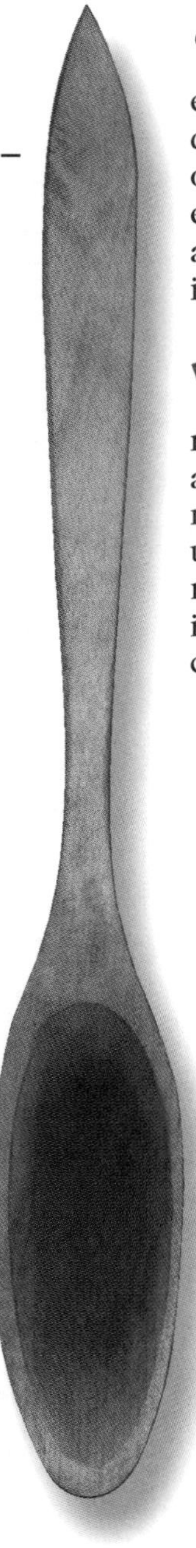

Spread the tops of three tortillas each with $\frac{1}{3}$ cup of the chutney, not quite to the edges. Sprinkle $\frac{1}{2}$ cup of the cheese over the chutney on each tortilla, and season with salt and pepper. Top with the remaining three tortillas.

Warm a heavy, dry skillet over medium heat. Add one filled tortilla and cook until the cheese starts to melt. Flip, and toast the other side until lightly browned. Repeat with remaining two tortillas. Cut each into wedges and serve with sour cream and salsa.

Kitchen Angels understands that even though we are disabled, we matter too, and they acknowledge that we have something to give also. In this community, Kitchen Angels is very special and so desperately needed. *A.*

Green Chile Chutney

MAKES ABOUT 5 CUPS

INGREDIENTS

4 tablespoons	olive oil
4 large	white onions – peeled and sliced
3	cloves of garlic – minced
2 cups	green chiles – roasted, peeled, seeded, and chopped *
1 tablespoon each:	mustard seeds, coriander seeds, and fennel seeds
1 teaspoon	ground cumin
1 teaspoon	cinnamon
1 cup	sugar
2 tablespoons	salt
1 cup	white vinegar

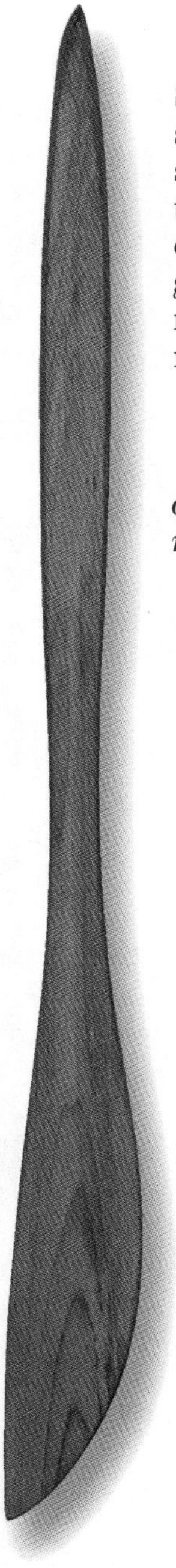

Heat oil in a medium skillet. Sauté the onions and garlic until soft. Add the green chiles and spices, and sauté for another 5 minutes. Add the sugar, stirring until dissolved, then the salt and vinegar. Reduce heat and simmer for 10 minutes. Cool, and store in the refrigerator.

**Can substitute 1 container (16 ounce) frozen green chiles – mild, medium, or hot.*

Chipotle Aïoli with Raw Vegetables

Makes 2 Cups

This version of the classic garlic aïoli takes on the smoky flavor of chipotle chiles. It is a delicious dip for crudités, or sauce for shrimp, chicken, or grilled fish. Use in place of hollandaise on steamed broccoli and asparagus, and substitute for mayonnaise in sandwiches and with tuna or chicken salad.

Ingredients

6	**egg yolks**
1/2 teaspoon	**salt**
1/2 cup	**fresh lime juice (about 2 limes) ***
1 tablespoon	**ground cumin**
1 small bunch	**cilantro - leaves only**
5	**cloves of garlic - crushed**
1 tablespoon	**tomato paste or ketchup**
2	**canned chipotle chiles ****
2 cups	**olive oil**

Raw vegetables, e.g. carrot, celery, and jicama sticks, broccoli or cauliflower florets, green beans, or whole mushrooms

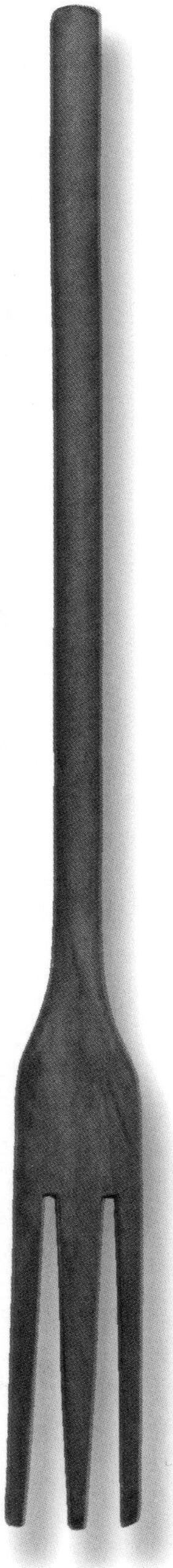

Place all ingredients, except olive oil, in a blender or food processor and purée until smooth. Add oil slowly, with motor running, until the sauce is thickened to a mayonnaise consistency. Serve with assorted raw vegetables. The aïoli will keep for a week in the refrigerator, tightly covered.

**Lemon juice may be substituted.*
*** Chipotle chiles are very hot, so start with two and add more for a spicier aïoli. Leftover canned chipotles will keep for weeks, tightly covered, in the refrigerator. Dried chipotles may be substituted: remove stems and seeds, if necessary, and soak in boiling water for 20 minutes, then drain.*

Verde Elote Soup

SERVES 6 TO 8

In Spanish, *elote* means an ear of corn. This piquant soup takes advantage of the fresh summer corn crop, although frozen or canned may be substituted.

INGREDIENTS

4 tablespoons	**butter**
1/4 medium	**white onion – finely chopped**
4	**cloves of garlic – minced**
4 1/2 cups	**fresh corn kernels, or frozen or canned**
2/3 cup	**fresh green peas, or frozen, thawed peas**
1 small bunch	**cilantro – leaves only**
2 small	**poblano chiles – seeded**
3 large	**romaine lettuce leaves – torn into large pieces**
2/3 cup	**tomatillos – peeled, halved, and steamed until soft**
5 cups	**chicken broth**
Salt, to taste	
6 tablespoons	**sour cream (garnish)**
2	**corn tortillas – cut into strips, fried, and drained (garnish)**

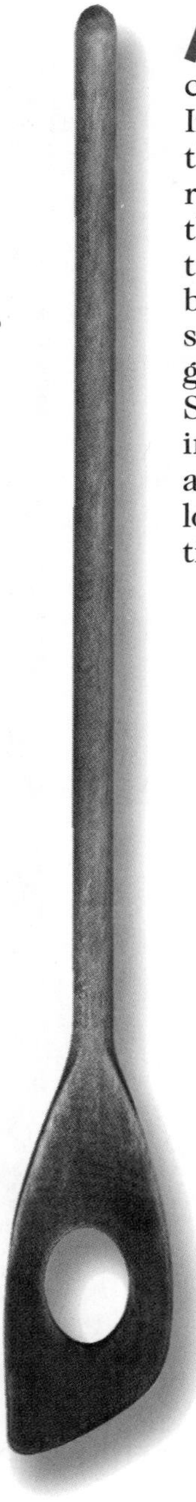

Melt butter in a large pot, and cook the onion and garlic until soft. In a blender or food processor, purée the corn, peas, cilantro, chiles, romaine, tomatillos, and 2 cups of the chicken broth. Strain this mixture by passing through medium blade of a food mill. Add the strained purée to the onions and garlic, along with remaining broth. Season with salt, and heat to serving temperature. Ladle into bowls and garnish each portion with a dollop of sour cream and some fried tortilla strips.

Blue Enchiladas with Red Chile

SERVES 6 TO 8

The sauce for this vegetarian entrée can be made ahead and used in other New Mexican dishes. For breakfast, top each enchilada with a soft fried egg.

INGREDIENTS

16 to 18	whole dried red chiles
2 cups	hot water
$^{1}/_{4}$ cup	shortening or olive oil
$^{1}/_{2}$ cup	flour
3	cloves of garlic – minced
Salt, to taste	
2 teaspoons	oregano
3 cans (8 ounce)	tomato sauce
Shortening or oil (enough to fry tortillas)	
18 to 24	blue corn tortillas (3 for each serving)
1 medium	onion –diced
$1^{1}/_{2}$ to 2 cups (6-8 ounces)	Longhorn cheese – grated
4 leaves	lettuce – shredded (garnish)

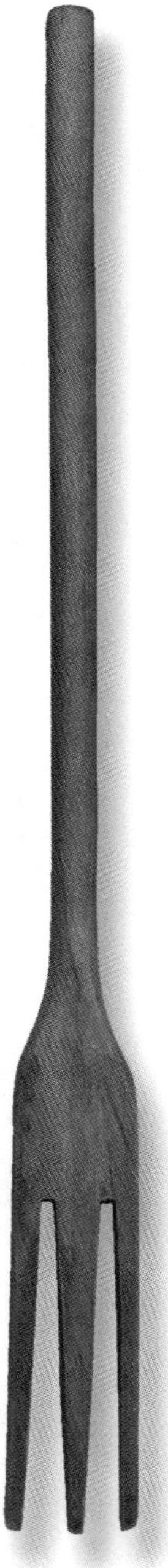

To make the sauce, remove stems, seeds, and veins from the chile pods. Rinse with cold water, then soak in hot water for about 30 minutes or until soft. Drain chiles and place in a blender. Add enough warm water to almost cover, leaving at least an inch of space in the container. Blend for 2 or 3 minutes. If the sauce seems too thick, add more water and blend until the chile skins disappear.

Melt shortening in a large saucepan. Add the flour and brown, stirring, as in making gravy. Remove from heat and slowly add 1 quart of the blended chile pods, stirring constantly until smooth. Place pan over medium heat. Add the garlic, salt, oregano, and enough water to give the mixture a medium-thick consistency. Cook until thickened, then add the tomato sauce. Reduce heat and simmer for $1^{1}/_{2}$ hours. *(Sauce can be prepared to this point and refrigerated until needed.)* When ready to make the enchiladas, heat the sauce and add more water, if needed, to give it the consistency of a light tomato sauce.

To make the enchiladas, preheat oven to 250 degrees. Heat shortening or oil in a heavy skillet, and fry each tortilla until soft. Drain on paper towels. Place one tortilla on each individual serving plate. Top with some sauce, then sprinkle with diced onion and cheese. Repeat the layering twice to make one complete enchilada for each serving. Top each enchilada with more sauce, then place each plate in the oven until the cheese melts. Serve immediately, garnished with shredded lettuce.

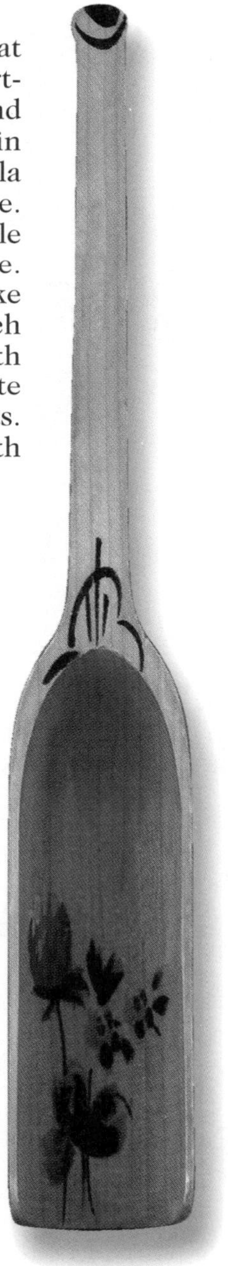

The meals continue to be superb...I often wonder how I would have managed these past two years trying to get my meals together 7 days a week, but thanks to all your wonderful volunteers – cooking and delivering – that problem was solved for me. Again, many thanks. I just want all of you to know how much I appreciate you. J.M.

Green Chile Chicken

SERVES 6 TO 8

Great for a party, this easy dish can be assembled ahead and baked before serving.

INGREDIENTS

5	**cloves of garlic – minced**
1 container (16 ounce)	**frozen diced green chiles, thawed ***
2 medium	**yellow onions – chopped**
$1^1/_2$ teaspoons	**ground cumin**
1 teaspoon	**chili powder**
1 teaspoon	**oregano**
6 to 8	**chicken breast halves, skinless and boneless**
2 to $2^1/_2$ cups (8 to 10 ounces)	**Monterey Jack cheese – shredded**

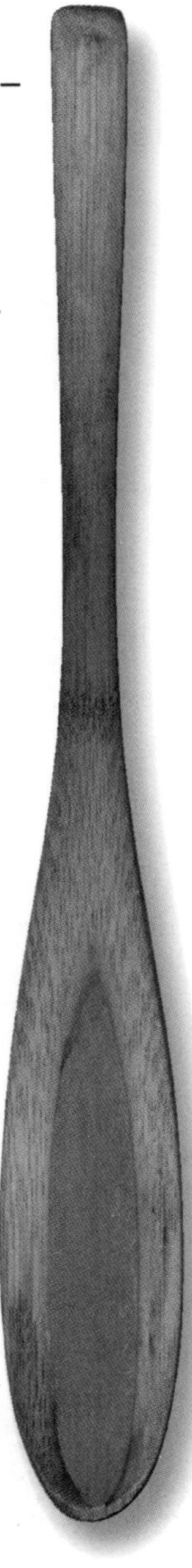

Preheat oven to 375 degrees. Lightly grease a baking dish.

In a mixing bowl, combine the garlic, green chiles, onion, cumin, chili powder, and oregano. Mix well. Place chicken breasts in the prepared baking dish in a single layer. Pour green chile sauce evenly over chicken. *(If making the dish ahead, cover and refrigerate until ready to bake.)* Bake the chicken, uncovered, for 30 minutes. Sprinkle with cheese, and bake for an additional 5 to 10 minutes, until the cheese is melted. Serve immediately.

**Frozen green chiles vary from mild to extra hot: choose the spiciness you wish. Canned chiles may be substituted.*

Tossed Green Salad with Buttermilk-Parsley Dressing

SERVES 6 TO 8

A cool counterbalance to spicy dishes.

INGREDIENTS

Buttermilk-Parsley Dressing
(makes $1\frac{1}{2}$ cups):

1 tablespoon	**sour cream**
$\frac{3}{4}$ cup	**buttermilk**
2 tablespoons	**lemon juice**
1	**clove of garlic – crushed**
3 tablespoons	**parsley – minced**
1 tablespoon	**fresh dill – minced, *or* $\frac{1}{2}$ teaspoon dried**
$\frac{1}{2}$ teaspoon	**celery salt**
Freshly ground pepper, to taste	
1 medium	**ripe tomato – seeded and diced (optional)**
4 to 5 cups	**assorted lettuces – washed, dried, and torn into bite-sized pieces**

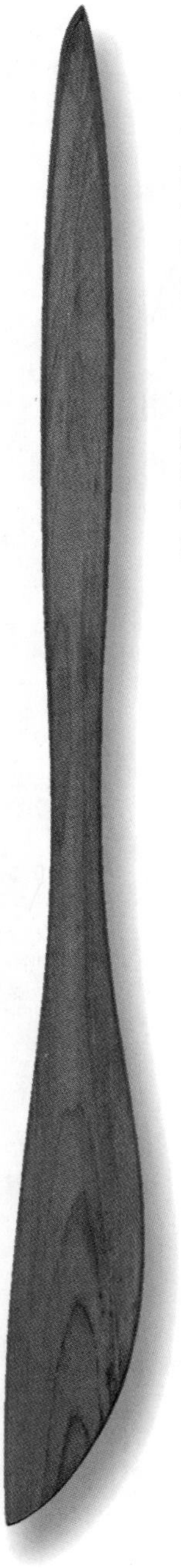

In a medium bowl, whisk together the sour cream and buttermilk until well blended. Add the remaining ingredients, except for the diced tomato, and mix well. Gently stir in tomato, if using. Refrigerate until ready to use.

At serving time, place assorted greens in a salad bowl. Add enough dressing to coat the greens, and toss well. Leftover dressing keeps well, refrigerated, for several days.

Jalapeño Cornmeal Muffins

Makes 12

These delicious muffins complement any meal from breakfast to dinner.

Ingredients

1	egg – at room temperature
$^1/_2$ cup	butter – melted
$^1/_4$ cup	vegetable oil
1 cup	milk – warmed
1 cup	cake flour
$^2/_3$ cup	yellow cornmeal
1 tablespoon	baking powder
$^1/_2$ teaspoon	salt
2 tablespoons	sugar
1 to 3 tablespoons	jalapeño peppers – seeded and minced *
2 tablespoons	scallions – diced (optional)

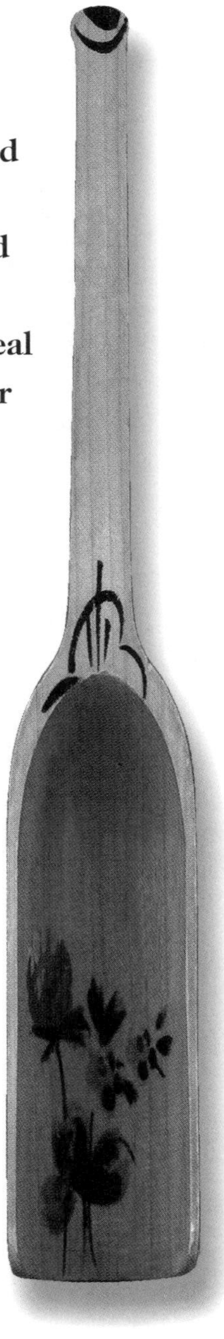

Preheat oven to 400 degrees. Line muffin tins with foil cupcake liners.

In a large bowl, beat or whisk the egg, melted butter, and oil until well blended. Stir in the warm milk. In a separate bowl, combine the cake flour, cornmeal, baking powder, salt, and sugar. Mix well, and add to the egg mixture, along with the jalapeños and scallions, if desired. Stir just until blended.

Spoon the batter into muffin tins so that each tin is three-quarters full. Bake for 15 to 20 minutes, or until the edges of muffins are slightly golden and a knife inserted into the center comes out clean. Cool on racks, or serve hot.

**Amount used depends on spiciness desired.*

Burnt Margarita Sorbet

SERVES 8

This sorbet delights the tongue with an appealing mix of sour, sweet, and bitter tastes.

INGREDIENTS

3 cups	**tequila**
1 cup	**fresh lime juice (about 6 to 8 limes)**
1 cup	**Triple Sec or orange-flavored liqueur**
1 teaspoon	**vanilla extract**
$^1/_4$ cup	**sugar**

Sugar
***or* coarse salt, to taste (garnish)**

1	**lime – cut into 8 thinly-sliced wedges (garnish)**
16 fresh	**juniper berries (optional garnish)**

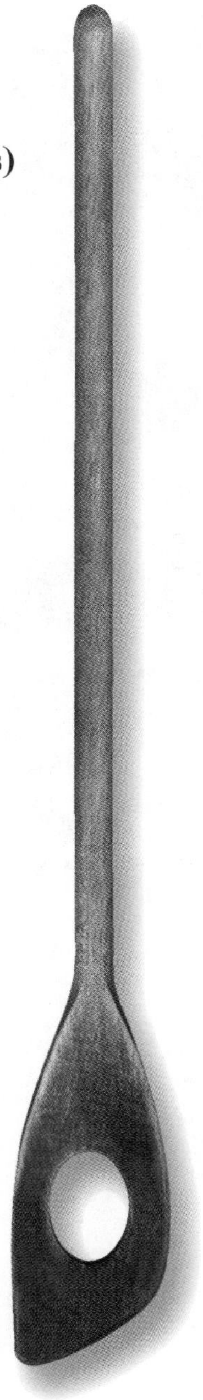

In a skillet, bring the tequila to the beginning of a boil. Just as it starts bubbling, *very carefully* tip the edge of the skillet toward the flames, to allow the tequila to catch fire. Alternatively, *carefully* light the tequila with a long match. Turn off the gas or move the skillet away from the heat source, and allow all the alcohol to burn away. This will take about 10 minutes, and should reduce the tequila by half.

In the meantime, grate the peel of 2 of the limes, and juice enough limes to yield 1 cup. Combine the grated peel, lime juice, Triple Sec, vanilla, and sugar in a bowl, stirring until the sugar has dissolved. Add the reduced tequila, and stir. Pour into an ice cream machine and process until frozen, according to the directions of your machine. Remove to a container and store in the freezer.

At serving time, dip the edges of 8 serving bowls or Margarita glasses with sugar or coarse salt and scoop sorbet into them. Garnish each serving with one lime slice and, if available, two juniper berries.

Photo by Jerry Harper

Al fresco Zozobra Dinner

In Memory of:
Barbara Fairbanks and Harvey Fite

The Fiesta de Santa Fe, held in early September since 1712, commemorates Don Diego de Vargas's reconquest of the territory in 1692 from the Pueblo Indians. Many activities pack Fiesta weekend. Everyone loves the Saturday morning Pet Parade around the Plaza, when costumed children walk their costumed dogs and cats, as well as birds, chickens, calves, ponies, even goldfish. On Sunday afternoon, people line the Paseo de Peralta for the Hysterical/Historical Parade. The Santa Fe Playhouse satirizes local politicians and issues to packed houses at its annual Fiesta Melodrama. The Plaza is filled with food and crafts booths, and lots of live music. There are also religious processions to observe the occasion, including a Sunday night Mass and candlelight walk from the Cathedral to the Cross of the Martyrs.

Fiesta starts officially with the burning of Zozobra, or Old Man Gloom. This unabashedly pagan tradition began in 1926 when Santa Fe artist Will Shuster created a large *papier maché* puppet, which he burned with friends in his backyard during Fiesta weekend to rid them of gloom for the year.

Zozobra has evolved into a 40-foot marionette that towers over Fort Marcy Park, and most of the town participates in the ritual burning. Zozobra, now made by the Kiwanis Club, moans and groans with his arms flailing, while mariachi music entertains picnickers. When the evening grows dark, the Fire Dancer appears and the crowd begins shouting, "Burn him! Burn him!" There is a spectacular display of fireworks and, finally, Old Man Gloom is ignited, to much cheering. "*Viva la Fiesta!*," the crowd shouts afterward as it disperses toward the Plaza in search of more merriment.

Celebrate the burning of Old Man Gloom with friends. Here is our menu for six.

Al Fresco Zozobra Dinner

Menu

Margaritas

Gay's Veggie Dip
with Crudités

Chilled Tomato-Mint Soup
with
Toasted Parmesan Rounds

Spinach and Chicken
Enchiladas

Fire and Ice Salad

Berry Shortcakes with
Tequila Whipped Cream

Iced Mint Tea and Coffee

Margaritas

1 Serving

A smashing version of the traditional Mexican cocktail.

Ingredients

Coarse kosher or sea salt

$^{1}/_{2}$	**lime**
2 ounces	**tequila**
2 tablespoons	**bottled sweetened lime juice**
$1^{1}/_{2}$ teaspoons	**Triple Sec or orange liqueur**

Ice cubes

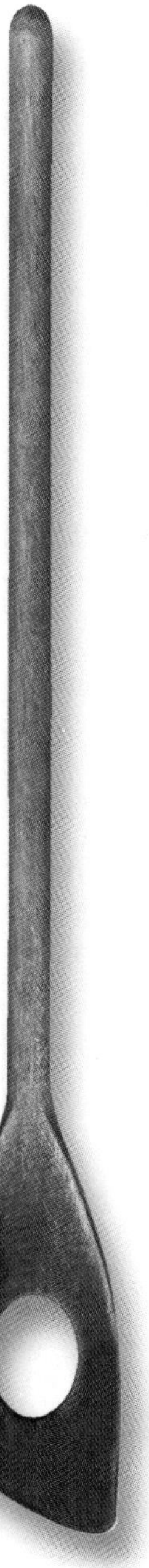

Pour enough salt into a flat dish to make a layer about $^{1}/_{8}$ -inch thick. Rub the lime around the rim of a glass, then dip rim into the salt, to form a crust.

Place tequila, sweetened lime juice, and Triple Sec in a cocktail shaker, along with several ice cubes. Shake until the shaker is frosted. Pour into the prepared glass and serve the margarita "up" or add ice cubes. Enjoy!

Variation: To make a Spicy Santa Fe Margarita, score 2 fresh jalapeño peppers with a fork. Stab peppers with a longer wooden skewer, and add to a quart bottle of tequila. Marinate for 3 days only, then discard the jalapeños. Replace the regular tequila in the recipe with the jalapeño tequila, and increase the sweetened lime juice by $1^{1}/_{2}$ teaspoons.

GAY'S VEGGIE DIP WITH CRUDITÉS

MAKES 2 CUPS

A savory dip for raw vegetables.

INGREDIENTS

1 cup	**mayonnaise**
$^1/_2$ cup	**sour cream**
2 tablespoons	**tarragon vinegar**
2 tablespoons	**garlic vinegar**
2 tablespoons	**white wine vinegar**
2 tablespoons	**onion powder**
1 tablespoon	**anchovy paste**
1 tablespoon	**fresh parsley leaves – minced**
1 tablespoon	**lemon juice**

Assorted raw vegetables for dipping

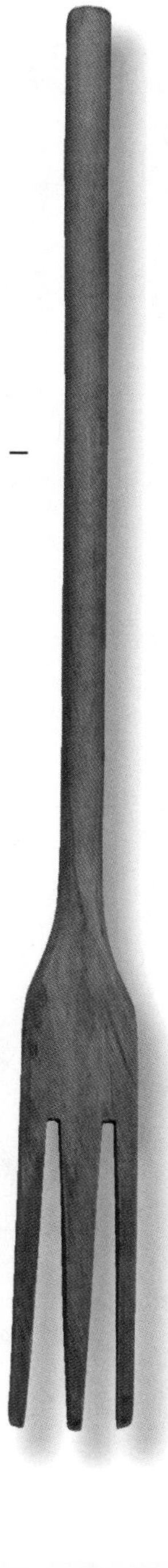

In a medium bowl, whisk together the mayonnaise and sour cream, then mix in the remaining ingredients. Chill until needed. Stir well before serving with raw vegetables. Keeps in the refrigerator for two days.

Thanks for the food! Thanks for the effort, thanks for the caring. It's not just the food that matters, but the care with which you prepare it, and the love we ingest with it. It is healing; it is a blessing. It makes me feel safer! A.G.

Chilled Tomato-Mint Soup

SERVES 6 TO 8

A delightful summer soup to use tomatoes and mint fresh from the garden.

INGREDIENTS

2 tablespoons	**olive oil**
1 medium	**onion – diced**
1	**clove of garlic – minced**
3 tablespoons	**flour**
2 pounds	**ripe tomatoes – cored, seeded, and cut into chunks**
3 cups	**chicken broth**
1 teaspoon	**ground ginger**

Salt and freshly ground pepper to taste

1/2 cup	**sour cream**
1	**cucumber – peeled, seeded, and diced**
1/2 cup	**fresh mint leaves – minced**

Mint sprigs (garnish)

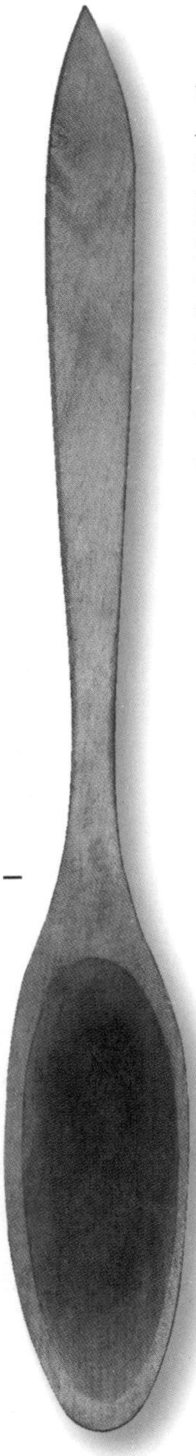

Heat oil in a soup pot and sauté the onion and garlic for 3 minutes. Add the flour, stirring, then the tomatoes, broth, ginger, salt, and pepper. Bring to a boil. Reduce heat and simmer for 20 minutes. Remove from heat and purée until smooth. Chill thoroughly in the refrigerator for at least 3 hours. Before serving, whisk in the sour cream until well blended. Then gently stir in the cucumber and mint. Ladle into individual bowls. Garnish with extra mint sprigs.

Toasted Parmesan Rounds

Makes 2 Cups

The cheese mixture keeps in the refrigerator for up to four days. It is great to have on hand to serve with drinks.

Ingredients

$^1/_3$ cup	**Parmesan cheese – grated**
$^3/_4$ cup	**mayonnaise**
$^1/_2$ cup	**onion – chopped**
$^1/_4$ teaspoon	**Worcestershire sauce**
$^1/_4$ teaspoon	**salt**
$^1/_4$ teaspoon	**pepper**

Party-sized rye or pumpernickel bread

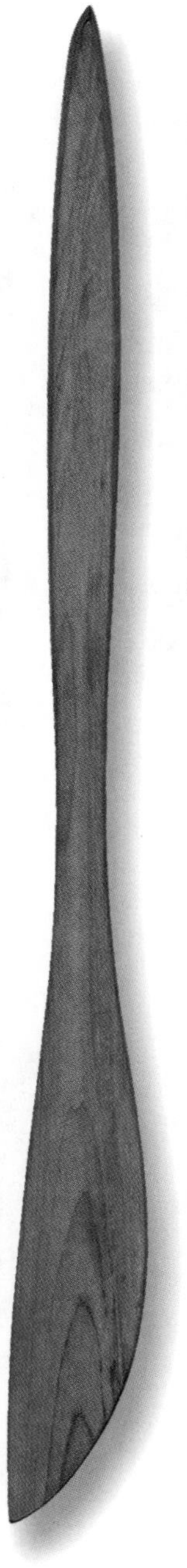

Combine all of the ingredients, except for the bread, in a small bowl. Mix well. Chill until ready to use.

At serving time, preheat the broiler. Lightly coat the bread slices with the Parmesan spread. Place on a baking sheet, and broil until brown and bubbly. Serve immediately.

Spicy variation: Add a dash of red chile powder or a tablespoon of chopped green chiles.

SPINACH AND CHICKEN ENCHILADAS

SERVES 6

A quick-and-easy version of a Southwestern favorite.

INGREDIENTS

1 tablespoon	**olive oil**
$^1/_2$ pound	**mushrooms – sliced**
1 pound	**fresh spinach – washed, rinsed, and chopped**
2 cups (8 ounces)	**Monterey Jack cheese – cubed**
6	**flour tortillas**
1 can (15 ounce)	**cream of chicken soup**
2 cups	**sour cream**
2 cups	**cooked chicken – cut in chunks**
1 can (4 ounce)	**diced green chile**
$^1/_2$ to 1 teaspoon	**garlic powder**

Salt and freshly ground pepper, to taste

Preheat oven to 350 degrees. Grease a shallow baking dish.

In a small skillet, heat oil and sauté the mushrooms for 3 minutes. Remove from heat. In a medium bowl, mix the mushrooms with the spinach and cheese. Line a sixth of this mixture down the middle of each tortilla. Roll the tortillas and place, seam side down, in the prepared baking dish.

Mix together the soup and sour cream in a medium bowl. Add the cooked chicken, green chile, and spices. Pour this mixture over the tortillas. Bake for 15 to 20 minutes, until the cheese is melted. Serve immediately.

Fire and Ice Salad

SERVES 6

A pretty summer salad. Chill for at least 4 hours before serving.

INGREDIENTS

Dressing:

$^{3}/_{4}$ cup	**vinegar**
$^{1}/_{4}$ cup	**water**
$1^{1}/_{2}$ teaspoons	**celery seed**
$1^{1}/_{4}$ teaspoons	**Dijon mustard**
Dash of	**cayenne pepper**
4 teaspoons	**sugar**
6 large	**ripe tomatoes – peeled and quartered**
1 large	**green pepper – cored and thinly sliced**
1 medium	**red onion – thinly sliced**
1	**cucumber – peeled and sliced**
1	**avocado – peeled, pitted, and sliced**
6 large	**butter lettuce leaves**

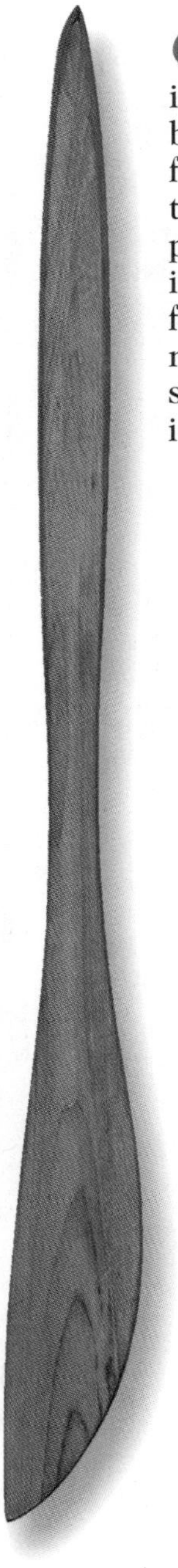

Combine the dressing ingredients in a small saucepan, and bring to a boil. Boil for 1 minute, and remove from the heat. In a medium bowl, toss the tomatoes with the green pepper and onion. Add the dressing and marinate in the refrigerator for 4 hours. Just before serving, mix in the cucumber and avocado slices. Serve on lettuce leaves on individual salad plates.

Berry Shortcakes with Tequila Whipped Cream

SERVES 6

Use any kind of berry to make this dessert.

INGREDIENTS

Shortcake:

2 cups	unbleached flour
$3/4$ tablespoon	double-acting baking powder
$1\,1/2$ tablespoons	sugar
$3/4$ teaspoon	salt
1 teaspoon	ground cloves
2 teaspoons	nutmeg
4 tablespoons	unsalted butter – at room temperature
$1/2$ cup	half-and-half

Filling:

6 cups	fresh berries
$1/2$ cup	brown sugar, or to taste

Topping:

2 cups	heavy cream
2 tablespoons	sugar
2 or more tablespoons	tequila, to taste

Preheat the oven to 425 degrees.

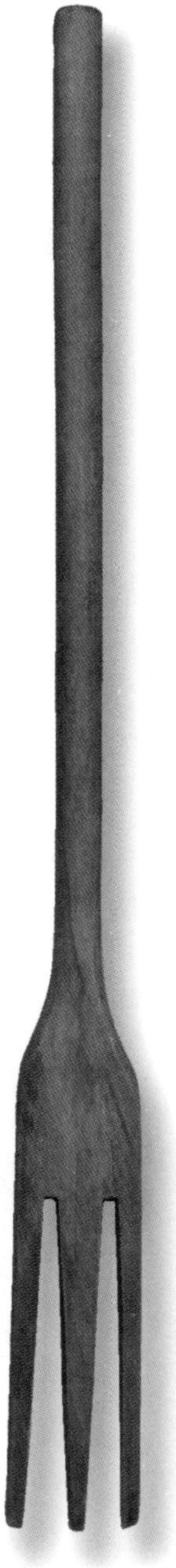

Mix the flour, baking powder, sugar, salt, ground cloves, and nutmeg in a large bowl. Cut the butter into small chunks and mix in, using two knives or a mixing fork. Slowly add the half-and-half and mix thoroughly. Roll out on a floured board to a thickness of about $1/4$-inch. Using a biscuit cutter or a small glass, cut out twelve 3-inch rounds, gathering and re-rolling the scraps as necessary. On a greased baking sheet, place the rounds in 6 stacks of two each. Bake for about 12 minutes, or until shortcakes are puffed and lightly browned.

Slice the berries, if necessary, reserving 6 perfect whole berries for garnish. Place in a bowl, and sweeten with brown sugar to taste. Take out one cup of the berries and mash or purée them.

Whip the cream. When it is firm, add the sugar and tequila, to taste.

For the assembly, split the shortcakes, and spread each of the bottom halves with whipped cream. Spoon the whole or sliced berries over the cream, and cover with the top half of the shortcakes. Top with remaining whipped cream. Spoon over the mashed berries, and top each shortcake with one berry.

AUTUMN

PHOTO BY JACK PARSONS

AUTUMN IN SANTA FE

THE AUTUMN SECTION IS SPONSORED BY
CAPITOL FORD – RAMONA BRANDT

PHOTO BY JACK PARSONS

SUPPER AFTER AN ASPEN ADVENTURE

SPONSORED BY:
CAPITOL CITY TITLE SERVICES

Supper after an Aspen Adventure

One can ride, bike, or hike the myriad meandering trails that thread through Santa Fe's Sangre de Cristo Mountains. And some of the most beautiful days for a Sangre adventure occur in late September and early October when the leaves of the quaking aspen trees change from ashy green to luminescent gold. Choose a crisp day, a trip to suit your abilities, and you are in for an exhilarating outdoor experience.

One option – the Aspen Vista Trail – begins three-quarters of the way up to the Santa Fe Ski Basin. The trail can be easy or strenuous, according to your preference. The hike to Tesuque Peak covers a varied uphill terrain full of bubbling creeks, lush vegetation, and open spaces that present spectacular views of both Santa Fe and the entire Rio Grande Valley. This trek covers twelve miles round trip and takes about six hours. For a shorter, but still soul-stirring excursion, hike for two or three miles among the aspens and then turn around. The easier Black Canyon Trail begins on Hyde Park Road, and during this two-mile walk you will be shaded by the aspens that edge the National Forest's pine stands. Along the way, pick juniper berries to flavor autumn venison or lamb dishes, or piñon nuts for Christmas sweets.

Lazier adventurers may wish to grab a seat on the ski lift near the Ski Basin's parking lot. This fall foliage attraction runs for ten days during aspen season. (Call the Ski Basin for the schedule.) The high-flying lift can take you above the treetops and back down again, but for a special experience hop off at the top and take a leisurely walk down along the edge of the basin.

After such a glorious day, you will need to ground yourself with a robust meal, so here is our supper for six.

Menu

Jalapeño and Corn Chowder
or
Sucha's Quick-and-Easy Vegetarian Chili

Chicken in a Paper Sack
or
Beef with Radishes

Michael's Caesar Salad

French Bread

Crunchy Oat-Apricot Bars

Herbal Tea or Red Wine

Jalapeño and Corn Chowder

SERVES 6

If available, substitute fresh corn kernels for the canned. This hearty vegetable soup is satisfying after a day outdoors.

INGREDIENTS

2 tablespoons	olive oil, or cooking oil spray
1 cup	onions – chopped
1 1/2 cups	vegetable broth
1 cup	cauliflower florets – chopped
1/2 cup	carrots – sliced
1/2 cup	celery – sliced
1/2 cup	green beans – sliced into 1/2 -inch pieces
1	jalapeño pepper – seeded and cut in half lengthwise *
1/4 cup	all-purpose flour
3 cups	lowfat milk
1/4 teaspoon	white pepper
Dash of	red chile powder, or cayenne
1 can (15 ounce)	corn kernels – drained
3/4 cup (3 ounces)	sharp Cheddar cheese – shredded (garnish)

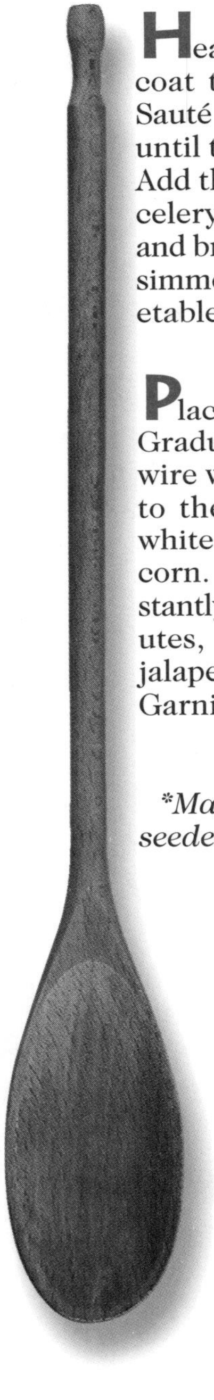

Heat oil in a large saucepan, or coat the pan with cooking spray. Sauté the onions over medium heat until translucent, about 5 minutes. Add the broth, cauliflower, carrots, celery, green beans, and jalapeño, and bring to a boil. Reduce heat and simmer for 20 minutes, or until vegetables are tender.

Place the flour in a medium bowl. Gradually add milk, stirring with a wire whisk until blended. Add this to the vegetables, along with the white pepper, ground red chile, and corn. Mix well. Cook, stirring constantly, over medium heat for 7 minutes, or until thickened. Discard jalapeño and ladle soup into bowls. Garnish with shredded cheese.

**May substitute one bell pepper, seeded and cut in half.*

Sucha's Quick-and-Easy Vegetarian Chili

SERVES 6

Very quick and easy! A meal in itself when served with salad and bread.

INGREDIENTS

1 can (15 ounce)	kidney beans – drained and rinsed
1 can (15 ounce)	Great Northern beans – drained and rinsed
1 can (15 ounce)	pinto beans – drained and rinsed
1 or 2 cans (14 ounce)	stewed tomatoes – cut in chunks
1 or 2 cups	tomato or vegetable juice (optional)
1 or 2 cans (4 ounce)	whole green chiles – sliced
1 can (4 ounce)	diced roasted jalapeño peppers *
2 to 4	cloves of garlic – minced, *or* garlic powder to taste
1 teaspoon	oregano, or to taste
1 teaspoon	basil, or to taste

Salt and freshly ground pepper, to taste

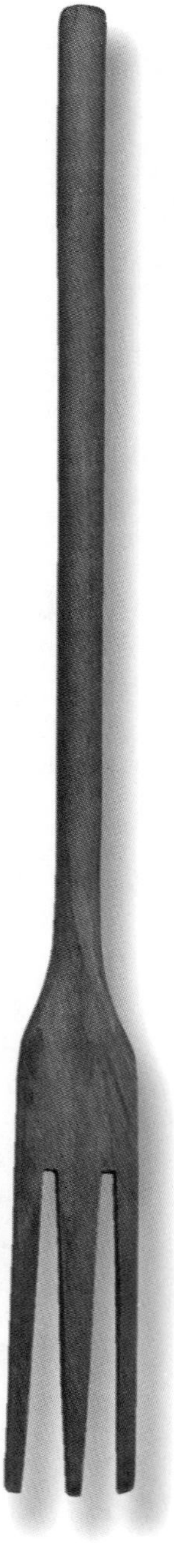

In a large saucepan or Dutch Oven, combine all ingredients over medium heat. Bring to a boil, then reduce heat and simmer for 10 to 20 minutes. Adjust seasonings, if necessary, and serve.

**Use half a can for a less spicy chili.*

Chicken in a Paper Sack

SERVES 2 OR 3

A simple recipe to double or triple, it makes perfect roasted chicken every time. It is also delicious cold. Bake half an hour longer at altitudes above 6500 feet.

INGREDIENTS

1 whole ($2^1/_2$ to $3^1/_2$ pounds)	**frying chicken**
2 tablespoons	**butter – at room temperature**
Salt and freshly ground pepper	
1 small bunch	**fresh parsley**
1	**celery rib – cut in half**
1	**onion**
2 tablespoons	**fresh tarragon, *or* 1 tablespoon dried**
Brown paper bag	
Paper clips, or string	

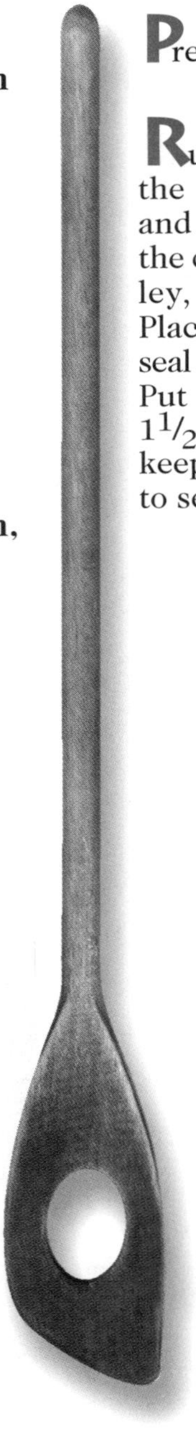

Preheat oven to 400 degrees.

Rub chicken inside and out with the softened butter. Sprinkle salt and pepper on the skin and inside the cavity. Fill the cavity with parsley, celery, onion, and tarragon. Place chicken in the paper bag and seal tightly with paper clips or string. Put in a roasting pan, and bake for $1^1/_2$ hours. Serve immediately, or keep chicken in the bag until ready to serve.

Beef with Radishes

SERVES 4 TO 6

This recipe's contributor learned it when she lived in Japan and studied Chinese cooking with French Benedictine nuns. An easy recipe to double or triple for a party.

INGREDIENTS

2 tablespoons	**soy sauce**
2 teaspoons	**cornstarch**
1 to $1\frac{1}{2}$ pounds	**beef steak – sliced very thin and cut into small pieces**
2 tablespoons	**olive or toasted sesame oil**
3 tablespoons	**vinegar**
6 tablespoons	**water**
$\frac{1}{2}$ cup	**sugar**
1 tablespoon	**cornstarch**
8 to 10	**radishes – sliced**

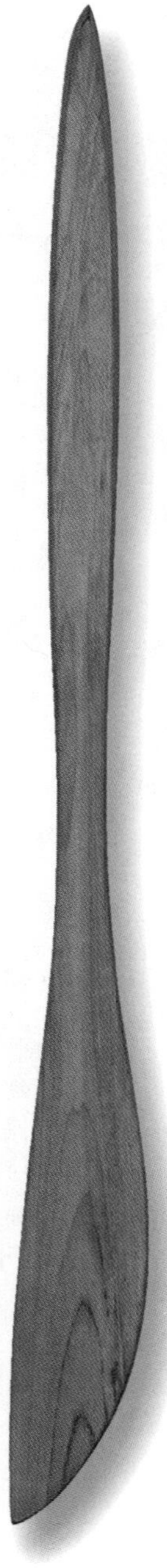

In a medium bowl, combine the soy sauce and 2 teaspoons cornstarch. Add beef and dredge well. Prepare a sweet-and-sour sauce by combining the oil, vinegar, water, sugar, and cornstarch in a small bowl. Add this mixture to a wok or heavy skillet and cook over medium heat for a few seconds. Add the dredged beef, and stir-fry until done. Add radish slices, and cook only long enough to heat thoroughly. Serve with rice, if desired.

Michael's Caesar Salad

SERVES 6

A classic!

INGREDIENTS

1	egg
2 cans (2 ounce)	anchovies, undrained
1/2 cup	extra virgin olive oil
4	cloves of garlic – minced
1	lemon – juiced
1/4 cup	vinegar
1 teaspoon	Worcestershire sauce
2 heads	romaine lettuce – washed, dried, and torn into pieces *
1 1/2 cups	croutons
1/2 cup	Parmesan cheese – grated

Freshly ground pepper, to taste

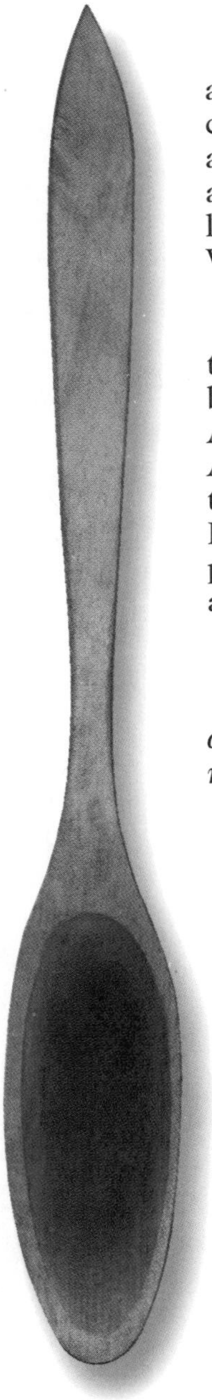

Break the egg into a salad bowl, and whisk lightly. In a small bowl, chop the anchovies in their oil and add the olive oil and garlic. In another small bowl, combine the lemon juice, vinegar, and Worcestershire.

Place the prepared lettuce into the salad bowl that contains the beaten egg, and toss until shiny. Add the anchovy mixture and toss. Add the lemon juice mixture and toss. Then add croutons, grated Parmesan, and freshly ground pepper. Toss again and serve immediately.

**May prepare ahead and keep in a plastic bag, refrigerated, until ready to use.*

French Bread

Makes 2 Baguettes

This recipe has been adjusted for high-altitude baking. Please note that preparation must begin at least 3 hours before serving time.

Ingredients

1 tablespoon	**active dry yeast**
$^{1}/_{2}$ teaspoon	**sugar**
$1^{1}/_{3}$ cups	**warm water**
4 cups	**unbleached all-purpose flour**
1 teaspoon	**salt**
2 tablespoons	**butter**
1 small	**onion – minced, *or* 6 cloves of garlic – minced (optional)**

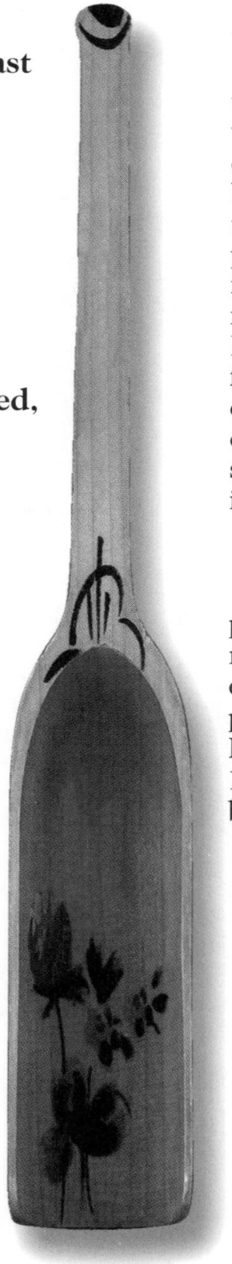

Dissolve the yeast and sugar in $^{1}/_{3}$ cup warm water. Allow 5 minutes to proof. Measure flour into the work bowl of a food processor equipped with the standard metal blade. Add salt and the yeast mixture. Process for 5 seconds. With processor running, add the remaining cup of water slowly (you may not need it all) until a dough ball forms. Remove the dough to a floured surface. Knead for about 10 minutes, occasionally slamming it down hard on the surface. If the dough is too sticky, add more flour while kneading, a little at a time.

Form the dough into a ball and place in a buttered or oiled bowl, rolling the ball lightly in the butter or oil. Cover the bowl tightly with plastic wrap or a damp dish towel. Put in a warm place to rise for about 1 hour, or until the dough has doubled in bulk.

(Continued on the next page)

French Bread - continued

Return the dough to the floured work surface. Punch it down, and knead for another 5 minutes. Place it back in the bowl, covered, and allow to rise a second time, for about 1 hour.

Melt butter in a small pan. Return the dough to the floured work surface. Punch it down again, and knead for 5 minutes. Form into two loaves. If desired, roll the loaves in the minced onion or garlic. Place on a baking sheet and coat them with melted butter. Cover loosely with plastic wrap, and allow to rise for another 45 minutes.

Preheat oven to 400 degrees. Put a pan of water or half a dozen ice cubes on the floor of the oven. With a sharp knife, slash three or four vents across the surface of the loaves. Place loaves, uncovered, on middle shelf of the oven. Bake for 30 minutes, or until golden brown. Serve immediately or at room temperature.

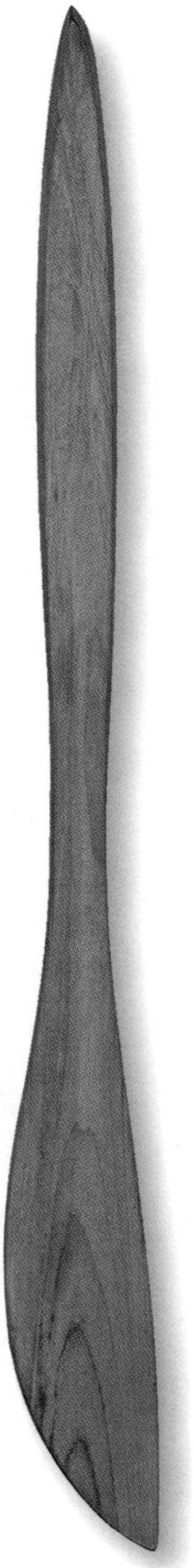

You have been supplying delicious and nutritious meals for a long time. The delivery people have been outstanding and very nice to me, and always managed to find me even though [my apartment] was very out of the way and confusing. I never missed a meal because they couldn't find me. The meals themselves have just been getting better and better, and I eat every bite. The cooks are, and have been, fabulous. B. M.

Crunchy Oat-Apricot Bars

MAKES 3 DOZEN

These yummy, quick-to-make bars are great to take along on a hike.

INGREDIENTS

$1\frac{3}{4}$ cup	**flour**
2 cups	**oats**
1 cup (well packed)	**brown sugar**
$\frac{2}{3}$ cup	**butter or margarine – at room temperature**
$1\frac{1}{2}$ teaspoons	**vanilla extract**
$1\frac{1}{2}$ cups	**apricot preserves**

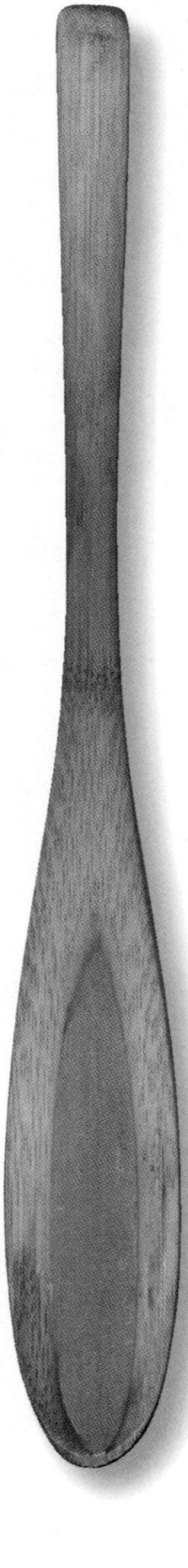

Preheat oven to 350 degrees.

Place the flour, oats, brown sugar, butter, and vanilla in a blender or food processor. Mix until ingredients resemble coarse meal. Press half of the mixture onto a greased 13 x 9-inch pan. Spread the preserves evenly over this layer. Sprinkle the remaining mixture on top and press it down lightly. Bake for 35 minutes, or until bubbly and golden brown. Cool completely before cutting.

Photo by Elliott McDowell

Box Lunch for the Kitchen Angels Road Rally

Sponsored by:
John Tyson

Box Lunch for the Kitchen Angels Road Rally

We at Kitchen Angels are quite proud of our Road Rally. This exciting event provides a day of fun and whirlwind adventure for all who participate. Not only does it raise money for our organization, but the lucky winners also go home with wonderful prizes!

The Road Rally resembles a treasure hunt and follows a circuitous route from Santa Fe along beautiful country mountain roads, winding up with a celebration of dinner, music, and dancing. At the start, participants are provided with a packet of clues – in the form of amusing riddles or clever math problems – to help them get from one checkpoint to another as expediently as possible. While adhering to additional rules and regulations, competitors are required to stop at each checkpoint, where their time and mileage are recorded. Every car must reach each consecutive destination within an estimated time limit, arriving from the correct direction and without having received a speeding ticket! Failure to meet any of the regulations seriously diminishes your chance of winning. The object, therefore, is to cross the finish line with the best score.

The spirit of competition always works up an appetite. Our delectable box lunch for four is great to take along in the car, as a snack when stomachs start to rumble or that competitive energy needs fueling. It works equally well for a cool-weather picnic with no agenda at all. So, what are you waiting for? Start your engines!

Menu

Pita Breads with
Hoisin Shrimp
or
Pita Breads with Curry-
Basil Chicken

Spicy Asian Rice Salad

Pumpkin Bars

Fresh Fruit

Santa Fe Hot Chocolate

Pita Breads with Hoisin Shrimp

SERVES 4

Filled pita breads make ideal pick-up meals. Pita pockets may be stuffed with tuna, chicken, or egg salad, falafel with tahini dressing, raw veggie salad, or whatever you fancy. Hoisin Shrimp makes an excellent pita filling. This Chinese dish also makes a fast and tasty dinner entrée when served with rice.

INGREDIENTS

4	**whole pita breads**

Hoisin Shrimp Pita filling:

3 tablespoons	**hoisin sauce**
2 tablespoons	**rice vinegar**
2 tablespoons	**water**
2 teaspoons	**sugar**
1/2 teaspoon	**ground ginger**
1/2 teaspoon	**cornstarch**
1/8 teaspoon	**crushed red pepper**
2 tablespoons	**peanut oil**
1 pound	**medium shrimp – shelled and deveined**
1	**clove of garlic – minced**
3	**scallions – cut diagonally into 1-inch lengths**

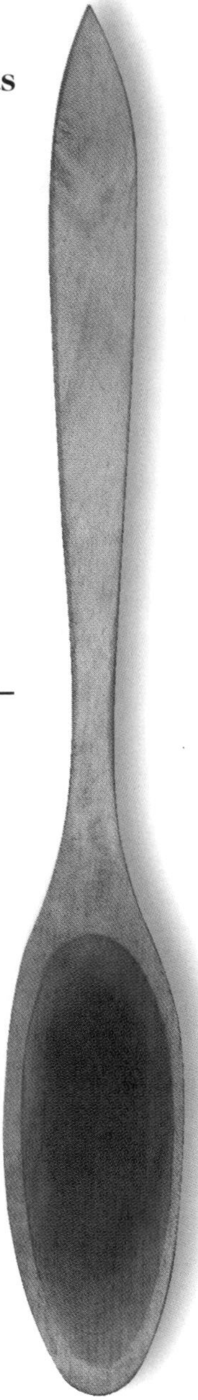

Preheat oven to 450 degrees. Place pita breads on a baking sheet, and bake for 1 minute or until the breads puff a bit. Remove from the oven. Cut the top third off of each bread, and discard. Alternatively, cut breads in half, and use both halves. Fill each pita with desired filling, being careful not to tear pita edges.

Combine the hoisin, vinegar, water, sugar, ginger, cornstarch, and crushed red pepper in a small bowl. Heat oil in a wok or frying pan over medium heat until almost smoking. Add the shrimp and garlic, and stir-fry about 2 minutes. Stir in scallions, and hoisin mixture. Cook for about 3 minutes, stirring constantly, until the shrimp are opaque. Cool the mixture a bit before filling the prepared pita breads.

If using this dish as a dinner entrée, serve with a side of rice.

Pita Breads with Curry-Basil Chicken

SERVES 4

This pita filling also makes a delicious entrée when served with rice.

INGREDIENTS

4	**whole pita breads**

<u>**Curry-Basil Chicken Pita filling:**</u>

2 tablespoons	**olive oil**
4	**chicken breast halves, boneless and skinless**
1 to 3	**cloves of garlic – minced**
2 teaspoons	**curry powder**
1 teaspoon	**dried chicken bouillon granules**
1 cup	**half-and-half, *or* evaporated skim milk**
1 bunch	**basil, leaves only – chopped**
4 large	**romaine leaves – julienned (optional)**

Prepare pita breads as in previous recipe.

Heat oil in a medium skillet and sauté the chicken breasts on both sides. Add the garlic and cook until the chicken is browned. Add the curry powder, bouillon, and half-and-half. Simmer for 10 minutes. Stir in the chopped basil and remove from heat.

To make a filling for pita, cool chicken in the sauce, then cut into strips. Add enough sauce to moisten the chicken and mix in the chopped lettuce, if desired. Fill the prepared pita pockets.

As a dinner main course, serve whole chicken breasts in their sauce, with a side dish of rice. Garnish with chopped scallions or radishes, and serve with chutney.

Spicy Asian Rice Salad

SERVES 4 TO 6

This crunchy salad rounds out any dinner or picnic menu. Prepare several hours ahead of time to allow flavors to marinate. It also makes an excellent vegetarian filling for pita breads.

INGREDIENTS

<u>Asian Vinaigrette:</u>

1/4 cup	**rice wine vinegar**
1	**lemon – juiced**
2	**shallots – minced**
2	**cloves of garlic – minced**
1 to 2 tablespoons	**fresh ginger – grated**
1/2 to 3/4 cup	**olive or vegetable oil**
2 teaspoons	**toasted sesame oil**
1/2 teaspoon	**Asian chili paste, *or* 1/4 teaspoon hot chili oil**

Salt and freshly ground pepper, to taste

2 cups	**water**
1/4 pound	**snow peas – strings removed**
2 cups	**cooked rice – cooled and fluffed**
1/2	**daikon (white) radish – julienned**
1	**red bell pepper – seeded, cored, and julienned**
1	**yellow bell pepper – seeded, cored, and julienned**
1/2 to 1 small	**red onion – julienned**

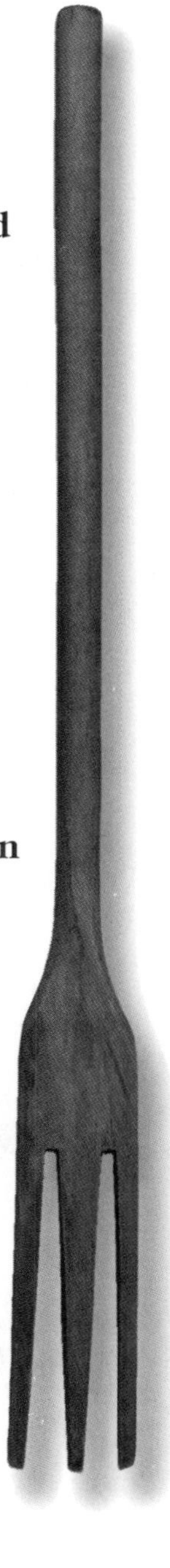

Combine the vinegar, lemon juice, shallots, garlic, and ginger in a small bowl. Whisk in oils and season with the chili paste, salt, and pepper. Set aside. In a medium saucepan bring water to a boil. Add the snow peas and blanch for 30 seconds. Drain and refresh with cold water. Cut into julienne strips. Refrigerate in a plastic bag.

In a large bowl, toss the cooked rice and julienned vegetables – except for the snow peas. Mix in the vinaigrette. Allow salad to marinate in the refrigerator for several hours. Bring to room temperature. Just before serving, mix in the snow peas.

Pumpkin Bars

MAKES 12 BARS

These healthy, delicious bars are low in fat, and contain no wheat or sugar.

INGREDIENTS

1/4 cup	oil
1/4 cup	apple, apricot, or other fruit nectar
2 cups	applesauce
2 cups	canned pumpkin
4	eggs
2 cups	barley, rice, or oat flour
2 teaspoons	cinnamon
1/2 teaspoon	salt
1 teaspoon	baking soda
2 teaspoons	baking powder

<u>Frosting</u> (optional):

1 package (8 ounce)	lowfat cream cheese – at room temperature
1/2 cup	applesauce
1/2 teaspoon	vanilla extract

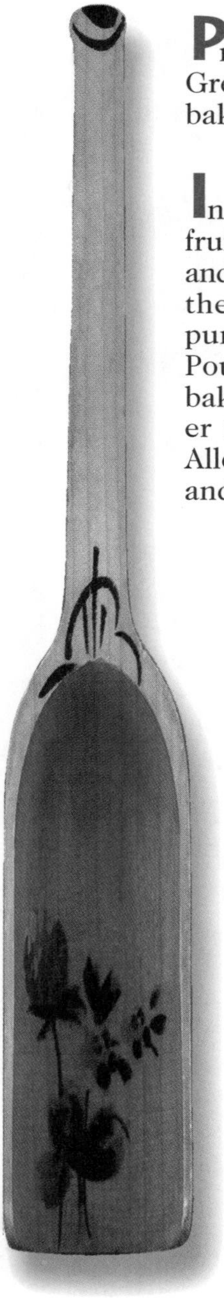

Preheat oven to 350 degrees. Grease and flour a 15 x 10 x 1-inch baking dish.

In a large bowl, mix together the oil, fruit nectar, applesauce, pumpkin, and eggs. In a second bowl, combine the dry ingredients, then add to pumpkin mixture, blending well. Pour into the prepared pan, and bake for 25 minutes. Beat together frosting ingredients, if desired. Allow the bars to cool, then frost, and cut into squares.

Santa Fe Hot Chocolate

8 Servings

To transport in a thermos, omit the instructions for beating until foamy. Use the foam method when serving at home.

Ingredients

3 ounces	**sweet chocolate – broken into small pieces**
$^{3}/_{4}$ cup	**boiling water**
6 cups (1 $^{1}/_{2}$ quarts)	**milk**
3 rounded tablespoons	**freeze-dried coffee crystals, *or* 5 tablespoons very strong, freshly brewed coffee**
2	**cinnamon sticks – broken in several pieces**
1$^{1}/_{2}$ teaspoons	**vanilla extract**
Pinch of	**salt**
Sprinkle of	**nutmeg (garnish)**

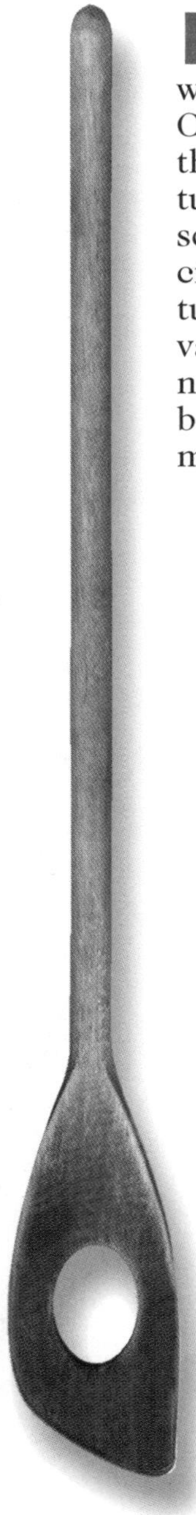

Place the chocolate and boiling water in a small heavy saucepan. Cook over low heat, stirring, until the chocolate is melted and mixture is smooth. In a large saucepan, scald the milk with the coffee and cinnamon. Add the chocolate mixture, blending well, and season with vanilla and salt. Remove the cinnamon sticks, and beat with a rotary beater until foamy. Pour into small mugs, and dust lightly with nutmeg.

Photo by Jack Parsons

Fall Feast from the Farmers' Market

Sponsored by:
The Marketplace Natural Grocery

Fall Feast from the Farmers' Market

On Tuesday and Saturday mornings, from early summer through fall, farmers, home gardeners, craftspeople, bakers, musicians, even dancers, come from all over northern New Mexico to our Farmers' Market next to the rail yard. They arrive early to set up stalls and tents or open the backs of their trucks to display their wares or harvests or talents. The restauranteurs are there to greet them, and throughout the morning locals and tourists mill about, sampling goodies and comparing prices.

Often you will hear fiddles as you cross the tracks and pass the stalls selling a variety of apples from Velarde. There will be chiles from Chimayó and Hatch, heirloom beans from Abiquiu, melons and squashes, homemade goat cheeses. Over there, a man offers tastes of fresh cider. Next to him, a woman snips sprouts with great big scissors. Beside her, a little girl clog dances on a crate, surrounded by the fiddlers you heard. There are stalls of dried flowers and wreaths, fresh herbs in pots, braids of garlic, and red chile *ristras*. "Turn around...," sings a woman in a shawl.

Along the next aisle you discover white eggplants and purple peppers and a tent filled with jars of fresh honey. The chicken guy yells, "Organic free rangers!" A fellow shopper you've seen all summer warns you that the man from Moriarty is almost out of corn, but you are busy tasting a sampler of salsas and jams. Across the aisle, there are chokecherry lollypops, freshly baked fruit pies, herbal vinegars, and the lamb man. His lambs, you've heard, are a breed brought here by early Spanish settlers.

Before buying, you stroll through the market, to take it all in. Then, as you make your purchases for our Farmers' Market menu, you muse to yourself, "This is the kind of excitement I want to bring to my guests."

Menu

Creamy Broccoli Soup

Butterflied Leg of Lamb with Chipotle Chutney

Sunshine Carrots

Gerry's Roadside Potatoes

Roasted Eggplant and Pepper Salad

Audrey's Apples
or
Heavenly Apple Pie

Fresh Apple Cider

Creamy Broccoli Soup

SERVES 4 TO 6

This puréed soup is delicious all winter long.

INGREDIENTS

2 cans (14.5 ounce)	**chicken or vegetable broth**
2 medium	**white potatoes – peeled and chopped**
2 medium	**white onions – chopped**
2	**cloves of garlic – minced**
2 small bunches	**broccoli – cut into stemmed florets**
$^1/_2$ to 1 cup	**skim, soy, or rice milk**
Salt and white pepper, to taste	
4 to 6 tablespoons	**sour cream (garnish)**
1 or 2 tablespoons	**chopped chives *or* dill weed (garnish)**

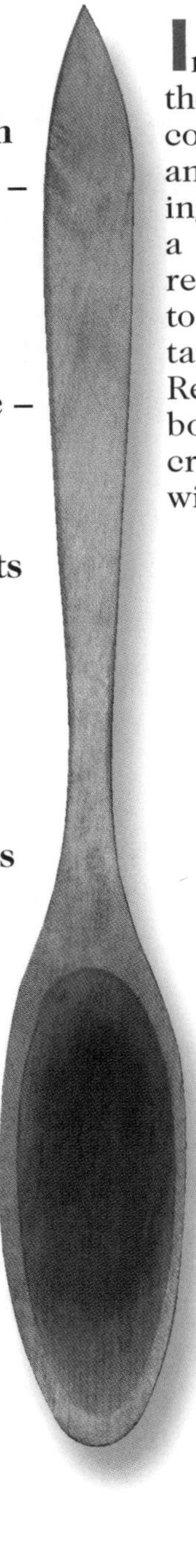

In a large saucepan, mix broth with the potatoes, onion, garlic, and broccoli. Bring to a boil. Reduce heat and simmer for 20 minutes, until ingredients are soft. Purée soup in a blender or food processor, and return to the saucepan. Add milk to desired consistency and season to taste with salt and white pepper. Reheat, but do not boil. Ladle into bowls and swirl a dollop of sour cream into each serving. Sprinkle with chives or dill.

Butterflied Leg of Lamb with Chipotle Chutney

SERVES 4 TO 6

The lamb should be marinated for 24 hours before grilling.

INGREDIENTS

<u>Marinade:</u>

$1^1/_2$ cups	red wine
$^3/_4$ cup	beef stock
$^1/_4$ cup	orange marmalade
2 tablespoons	red wine vinegar
2 tablespoons	onion – finely chopped
1 tablespoon	marjoram
1 tablespoon	dried rosemary
2	bay leaves – crumbled
$^1/_2$ teaspoon	ground ginger
$^1/_2$ teaspoon	seasoning salt
2	cloves of garlic – crushed
1 whole small (3 to 4 pound)	leg of lamb, boned and butterflied
2 more tablespoons	orange marmalade

Chipotle Chutney – *recipe follows*

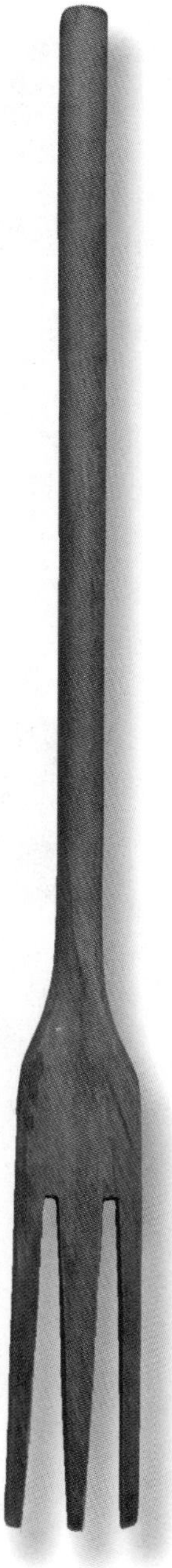

The day before grilling, combine the marinade ingredients in a saucepan and simmer for 20 minutes over low heat. Cool to room temperature.

Lay the leg of lamb flat in a roasting pan and cover with marinade. Refrigerate, covered, turning the lamb four times while marinating. Two hours before cooking, bring lamb to room temperature.

If using a charcoal grill, light the briquettes 45 minutes before cooking. For a gas grill, preheat on the highest setting for 15 minutes. Remove the lamb from the marinade and pat dry with paper towels. Reserve 1 cup of the marinade.

Place the lamb flat on the grill. If a gas grill is being used, adjust the setting to medium. Put the reserved marinade into a saucepan on the stove over high heat and reduce it by half. Stir in the additional 2 tablespoons marmalade.

For medium rare, grill the lamb for 10 minutes on each side. Turn again and brush the top with half of the reduced marinade glaze. Cook for 5 minutes. Turn, brush with remaining glaze, and grill 5 more minutes. A meat thermometer, inserted into one of the thicker parts, should read 140 to 150 degrees. When done, allow the lamb to sit for 10 minutes on a heated platter. Slice into strips before serving.

CHIPOTLE CHUTNEY

SERVES 4

This spicy relish can be easily increased for a crowd. It is a tangy accompaniment for lamb, pork chops, or chicken.

INGREDIENTS

1 can (7 ounce)	**chipotle chiles – diced**
1 medium	**Granny Smith apple – unpeeled and diced**
1/2 cup	**sherry vinegar**
1/2 cup	**light brown sugar**
1/4 cup	**white sugar**
1 to 2	**cloves of garlic – minced**
3	**Anaheim or Poblano chiles – roasted, peeled, and diced**

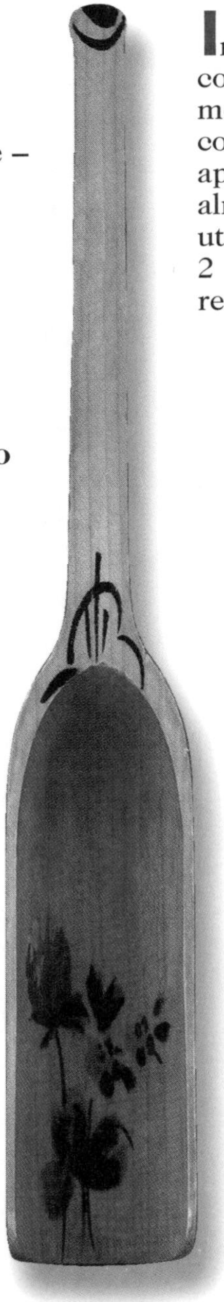

In a medium nonreactive saucepan, combine all of the ingredients over moderately low heat. Cover and cook, stirring occasionally, until the apple is tender and the liquid is almost evaporated, about 25 minutes. Cool before serving. Keeps for 2 weeks, tightly covered, in the refrigerator.

Sunshine Carrots

SERVES 4 TO 6

These sweet carrots can be assembled quickly.

INGREDIENTS

3/4 cup	**orange juice**
1/2 cup	**maple syrup**
1/4 cup	**English orange marmalade**
1 pound	**whole baby carrots – peeled, *or* 2 cans or jars (16 ounce) small whole carrots – drained**

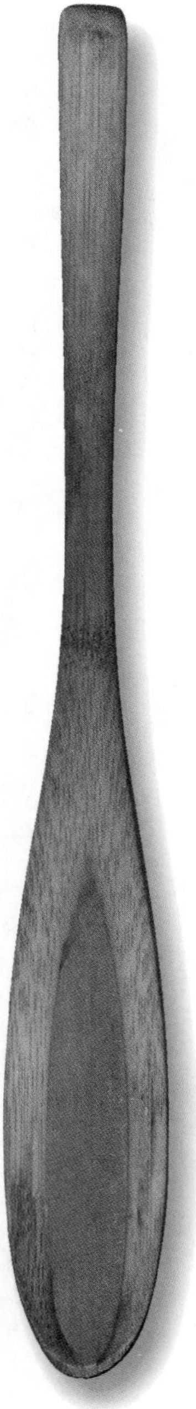

In a heavy saucepan, over low heat, mix together all ingredients. Cover and cook, stirring occasionally, until the carrots are tender, or cooked though.

GERRY'S ROADSIDE POTATOES

SERVES 4 TO 6

An all-time favorite from one of the initial members of the Wednesday cooking crew at Kitchen Angels. She used to say, "This is one of those recipes that's hard to mess up, and everyone loves these potatoes." An easy dish to increase for large parties.

INGREDIENTS

12 to 14 ounces	**Cheddar cheese**
4	**potatoes – peeled ***
2	**onions – diced**
Salt and freshly ground pepper, to taste	
4 to 5 tablespoons	**flour**
$^{1}/_{4}$ cup	**milk**

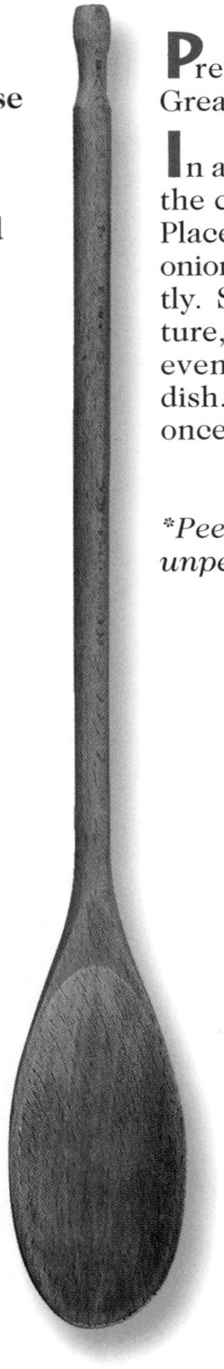

Preheat oven to 350 degrees. Grease a shallow baking dish.

In a food processor, grate or shred the cheese, and then the potatoes. Place both in a large bowl. Add the onions, salt, and pepper, mixing gently. Sprinkle the flour over the mixture, and stir in the milk. Scrape evenly into the prepared baking dish. Bake for 1 hour, and serve at once.

**Peeling is optional; if using unpeeled, scrub potatoes well.*

Roasted Eggplant and Pepper Salad

SERVES 4

This antipasto-type salad may be made up to a day ahead of time. It can be increased easily for a larger crowd.

INGREDIENTS

1 medium	**eggplant**
2	**red bell peppers**
1	**green bell pepper**
$^1/_4$ cup	**shallots – minced**
1	**clove of garlic – minced**
2 tablespoons	**olive oil**
2 tablespoons	**fresh lemon juice**
1 tablespoon	**red wine vinegar**

Salt and freshly ground pepper, to taste

1 can (3.75 ounce)	**sardines in oil – drained**

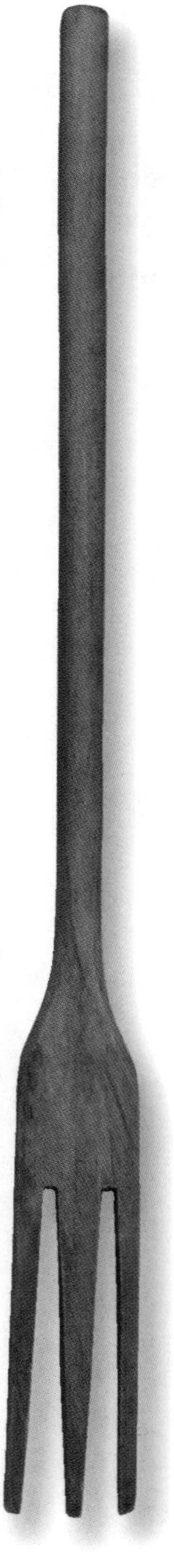

Roast the eggplant and bell peppers in a very hot oven, under a broiler, or on a grill over hot coals, turning often until the skins are blistered and charred. Transfer to a plate, and cover tightly with plastic wrap. Allow to sweat and cool, then peel the eggplant and cut into narrow strips. Remove scorched skins of the peppers, discard seeds and membranes, and cut into narrow strips.

In a medium bowl, combine the eggplant and peppers with the shallots, garlic, oil, lemon juice, and vinegar. Mix well, and season with salt and pepper. Gently toss in the sardines. Cover and refrigerate for several hours or overnight.

AUDREY'S APPLES

SERVES 4 TO 6

For this easy recipe, the apples are sliced and cooked on the stove top.

INGREDIENTS

1 stick (4 ounces)	**butter**
6 to 8	**Rome baking apples unpeeled, cored, and sliced thickly**
$^3/_4$ to 1 cup	**walnuts – chopped**
1 cup	**raisins or currants**
$^1/_2$ teaspoon	**nutmeg**
2 tablespoons	**cinnamon**
1 pint	**vanilla ice cream (optional)**

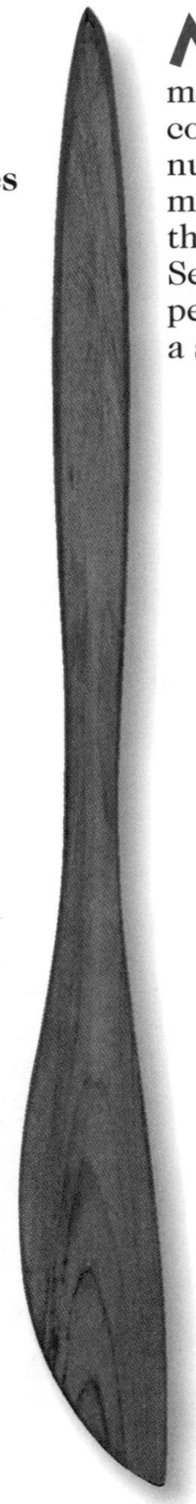

Melt butter in a large skillet over medium heat. Add the apples and cook until fork tender. Stir in the nuts, raisins, nutmeg, and cinnamon, and continue cooking until the apples are soft but not mushy. Serve either hot or at room temperature, alone or accompanied by a scoop of vanilla ice cream.

Heavenly Apple Pie

SERVES 6 TO 8

This recipe is adjusted for high altitude. *

INGREDIENTS

8 large or 14 small	**Red Delicious apples – peeled, cored, and sliced**
$1/2$ cup	**raisins**
$1/3$ cup	**white sugar**
2 tablespoons	**brown sugar**
2 tablespoons	**flour**
1 to 2 teaspoons	**cinnamon**
$1/2$ to 1 teaspoon	**almond extract**

Additional cinnamon, to taste

Uncooked bottom and top crust for a 9-inch pie shell

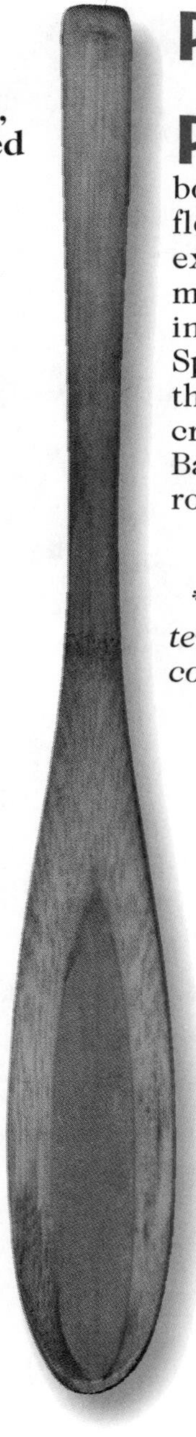

Preheat oven to 375 degrees.

Place the apple slices in a large bowl. Add the raisins, both sugars, flour, cinnamon, and almond extract. Toss well. Arrange the mixture in the bottom crust of a 9-inch pie shell, and pile high. Sprinkle additional cinnamon over the top. Cover with the top crust, crimp edges, and prick with a fork. Bake for $1\frac{1}{2}$ hours. Serve hot or at room temperature.

**For lower altitudes, lower oven temperature to 350 degrees, and cook for 1 hour.*

Photo by Jack Parsons

Heirloom Recipes to Honor the Day of the Dead

Sponsored by:
Marilyn Seckler and Ted Ore

All Souls' or All Saints' Days were originally Catholic days of commemoration, upon which intercessions were made for the souls of the departed. The custom of decorating graves or laying tables of favorite foods near them still exists in many European Roman Catholic countries. In Latin American cultures, the Day of the Dead is a more homey event where bouquets of flowers and elaborate meals are prepared and taken to cemeteries. Relatives and friends celebrate by eating at the grave sites of those family members who are gone but not forgotten. In Mexico, the celebration – El Día de los Muertos – begins on the evening of October thirty-first and continues through November second. It is considered the most important holiday of the year and is a time of joy, remembering, and much feasting.

Preparing food is an intimate act. Preparing a dish well – an old favorite, for example – not only nourishes the bodies of our families and friends, it also lifts our spirits and creates a sense of community around the table. It is that feeling, in regard to those who are departed, which is sought in the informal Day of the Dead celebrations here in northern New Mexico.

Our menu seeks to honor our loved ones in yet another aspect. All the dishes here were handed down to us by them. Some are from relatives and friends still living, some are from those who have departed. How wonderful to recall them, not only in eating the food, but in preparing it. How intimate to remember, in the act of stirring ingredients, that your loved ones have made the same motions that you now make.

Stop, and say to yourself, "They did this." Bring their cherished dishes to your table. You are their link to life and tradition.

Heirloom Recipes to Honor the Day of the Dead

Menu

Mama's Pimiento Spread with Crackers

Grandma's Mac & Cheese
or
Rose's Pot Roast
or
Nonna's Baked Pumpkin

Maggie's and Charlie's Corn Pudding

Mamie's Autumn Salad

Irish Oat Cakes

Gran's Scottish Shortbread

Red Wine and Coffee

Mama's Pimiento Spread with Crackers

MAKES 2 CUPS

This piquant spread may also be used as a topping for baked potatoes or any favorite cooked vegetable.

INGREDIENTS

1 pound	**Wisconsin Cheddar cheese – grated**
1/2 pound	**extra sharp Cheddar cheese – grated**
1 jar (4 ounce)	**chopped pimiento – drained**
1/2 can (4 ounce)	**diced jalapeño peppers – seeds removed**
1/3 cup	**mayonnaise**
2 tablespoons	**sweet pickle relish**
1 tablespoon	**sugar**
Assorted crackers	

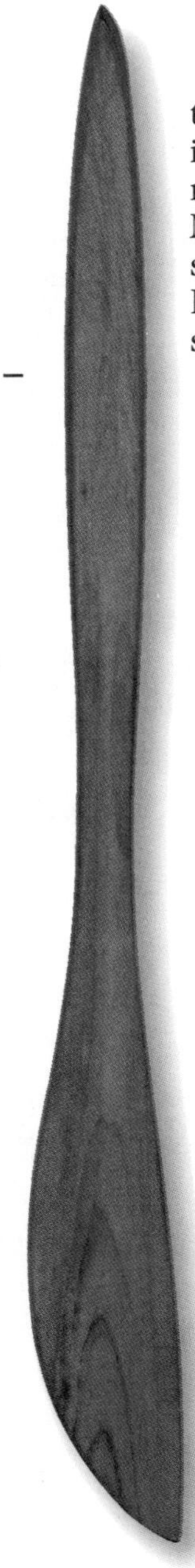

Put the cheeses, chopped pimientos, and diced jalapeños into a mixing bowl. With a fork, stir in the mayonnaise, pickle relish, and sugar. Mash and blend the mixture until smooth. Cover and refrigerate. Bring to room temperature before serving with crackers.

Grandma's Mac & Cheese

SERVES 4 TO 6

Everyone's favorite comfort food and an easy recipe to increase. Be sure to try the spicy Santa Fe variation, noted below, when you're feeling adventurous.

INGREDIENTS

1 pound	**macaroni (elbows or another shape)**
1 tablespoon	**olive oil**
1 large	**yellow onion – chopped**
1 quart	**stewed tomatoes, or whole tomatoes – chopped with juice**
1/2 to 1 teaspoon	**oregano**
Salt and freshly ground pepper, to taste	
2 cups (8 ounces)	**Cheddar cheese – shredded ***

Topping:

1/2 cup	**bread crumbs**
1 tablespoon	**butter – melted**
1/4 cup	**Parmesan cheese – grated**

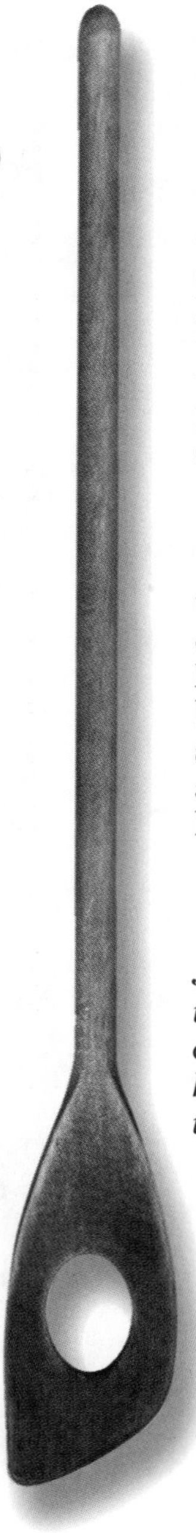

Preheat oven to 350 degrees. Butter a 2-quart casserole.

Bring water to a boil in a large pot and add the macaroni. Cook until done, and drain. In the meantime, heat oil in a large skillet and sauté the onions until translucent. Add the tomatoes and cook until slightly thickened. Season with oregano, salt, and pepper.

In the buttered casserole, layer the tomato sauce, macaroni, and shredded Cheddar, ending with pasta. Mix the bread crumbs with melted butter and grated Parmesan in a small bowl. Sprinkle over the macaroni. Bake about 45 minutes, until hot and bubbly.

**For a Santa Fe touch, substitute Jalapeño Monterey Jack cheese for the Cheddar, and/or add a 4-ounce can of diced green chiles – mild to hot, according to taste – to the tomato sauce.*

Rose's Pot Roast

SERVES 8 TO 10

In this elegant version of a wonderfully comforting main dish, the roast is marinated for 24 hours before cooking. Leftovers are fought over the next day.

INGREDIENTS

1 whole (3 to 4 pound)	lean beef roast
2	onions – sliced
1	lemon – sliced
2 tablespoons	sugar
1 tablespoon	salt
1 teaspoon	ground ginger
12 whole	black peppercorns
1 to 2 cups	red Burgundy wine
2 tablespoons	olive oil
Water, as needed	
1 to 2 tablespoons	flour
1/4 cup	water

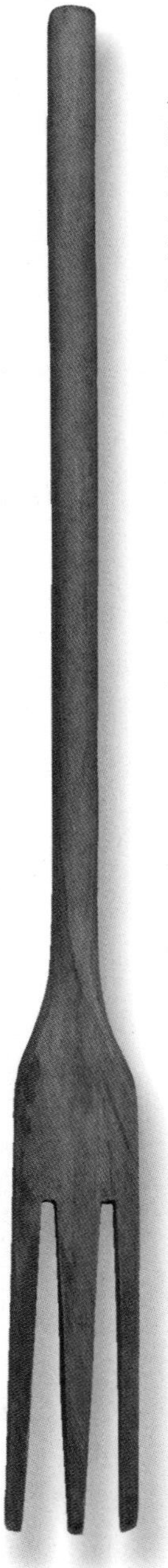

Place the roast in a deep bowl. Add the onion and lemon slices, sugar, salt, ginger, peppercorns, and enough wine to cover more than half of the roast. Marinate in the refrigerator for 24 hours, turning occasionally.

When ready to cook, drain the roast and pat it dry, reserving the marinade. Heat oil in a large Dutch oven or deep pot and brown the roast on all sides. Strain the reserved marinade and add it to the pot. Cover and simmer for 3 to 4 hours, adding water as necessary. When tender, remove the roast to a platter.

Mix the flour and water in a small bowl and add it to the remaining liquid in the pot. Cook, stirring, until the sauce is thickened. Return the roast to the pot for a quick reheat. Serve the roast and gravy with either cooked noodles or baked potatoes.

Nonna's Baked Pumpkin

SERVES 4

The size of the pumpkin you need depends upon how many people you want to feed; the ingredient amounts can be flexible. A smallish pumpkin, about 8- to 10-inches in diameter, will feed 4 as a vegetarian main dish, or 6 to 8 as a side dish.

INGREDIENTS

1 whole	**pumpkin, about 8- to 10-inches in diameter**
Salt and freshly ground pepper, to taste	
1 baguette	**French bread – cut into 1/2 -inch slices ***
3 medium	**onions – sliced**
1 pound	**Cheddar or Jalapeño Monterey Jack cheese – thinly sliced**

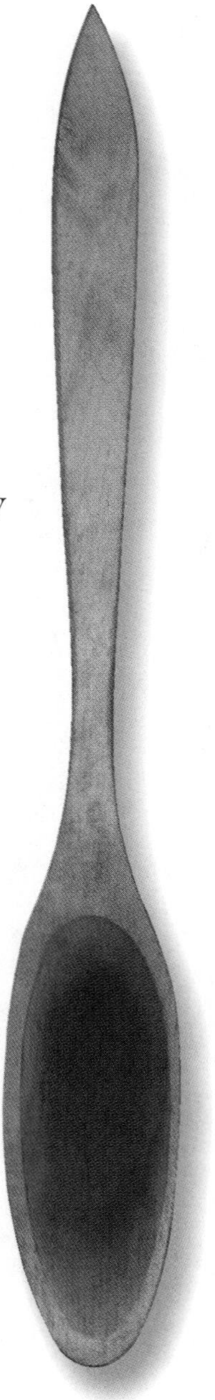

Preheat oven to 400 degrees. Grease a shallow baking dish.

Prepare the pumpkin exactly as if you were going to carve a face on it for Halloween: Slice it across the top, reserving the lid, and scoop out all of the seeds and strings.

Sprinkle salt and pepper into the pumpkin's cavity. Arrange alternating layers of bread, onion, and cheese slices inside the pumpkin, ending up with a layer of cheese. Cover with the pumpkin lid. Place on the prepared baking dish, and add about 1/2-inch of water. Bake until the pumpkin meat is soft and the cheese is melted, about 1 hour. Remove the pumpkin lid, and use a large spoon to scoop out servings, being careful not to puncture the softened pumpkin shell.

**It is fine to use bread that is slightly stale for this recipe.*

Maggie's and Charlie's Corn Pudding

SERVES 6 TO 8

Maggie used to say, "There's no point in making this if your corn's not fresh-shucked."

INGREDIENTS

2 teaspoons	**unsalted butter – at room temperature**
9 ears	**fresh corn – shucked and cleaned**
3 tablespoons	**flour**
2 tablespoons	**sugar**
$^1/_2$ teaspoon	**freshly ground black pepper, or to taste**
2	**eggs – beaten**
2 tablespoons	**unsalted butter – cut in slivers**
1 cup	**milk**

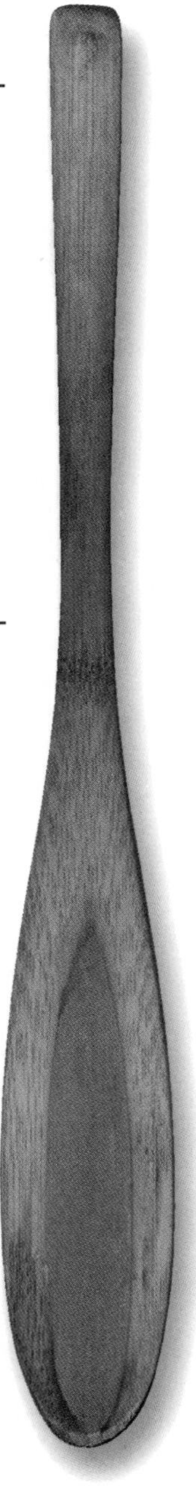

Preheat oven to 350 degrees. Rub 2 teaspoons butter over the inside of a medium-sized ovenproof casserole.

Into a mixing bowl, slice the kernels off the shucked corn. With the back of the knife blade, scrape each cob thoroughly, releasing as much of the "milk" into the bowl as possible. Add half of the flour and mix into the corn. Add remaining flour and mix again, coating each kernel. Add the sugar and freshly ground pepper, coating the kernels well, then thoroughly mix in the beaten eggs.

Pour the corn into the baking dish, spreading it evenly. Setting four or five slivers of butter aside, distribute the rest across the top. Using your finger, push each one down approximately halfway into the pudding. Pour the milk slowly over the mixture. It should settle just at the top. Lay the remaining butter slivers across the pudding. *(The pudding may be set aside for an hour at this point before baking.)* Bake for 1 hour, or until the sides are bubbling and the top is golden brown. Serve immediately.

Mamie's Autumn Salad

SERVES 4 TO 6

This raw vegetable salad may be prepared and chilled for several hours before serving.

INGREDIENTS

2 cups	white turnips – julienned
1 cup	carrots – julienned
1/2 cup	celery root or fennel – julienned
1 small	red onion – sliced thin
1/4 cup	fresh cilantro *or* parsley leaves – chopped

Autumn Dressing:

2 tablespoons	white wine vinegar
1	clove of garlic – minced
1	shallot – minced
1/2 teaspoon	sugar
1/2 teaspoon	ground cumin
Dash of	hot pepper sauce

Salt and freshly ground pepper, to taste

6 tablespoons	olive oil

Romaine or butter lettuce leaves (garnish)

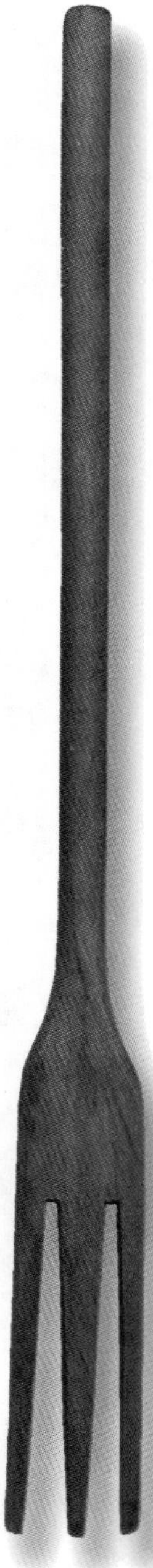

Julienne the vegetables by hand or by using a food processor fitted with a julienne blade, and put them into a large mixing bowl along with the sliced onion and chopped cilantro or parsley.

In a small bowl, mix together all of the dressing ingredients, except the oil. Whisk in the oil until well blended, and pour over the vegetables, tossing well. *(The salad can be refrigerated for several hours before serving.)* At serving time, line a serving platter or individual salad plates with lettuce leaves and arrange the vegetable salad on top.

Irish Oat Cakes

SERVES 6

These easy-to-make biscuits are also delicious for breakfast.

INGREDIENTS

$^{1}/_{4}$ teaspoon	**baking powder**
1 teaspoon	**salt**
$^{1}/_{2}$ cup	**flour**
1 tablespoon	**sugar**
$^{1}/_{2}$ cup	**boiling water**
$^{1}/_{2}$ cup	**shortening or lard**
2 cups	**fine- or medium-cut oatmeal**

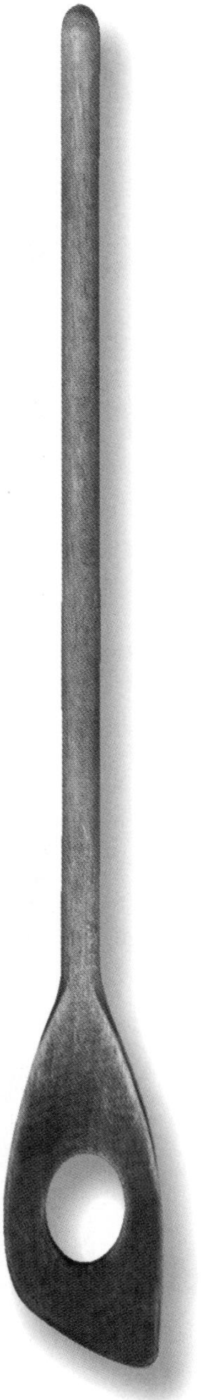

Preheat over to 400 degrees. Very lightly grease a baking sheet.

Sift the baking powder, salt, and flour into a small bowl. Stir in sugar, and set aside

Mix together the boiling water and shortening in a large bowl until well blended. Add the oatmeal, stirring well. Add the flour mixture, and blend together. Shape the dough into a loose ball. Roll on a lightly-floured surface to a thickness of $^{1}/_{4}$ to $^{3}/_{8}$-inch. Cut the dough into 4-inch squares, or use large cookie cutters to make decorative shapes. Place on the prepared cookie sheet, and bake for 12 to 15 minutes. Remove the oat cakes to a wire rack, and cool. Serve warm or at room temperature with butter, and jam if serving for breakfast.

Gran's Scottish Shortbread

MAKES 64 PIECES

Easy and delicious...what more could we want from our grandmothers?

INGREDIENTS

1 pound	unsalted butter – at room temperature
1 cup	sugar
4 cups	all-purpose flour

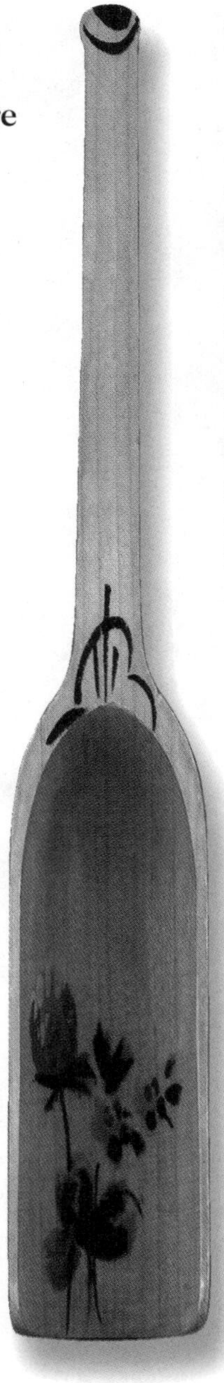

Preheat oven to 350 degrees.

In a medium bowl, cream together the butter and sugar. Add one cup of flour at a time, blending well. Mix until a stiff ball forms. Press the dough evenly onto an ungreased 10 x 15-inch baking pan. Prick the entire top with a fork. Bake for 35 or 40 minutes, or until golden brown. Remove from the oven. Cool for 5 minutes, and slice while still in the pan. Cool for 30 minutes more, and remove to a tin or serving platter.

Photo by Tom Parrish

A Santa Fe Thanksgiving Gathering

Special Thanks to:
New Mexico State Representative Max Coll

A Santa Fe Thanksgiving Gathering

Thanksgiving is a day to bring together family and friends, to reminisce, laugh, feast, and – most of all – count our blessings. The long weekend marks the opening of the Santa Fe Ski Basin, and we often look out our windows onto a white Thanksgiving. The day after, the city traditionally turns on its Christmas lights and crowds gather in the Plaza at dusk to drink hot chocolate and munch biscochitos while waiting for *La Luz de la Plaza.*

On Thanksgiving Day itself, after a bracing walk in the crisp impending winter air, we gather inside our warm adobe homes and hover around the kitchen, talking and helping with last-minute preparations. The combinations of New Mexican chiles and spices with our local produce bring savory new twists to favorite Thanksgiving classics as well as a piquant fragrance to the house that would be unrecognizable outside of the region. The result is a feast for the eyes and the taste buds.

And after the last plate has been licked clean and the turkey coma begins to settle over us, we nestle down in front of the fire and fantasize...about leftovers.

Menu

Harvest Empanaditas

Apple Soup with Green Chiles

Red Chile-Dusted Roast Turkey

Santa Fe Chorizo and Jalapeño Dressing

An Assortment of Cranberry Chutneys and Relishes

Chipotle-Garlic Mashed Sweet Potatoes

Celery Root au Gratin

Spinach, Mushroom, and Orange Salad

Sweet Cherry Clafouti

Spiced Pumpkin Pie

Sparkling Cider and Wine and Coffee

Harvest Empanaditas

MAKES 2 TO 3 DOZEN

These delicious filled turnovers may also be served for dessert.

INGREDIENTS

Pastry:

2 cups	**whole wheat pastry flour**
1 cup	**unbleached white flour**
$^1/_2$ teaspoon	**baking powder**
$^3/_4$ teaspoon	**salt**
$^2/_3$ cup	**butter – at room temperature**
$^1/_2$ to $^3/_4$ cup	**cold water**
2 tablespoons	**butter – melted**

Filling:

2 cups	**cooked butternut squash *or* pumpkin – mashed**
$^1/_2$ cup	**sugar**
1 teaspoon	**cinnamon**
$^1/_2$ teaspoon	**nutmeg**
$^1/_2$ teaspoon	**ground cloves**
$^1/_2$ teaspoon	**ground ginger**
$^1/_2$ teaspoon	**medium or hot red chile powder (optional)**

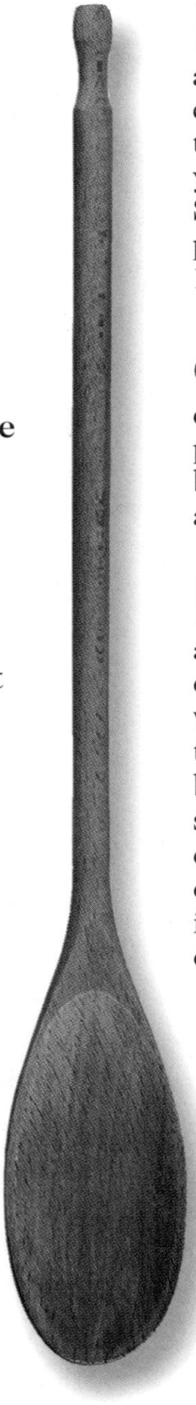

Place both flours, baking powder, and salt in a large bowl. Cut in $^2/_3$ cup of butter. Sprinkle water over the flour and work with a fork or your hands to form a solid dough. Shape into a ball, and cover with plastic wrap. Refrigerate for at least 1 hour.

Combine all of the filling ingredients in a bowl, including the chile powder if you wish to add a spicy bite when serving the empanaditas as an hors d'oeuvre.

Preheat oven to 375 degrees. On a floured board, roll out the chilled dough $^1/_8$ - to $^1/_4$ -inch thick, and cut with 2- or 3-inch round biscuit cutters. Brush 2 tablespoons melted butter over the pastry circles. Place some filling in the center of each circle. Fold the dough in half, and seal edges with fork tines. Place on baking sheets and bake for 20 minutes, or until golden brown.

Apple Soup with Green Chiles

SERVES 6

This puréed soup is also delicious served chilled. An easy recipe to double or triple.

INGREDIENTS

2 large	**apples – peeled, cored, and coarsely chopped**
1 medium	**onion – coarsely chopped**
2 cans (14.5 ounce)	**chicken or vegetable broth**
1 can (4 ounce)	**diced green chiles**
1 teaspoon	**garam masala ***
1 cup	**light cream**
1	**lemon – juiced**

Salt and freshly ground pepper, to taste

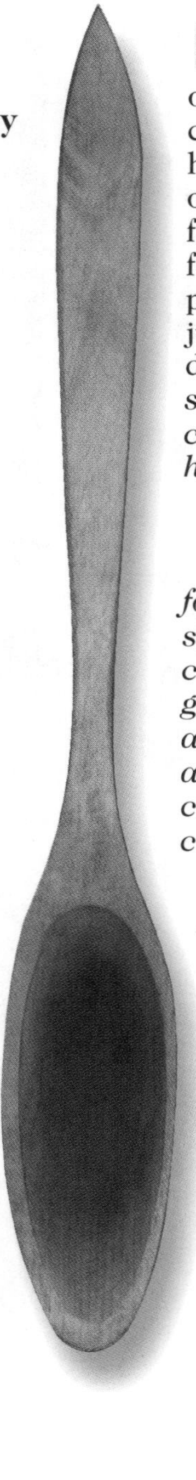

In a soup pot, bring the apples, onion, and broth to a boil. Add the chiles and garam masala. Reduce heat and simmer for 20 minutes, or until the apples are soft. Remove from heat and purée in a blender or food processor. Return soup to the pot, and stir in the cream, lemon juice, salt, and pepper. Reheat, but do not boil. Serve immediately. *(If serving chilled, place in a covered container and refrigerate for 4 hours or overnight.)*

**Garam masala spice may be found at East Indian grocers or specialty stores. It contains ground cumin, black pepper, cinnamon, ground cloves, ground coriander, and ground cardamon. If unavailable, substitute 3/4 teaspoon ground cinnamon and 1/4 teaspoon ground cloves.*

Red Chile-Dusted Roast Turkey

SERVE 10 TO 12

The red chile dusting adds flavor, but does not make the turkey and gravy too spicy because the initial high temperature seals the flavor into the skin.

INGREDIENTS

1 (16 to 18 pound)	**turkey – giblets removed and saved for dressing**
Salt and freshly ground pepper	
Santa Fe Chorizo and Jalapeño Dressing – *recipe follows*	
1 large	**onion – cut in half (optional)**
1	**lemon – cut in half (optional)**
1 small bunch	**parsley (optional)**
1 to 2 tablespoons	**mild to hot red chile powder**
2 to 3 cans (14.5 ounce)	**chicken broth**
2 tablespoons	**flour**
$1/2$ cup	**water**

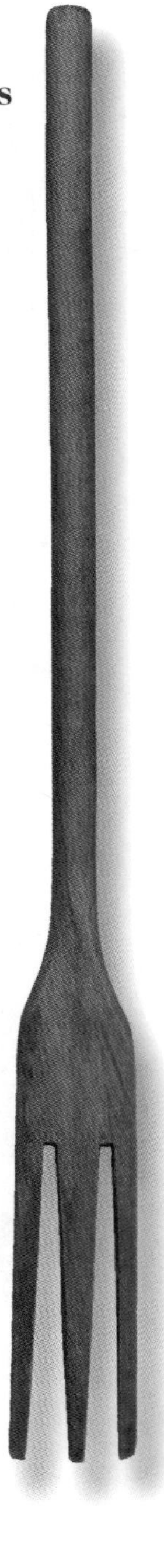

Preheat oven to 500 degrees.

Rinse the turkey inside and out; pat dry. Sprinkle the skin and cavity with salt and pepper, and stuff the turkey with dressing. *(Alternatively, stuff turkey cavity with the onion, lemon, and parsley, and bake the dressing separately.)* Massage the red chile powder into the skin. Put the turkey in a large roasting pan and insert a meat thermometer into the thickest part of the thigh. Cook at 500 degrees, uncovered, for 15 minutes.

Lower heat to 350 degrees. Baste the turkey with some of the chicken broth. Cook for 30 minutes, then baste again. Tent the turkey loosely with foil. Roast until the meat thermometer registers 180 degrees, about another $3^1/_2$ hours, basting every half hour with more broth or pan juices. When the turkey is done, transfer to a serving platter, and tent with fresh foil.

Pour the pan juices into a heavy saucepan and spoon off the fat. Add more chicken broth, if necessary, and bring to a boil over medium-high heat. In a small bowl, mix the flour and water until smooth. Add to the gravy, whisking well. Lower heat, and cook, stirring, until the gravy is thickened. Season with salt and pepper. Transfer to a gravy bowl. Remove foil from the turkey and serve with a grand flourish.

Santa Fe Chorizo and Jalapeño Stuffing

Makes about 10 to 12 servings

The best turkey stuffings are often improvised, usually by substituting an ingredient you have on hand for one that you don't. Mexican chorizo sausage adds spice but, if unavailable, hot Italian sausage works well.

Ingredients

1 stick (4 ounces)	**butter**
Turkey giblets	**chopped**
1 large	**onion – chopped**
5 large stalks	**celery – chopped**
1	**red or green bell pepper – seeded and chopped**
3/4 pound	**Mexican chorizo, *or* spicy Italian sausage – casings removed**
4 cups	**day-old white, whole wheat or corn bread – crusts removed, and diced**
1 to 2 cans (14.5 ounce)	**unsalted chicken broth**
1 large	**apple – peeled, cored, and chopped**
1 large	**Valencia orange – peeled, membranes removed, and chopped**
1/2 cup	**raisins or currants**

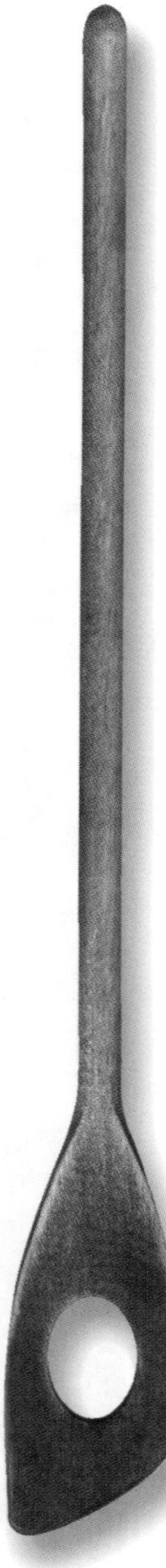

1/2 to 1 cup	**piñon nuts, chopped pecans or walnuts**
1 can (4 ounce)	**diced jalapeño peppers ***
1/2 cup	**fresh parsley leaves – chopped**
1 teaspoon each:	**oregano, marjoram, celery seeds, cinnamon and ground cumin**
1/2 teaspoon	**ground sage**
1/2 teaspoon	**ground cloves**
1/2 teaspoon	**ground coriander**
1/2 teaspoon	**sweet paprika**
1/8 teaspoon	**nutmeg**

Salt and freshly ground pepper, to taste

(Continued on next page)

Melt butter and add the chopped giblets, onion, celery, and bell pepper. Sauté for 5 minutes, stirring. Remove from heat.

In a large skillet over medium-high heat, cook the sausage until browned, stirring often and crumbling with the back of a spoon. Drain on paper towels.

In a large bowl, add the diced stale bread and cooked giblet mixture, including the butter in which the giblets were cooked. Mix in the drained sausage, 1 can of the chicken broth, and the remaining ingredients. Combine well. If dressing is not moist enough, add additional chicken broth or warm water. Stuff into the cavity of the turkey. Any leftover dressing – or *all* of the dressing, if you prefer – may be baked in a greased baking dish, for 45 minutes in a preheated 375-degree oven.

**For a less spicy dressing, substitute 2 cans (4 ounce) diced mild green chiles.*

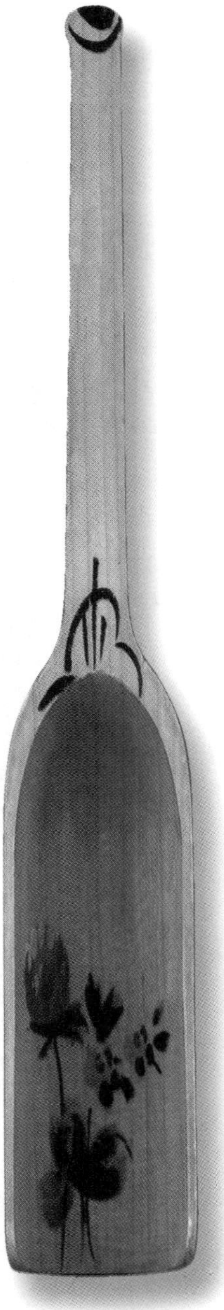

Thank all the Kitchen Angels for the excellent meals you provide us. My little girl and I always look forward to seeing the cheery Angels' faces each evening. You do an outstanding job, and I thank you for helping me on the way to recovery. B.H.

Cranberry Chutney

SERVES 12 OR MORE

This cranberry chutney is a great change from the usual jellied cranberry sauce. It keeps well, refrigerated, for up to 3 weeks. It is excellent with ham, chicken, and game as well as turkey. Put in decorative glass jars for a nice kitchen gift.

INGREDIENTS

2 cups	**fresh cranberries**
$^1/_2$ cup	**fresh-squeezed orange juice**
$^1/_2$ cup	**raisins**
1 small	**onion – chopped**
1 cup	**sugar**
$^1/_4$ teaspoon	**ground ginger, or $^1/_2$ teaspoon grated fresh ginger**
$^1/_4$ teaspoon	**cinnamon**
$^1/_8$ teaspoon	**ground allspice**
$^1/_8$ teaspoon	**salt**
1 can (8 ounce)	**crushed pineapple, undrained**
$^1/_4$ cup	**celery, *or* water chestnuts – diced**
$^1/_4$ cup	**pecans or walnuts – chopped**
1 or 2	**apples – peeled, cored, and chopped, to yield $^1/_2$ cup**
1 to 2 tablespoons	**fresh lemon juice ***
1 large	**orange – grated zest only**

Combine the cranberries, orange juice, raisins, onion, sugar, ginger, cinnamon, allspice and salt in a Dutch oven. Cook, uncovered, over medium heat for 15 -17 minutes, or until the cranberry skins pop. Stir in the undrained pineapple, celery, nuts, apples, and orange zest. Reduce heat to a low simmer. Cook, uncovered, for 30 minutes, stirring frequently. Serve at room temperature or slightly warmed.

**Sprinkle lemon juice over the chopped apple if using Red or Golden Delicious or other "sweet" apples; no lemon juice needed for Granny Smith Apples.*

Brandied Cranberries

SERVES 12 OR MORE

Wonderful as a side dish for turkey or game, or as a topping for ice cream. Keeps for months in the refrigerator.

INGREDIENTS

2 cups	**sugar**
$^{1}/_{2}$ cup	**water**
4 cups	**fresh cranberries**
3 whole	**cloves**
1 stick of	**cinnamon**
1 teaspoon	**grated orange zest (about $^{1}/_{2}$ orange)**
$^{1}/_{2}$ cup	**Cognac, brandy, or apple brandy**

Cook the sugar and water for 3 minutes in a heavy saucepan over medium heat, until the sugar is dissolved. Add all of the other ingredients, except for the Cognac. Cook for 15 to 20 minutes, or until the cranberries pop. Cool. Add the Cognac, and refrigerate until ready to use.

Cranberry Relish

SERVES 10 TO 12

Freezes well.

INGREDIENTS

1 pound	**fresh cranberries**
2	**oranges – peeled, membranes removed, and chopped**
2	**Golden Delicious apples – peeled, cored, and chopped**
1 to 2 cups	**sugar**

In a food processor, process the cranberries, oranges, and apples until finely chopped. Pour into a large bowl. Mix in 1 cup sugar, and let stand for 30 minutes. Add additional sugar to taste. Mix well, and let stand another 30 minutes before serving.

Jellied Cranberry Relish Ring

SERVES 8 TO 10

Serve on a beautiful platter for any festive occasion.

INGREDIENTS

2 packages (3 ounce)	**raspberry *or* cherry gelatin (or one of each)**
$2^1/_2$ cups	**hot water**
2 cups	**fresh cranberries**
1 small whole	**orange – washed, ends removed and cut in chunks**
1 small	**apple – washed, cored and cut in chunks**
$^3/_4$ cup	**sugar**

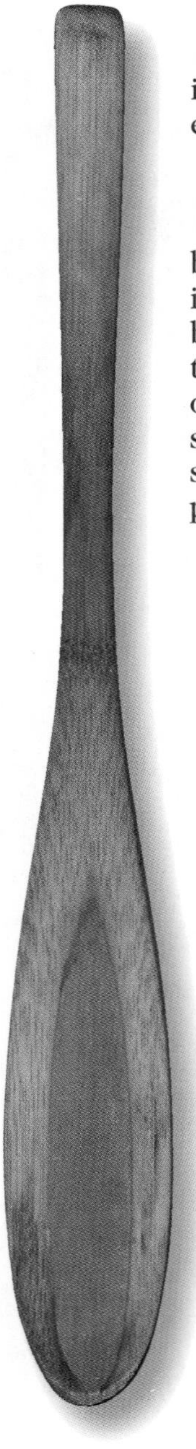

In a large bowl, dissolve the gelatin in the hot water. Chill in the refrigerator until slightly thickened.

In a food processor, chop the cranberries, unpeeled orange, and apple into a coarse purée. Remove to a bowl and stir in the sugar. Fold into the thickened gelatin. Pour into an oiled ring mold, or any festively-shaped mold, and chill until firm. At serving time, unmold onto a serving platter.

Chipotle-Garlic Mashed Sweet Potatoes

SERVES 6 TO 8

The chipotle chiles add a smoky, spicy taste that contrasts nicely with the sweetness of the potatoes.

INGREDIENTS

1 large pot	**boiling water**
3 large	**sweet potatoes *or* garnet yams – peeled and chopped**
6 to 8	**cloves of garlic – minced**
2 tablespoons	**butter**
1/2 teaspoon	**salt**
1/4 cup	**milk *or* light cream**
1 to 2 whole	**chipotle chiles – minced ***
1/4 cup	**fresh parsley *or* cilantro leaves – minced (garnish)**

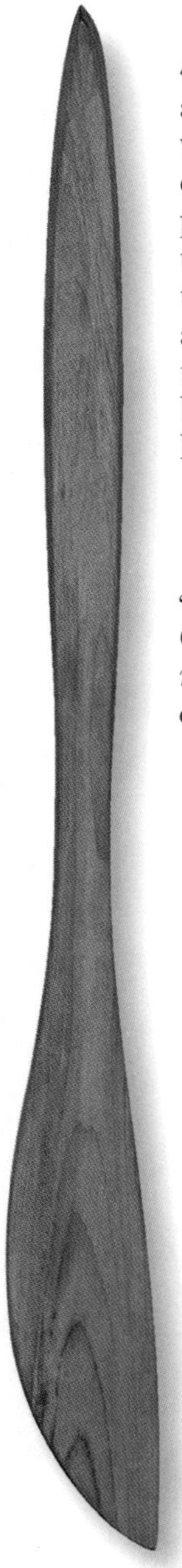

Add the chopped sweet potatoes and minced garlic to the boiling water. Reduce heat to medium and cook for 15 to 20 minutes, until the potatoes are soft. Drain and return to the cooking pot. Turn the heat to low and add the butter, salt, milk, and chiles. Mash well with a potato masher. Transfer to a serving bowl and garnish with chopped parsley or cilantro.

**Chipotle chiles are hot! Start with one and add more, if desired. Canned chipotles may be found in most supermarkets. Diced green chiles may be substituted.*

Celery Root au Gratin

SERVES 6 TO 8

Celery root or celeriac, an underused vegetable, is exquisite when prepared this way.

INGREDIENTS

2 whole large	**celery roots – peeled**
3 cups	**milk**
1/2 teaspoon	**nutmeg**
1/2 teaspoon	**salt**
1/4 teaspoon	**pepper**
2 cups	**crème fraîche, *or* 1 1/2 cups heavy cream**
1 cup (4 ounces)	**Parmesan or Asiago cheese – grated or shredded**

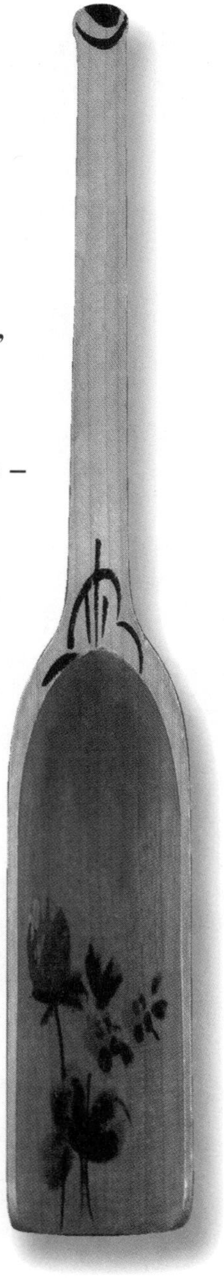

Preheat oven to 350 degrees. Butter a 2-quart casserole.

Slice the peeled celery root so that it will fit through the feed tube of a food processor and slice, using the slicing blade. Pour the milk into a large saucepan. Add the sliced celery root, nutmeg, salt, and pepper. Bring to a boil. Reduce heat and cook for about 15 minutes, until the celery root is slightly more tender than *al dente,* but not soft. Drain.

In the prepared casserole, layer half of the ingredients in the following order: celery root, crème fraîche, and cheese. Repeat, ending up with the cheese. Bake for 30 to 40 minutes, until browned and bubbly.

Spinach, Mushroom, and Orange Salad

SERVES 8

This Kitchen Angel's recipe appeared in Bon Appetit, and is perfect any time of year. Prepare dressing ahead of time, to allow flavors to blend.

INGREDIENTS

Dressing:

1/2 cup	**olive oil**
1/3 cup	**red or white wine vinegar**
2 tablespoons	**honey**
1 tablespoon	**yellow onion – finely grated**
1/2 teaspoon	**salt**
1/2 teaspoon	**powdered mustard**
1/8 teaspoon	**freshly ground black pepper**
1 pound	**tender young spinach leaves – stems removed, and washed**
3/4 pound medium-sized	**mushroom caps – wiped clean and thinly sliced**
1 large	**navel orange – peeled, sectioned, and cubed**

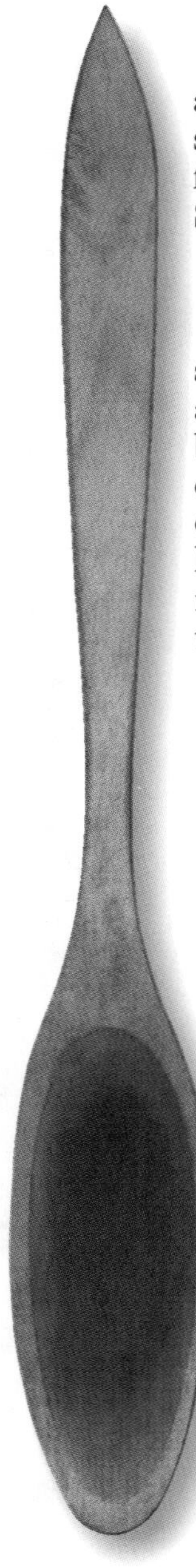

Place the dressing ingredients in a pint jar with a screw top, and shake well. Let the dressing mellow for several hours or overnight. Shake well before using.

Before serving, toss together the spinach leaves, sliced mushrooms, and cubed orange in a large salad bowl. Drizzle with about half the dressing, and toss lightly. Add more dressing, if needed, coating the leaves lightly. Let the salad stand at room temperature for 10 or 15 minutes. Toss again, and serve.

Sweet Cherry Clafouti

SERVES 6

A wonderful cold weather dessert that is quick to put together. An easy recipe to double or triple for a crowd.

INGREDIENTS

4 large	**eggs**
$^{1}/_{2}$ cup	**sugar**
Pinch of	**salt**
$^{1}/_{3}$ cup	**flour**
1 cup	**whole milk**
$^{1}/_{4}$ cup	**butter – melted**
1 teaspoon	**vanilla extract**
1 teaspoon	**grated lemon peel**
1 bag (1 pound)	**frozen pitted dark sweet cherries – thawed and drained**

Powdered sugar, to taste

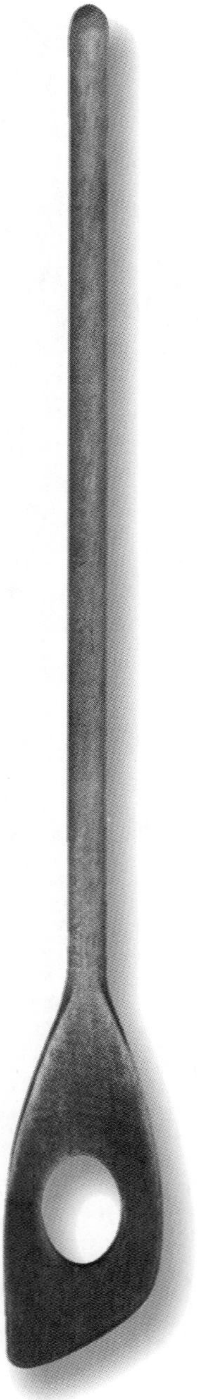

Preheat oven to 325 degrees. Butter an 8 x 8 x 2-inch baking dish.

In a medium bowl, whisk together the eggs, sugar, and salt. Stir in the flour. Add the milk, melted butter, vanilla, and lemon peel. Blend until smooth. Arrange the cherries in the bottom of the prepared baking dish, and spoon the batter evenly over them. Bake until set and golden on top, about 50 minutes. Remove from the oven. When cool, sift powdered sugar over the top.

Spiced Pumpkin Pie

SERVES 8 TO 10

What distinguishes a great pumpkin pie from that bland dish you often push aside at holiday dinners is the amount of spice. Taste the filling after it is mixed; if it is not right, add more spices until you're satisfied. Be bold!

INGREDIENTS

Pastry:

$1/4$ cup	**sugar**
1 tablespoon	**cinnamon**
1 cup	**all-purpose flour**
6 tablespoons	**butter or margarine**
$1/4$ teaspoon	**salt**
$1/4$ cup	**cold water**

Filling:

2 cups	**pumpkin, fresh or canned**
$3/4$ cup	**brown sugar**
$1/4$ cup	**molasses**
2 teaspoons	**nutmeg**
1 tablespoon	**cinnamon**
2 teaspoons	**ground ginger**
1 teaspoon	**ground cloves**
$1/2$ teaspoon	**salt**
3	**eggs – beaten**
$1\,1/2$ cups	**evaporated milk, *or* 1 cup milk and $1/2$ cup cream**

Preheat oven to 450 degrees. Lightly grease a 9-inch pie plate.

Mix the sugar and cinnamon in a small bowl, and set aside. Put the flour, butter, and salt into a food processor equipped with a metal blade, and mix until blended. With the motor running, add the water slowly through the feed tube until the dough forms a ball. Remove the dough to a floured surface and flatten into a disc with your hands. Roll out to a 12-inch diameter, turning and sprinkling with the cinnamon sugar as you roll, so that it is worked into the dough. Roll the dough loosely around the rolling pin, and unroll onto the prepared pie plate. Fold back the edges of the dough and crimp to a height of about $1/2$-inch above the rim of the plate. Line the dough with waxed paper and fill evenly with pie weights (chickpeas or dried beans will do). Partially bake for about 6 minutes. Remove from oven, and remove the weights and waxed paper. Leave the oven on.

If using fresh pumpkin for the filling, peel and cut it into chunks, then steam it until soft, and purée in a food processor. In a large bowl, mix the fresh purée or canned pumpkin with the brown sugar, molasses, spices, and salt. Add the beaten eggs and evaporated milk. Taste and continue to add spices, if desired. Pour into the partially baked pie crust and return to the 450-degree oven. Bake for 15 minutes, then reduce heat to 325 degrees. Bake for another 30 minutes, or until center of pie is firm.

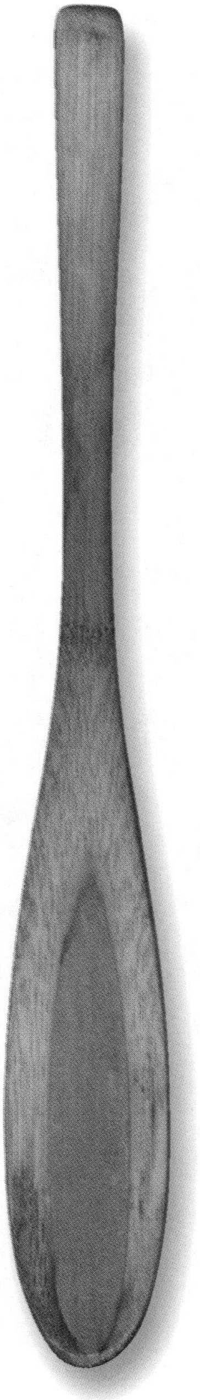

On Thanksgiving I was eating my dinner and thinking of all the things I had to be thankful for. Very high among those things is the service and courtesy provided by Kitchen Angels. I have no adequate way to say how much I appreciate your help. I simply could not make it without you. J.W.

Winter

PHOTO BY JACK PARSONS

WINTER IN SANTA FE

THE WINTER SECTION IS
IN MEMORY OF LOUISE M. LARKINS

PHOTO BY JACK PARSONS

AN OPEN HOUSE FOR THE CHRISTMAS EVE FAROLITO WALK

SPONSORED BY:
TOWN & RANCH INC., A REAL ESTATE BROKERAGE
MICHAEL UMPHREY, OWNER

An Open House for the Christmas Eve Farolito Walk

It always snows on Christmas Eve, at least that is the way it seems. And though Santa Fe abounds with wonderful traditions for every season, the Farolito Walk on the evening before Christmas is one of the most special. As darkness settles, families and friends get together and stroll along Acequia Madre, up Canyon Road, and down the surrounding narrow streets and dead-end lanes of the East Side. The air is often filled with snowflakes as groups of carolers gather around cheerful little bonfires, known as luminarias, to sing more verses of Christmas carols than most people have ever heard.

The whole scene is made magical by farolitos, or "little lanterns" – many thousands of paper bags, each filled with a glowing votive candle set in an inch or two of sand. These adorn the sidewalks and adobe walls, tree branches, even entire houses. Locals and visitors bundle up in sweaters and parkas and stocking caps to admire the creative displays exhibited by homes, galleries, and shops along the route. Arms linked, heads held high, these happy groups greet each other with smiles and song. A genuine feeling of peace and goodwill fills the air. Those who participate in this charming festival of lights are reminded that this is, indeed, the Land of Enchantment.

There is a debate within the state regarding the definitions of farolito and luminaria. In northern New Mexico, the farolito is the paper bag with the candle, and the luminaria is the bonfire. In the southern part of the state it is just the opposite. Whichever. By any name, the scene is dazzling.

A merry way to join in on the festivities is to host a Christmas Eve open house. This makes it easy for you to celebrate with everyone and at the same time gives your guests a chance to warm up and refuel. Happy holidays!

Menu

Spiced Pecans

Smoked Salmon and Dill Tart

Spicy Artichoke Dip

Mexicitos

Strudel of Leeks and Feta

Spiced Plum Soup

New Mexican Meatball Soup

Posole

Best Ever Cake

Kringle Pastry

"I Hate Fruit Cake" Fruit Cake

Chocolate Chile Truffles

Hot Mulled Cider or Wine

Santa Fe Hot Chocolate *(page 148)*

Spiced Pecans

MAKES 2 CUPS

A treat any time of the year. In pretty jars or tins, they make a lovely holiday gift.

INGREDIENTS

1 pound	**pecan halves**
1 quart	**boiling water**
1/2 cup	**sugar**
2 1/2 tablespoons	**corn oil**
1 teaspoon	**salt**
1/2 teaspoon	**pepper**
1/4 teaspoon	**cayenne pepper**
2 1/2 teaspoons	**ground cumin**
1 teaspoon	**ground ginger**
1 teaspoon	**chili powder**
1/2 teaspoon	**ground coriander**
1/2 teaspoon	**ground cloves**

The potted plant and the basket of goodies are just the 'topping-on-the-cake' to your regular food service and sense of caring and compassion.
N.T.

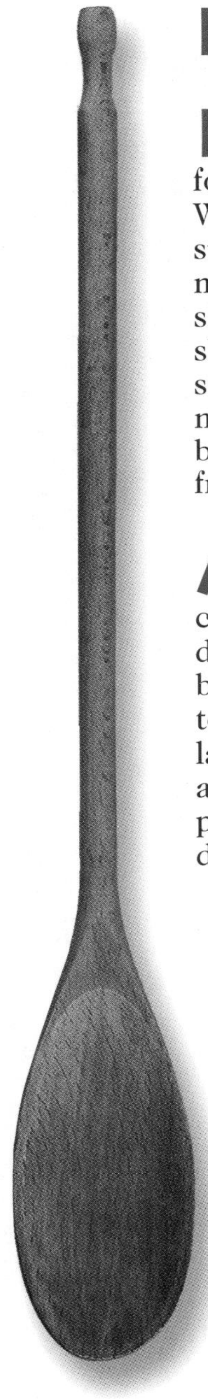

Preheat oven to 325 degrees.

Blanch the pecans in boiling water for 1 minute. Drain thoroughly. While still hot, toss them with the sugar and corn oil. Let stand for 10 minutes. Arrange the pecans in a single layer on a rimmed baking sheet. Bake for 30 to 35 minutes, stirring and turning every 5 to 10 minutes. When the pecans are brown and crispy, remove them from the oven and place in a bowl.

Mix together the salt, pepper, cayenne, cumin, ginger, chili powder, coriander, and cloves in a small bowl. Add to the warm pecans and toss well. Spread pecans in a single layer on the cooled baking sheet or a sheet of waxed paper. Cool completely before storing in a tightly-lidded container.

Smoked Salmon and Dill Tart

MAKES 70 HORS D'OEUVRES OR SERVES 15 FOR BRUNCH

Make several hours ahead. Great for a cocktail party or as a brunch dish.

INGREDIENTS

Pastry:

6 tablespoons	**butter or margarine – cut in chunks**
1 1/4 cups	**flour**
1 large	**egg**

Filling:

3	**cloves of garlic**
3 large	**eggs**
1 cup	**sour cream**
3/4 pound	**cream cheese – cut in chunks**
1/2 cup	**heavy cream**
1/2 pound	**smoked salmon – finely chopped**
1/2 cup	**scallions – diced**
3 tablespoons	**fresh dill – minced**
1/2 cup	**red bell pepper – seeded and diced**
Salt and freshly ground pepper, to taste	
1/2 cup	**Parmesan cheese – grated**

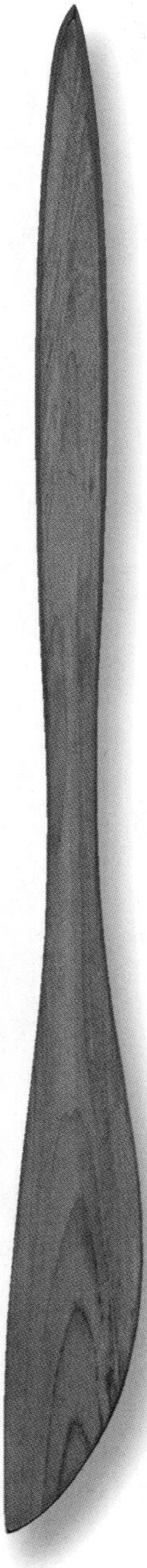

Preheat oven to 350 degrees. Line a 10 x 15-inch baking pan with heavy foil and lightly grease.

In a food processor or with your fingers, whirl or rub the butter and flour until it resembles coarse meal. Whirl or stir in the egg until the dough holds together. Press the dough evenly over bottom of the prepared baking pan. Bake until lightly browned, about 10 to 15 minutes. Use hot or cool. *(If making ahead, cover and chill until the next day.)*

For the filling, mince the garlic cloves in a food processor or blender, then add the eggs, sour cream, cream cheese, and heavy cream. Process until smooth. Remove to a bowl and stir in the salmon, scallions, dill, and red pepper. Season with salt, depending upon the saltiness of the salmon, and pepper. Spread evenly over the pastry and sprinkle the top with Parmesan. Bake at 350 degrees until puffed and lightly browned, about 35 minutes. Let cool. Cover and keep at room temperature or chill for at least 2 hours. With a sharp knife, cut the tart into fifteen pieces, if serving for brunch. For hors d'oeuvres, cut into 2-inch squares, then slice each square in half diagonally.

Spicy Artichoke Dip

MAKES 20 TO 25 APPETIZER SERVINGS

This recipe adds Southwestern zip to an old favorite. May be made up to 3 days ahead and baked before serving. Leftover dip keeps well, refrigerated; reheat in oven or microwave.

INGREDIENTS

3 cans (15 ounce)	**artichoke hearts in water, drained**
3 or 4	**cloves of garlic – minced**
1 can (4 ounce)	**diced jalapeño peppers, drained ***
1 can (4 ounce)	**diced mild green chiles, drained**
$^1/_2$ teaspoon	**cumin powder**
1 cup	**mayonnaise**
1 cup (4 ounces)	**Parmesan cheese – grated**

Paprika (garnish)

Wheat thins or tortilla chips

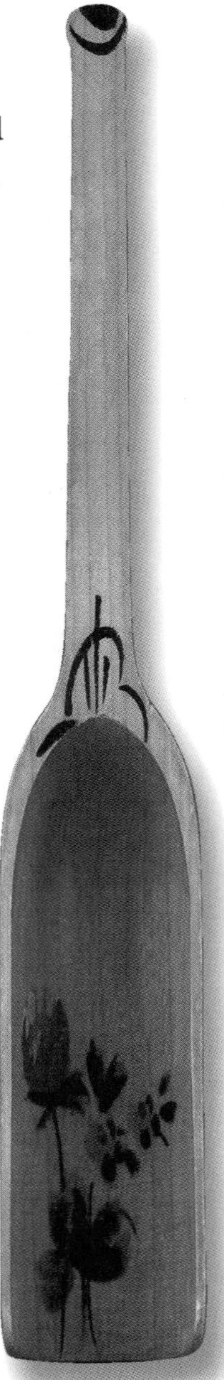

Preheat oven to 350 degrees.

In a food processor, coarsely chop the drained artichoke hearts and garlic; do not purée. Transfer to a medium bowl, and mix with the remaining ingredients. Pour mixture into a baking dish that can be used for serving, and sprinkle the top with paprika. *(Can be made to this point and refrigerated until ready to bake.)* Bake for 30 minutes, or until hot and bubbly. Serve with wheat thins or tortilla chips.

**For a less spicy dip, omit jalapeños and use 2 cans mild green chiles.*

Mexicitos

MAKES 40 PIECES

Very easy! A wonderful party hors d'oeuvre.

INGREDIENTS

1 pound	**ground round steak**
2 teaspoons	**garlic powder**
2 teaspoons	**oregano**
2 teaspoons	**chili powder**
2 teaspoons	**fresh cilantro leaves – chopped**
1 can (8 ounce)	**tomato sauce**
1 can (8 ounce)	**refrigerated buttermilk biscuits**

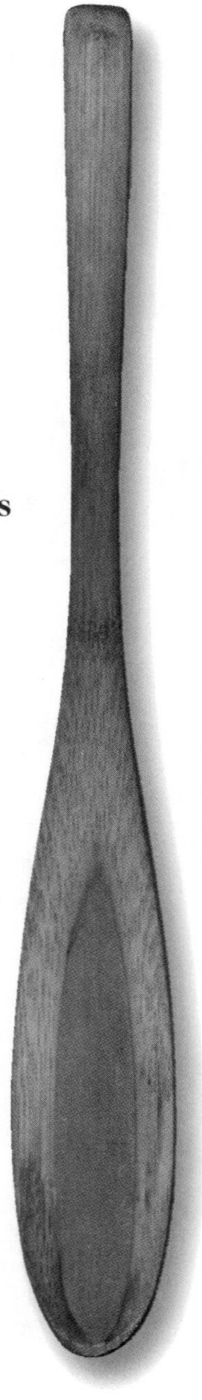

Preheat oven to 350 degrees.

Brown the meat in a skillet over medium-high heat. Add the garlic powder, oregano, chili powder, and cilantro, and stir well. When the meat is done, drain it, then return it to the skillet and stir in the tomato sauce. Simmer for 5 or 6 minutes.

Cut each biscuit into quarters and flatten pieces with a rolling pin. Place a heaping teaspoon of the meat mixture in the center of each piece. Fold in half to form a crescent and seal the edges with fork tines. Place on an ungreased baking sheet and bake for 8 to 10 minutes. Serve immediately. *(Can be assembled and refrigerated ahead of time. Bring to room temperature before baking.)*

Strudel of Leeks and Feta

SERVES 20 OR MORE

Assembly takes a bit of time, but the result is well worth it!

INGREDIENTS

3 tablespoons	**canola oil**
6 to 8 large	**leeks – split, washed, and chopped**
3	**eggs – lightly beaten**
Salt and freshly ground pepper, to taste	
1 box (1 pound)	**frozen *phyllo* pastry – defrosted**
1/4 cup	**skim milk**
1/2 cup	**canola oil**
1 1/2 pounds	**Feta cheese – crumbled**
Water or club soda	

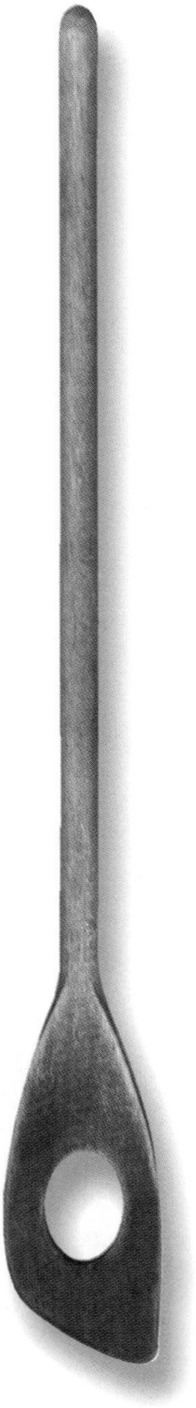

Preheat oven to 350 degrees.

In a large skillet, heat 3 tablespoons oil. Sauté the leeks until soft. Let cool, then mix in the beaten eggs. Season with salt and pepper. On a work surface, lay out one sheet of *phyllo,* keeping the unused pastry sheets covered with a dampened kitchen towel. Sprinkle the *phyllo* sheet with some milk. Place another sheet on top and sprinkle it with oil. Then add some of the leek mixture and crumbled Feta. Top with another pastry sheet, more oil, leeks, and Feta. Repeat once more.

Fold in a 3/4-inch pleat along the long end and sprinkle with some more milk and Feta. Roll, jelly roll fashion, and place on a lightly oiled baking sheet. Repeat this process with the remaining *phyllo* sheets and filling, to make a total of 5 rolls. Brush the tops of the rolls with oil and bake for 30 minutes, or until browned. Remove from the oven. Sprinkle lightly with water or club soda, and cover with a clean dish towel until cool. Cut into 4-inch pieces, or 1- or 2-inch thick slices if serving more people.

Spiced Plum Soup

SERVES 8

A perfect soup for the holidays, but also a refreshing warm weather soup when served chilled. The recipe is easily increased for a crowd.

INGREDIENTS

4 cans (16 ounce)	**plums in syrup**
1 bottle	**red Burgundy wine**
1 teaspoon	**cinnamon**
1/2 teaspoon	**nutmeg**
1/2 teaspoon	**ground cloves**
2 tablespoons	**sugar**
2	**oranges – grated zest only**
2	**lemons – grated zest only**
1/4 cup	**Cointreau or other orange liqueur**
8 tablespoons	**sour cream (garnish)**
8	**mint sprigs (garnish)**

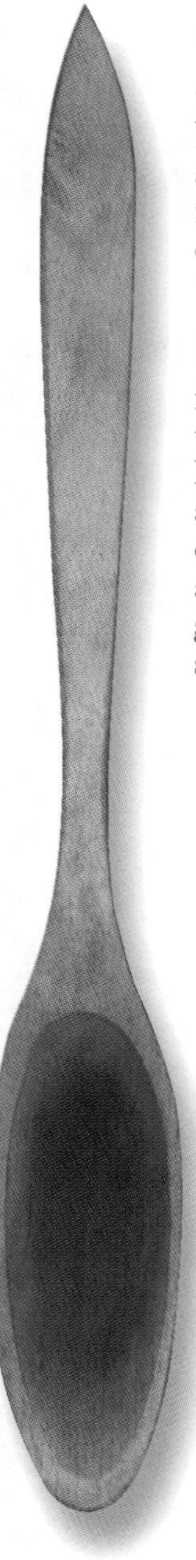

Drain and pit the plums, reserving the syrup. In a large saucepan, combine the plums, syrup, wine, spices, and sugar. Bring to a boil, then reduce heat and simmer, uncovered, for 30 minutes.

Purée the soup in small batches in a blender or food processor. Add the orange and lemon zests and liqueur. Return to the saucepan and reheat before serving, or refrigerate for several hours or overnight, and serve chilled. Before serving, garnish each bowl with a dollop of sour cream and a mint sprig.

I have been astounded on so many occasions by the thoughtfulness of all the goodies, especially around each holiday. Besides the wonderful nourishing foods, I am always in awe and have deep appreciation for the homemade cards, plants, etc. that come with each holiday. N.T.

New Mexican Meatball Soup

SERVES 6 TO 8

A robust soup for a cold winter night. May be served as a main course, along with cornbread and salad. Easy to increase for a crowd.

INGREDIENTS

1 tablespoon	**olive oil**
1 medium	**onion – chopped**
1 can (15.5 ounce)	**diced tomatoes**
4 cups	**water**
1 can (4 ounce)	**diced green chiles**
1 teaspoon	**oregano**
1 teaspoon	**red chile or chipotle chile powder**
1/2 teaspoon	**ground cumin**

Salt and freshly ground pepper, to taste

Meatballs:

1/2 pound	**lean ground beef**
1/2 pound	**lean ground pork**
3/4 cup	**blue or yellow cornmeal**
2 large	**eggs – beaten**
1 medium	**onion – diced**
2	**cloves of garlic – minced**
1/2 teaspoon each:	**oregano, ground cumin, and ground coriander**
1 teaspoon	**salt**

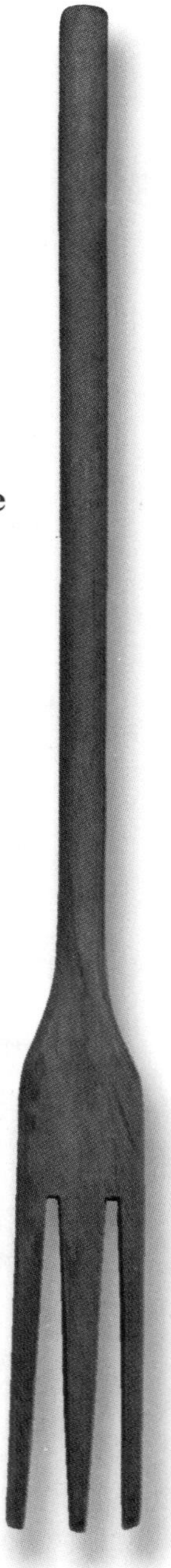

Dash of	**cayenne pepper**
1/2 cup (2 ounces)	**Monterey Jack cheese – shredded (garnish)**
1/4 cup	**fresh cilantro leaves – chopped (garnish)**

Heat oil in a soup pot, and sauté the onion until translucent. Add the tomatoes and water. Bring to a boil, and add the green chiles, oregano, chile powder, cumin, salt, and pepper. Reduce heat and simmer for 20 minutes.

While the soup is simmering, combine all of the ingredients for the meatballs in a large bowl. Mix well with your hands and shape into balls about the size of a walnut. Drop the meatballs carefully, one by one, into the soup. Cover the pot, and simmer for 45 minutes, until the meatballs are done. Garnish each serving with cheese and cilantro.

Posole

SERVES 8 TO 10

Posole is dried whole hominy, and it – and only it – can give this pork stew its special flavor and character. It is a feast day favorite among the Pueblo Indians who live in the Rio Grande Valley near Santa Fe. There are many versions of *posole*; this one was featured in *Bon Appetit*. Allow approximately 7 hours from start to finish.

INGREDIENTS

1 pound	***posole* – washed and sorted ***
6 cups	**cold water**
3 to 4 tablespoons	**oil**
5 medium	**yellow onions – coarsely chopped**
4 large	**cloves of garlic – crushed**
3 pounds	**boned pork shoulder – cut into $\frac{3}{4}$ to 1-inch cubes**
1 teaspoon	**oregano**
$\frac{1}{2}$ teaspoon	**thyme**
2 teaspoons	**salt, or to taste**
$\frac{1}{8}$ teaspoon	**freshly ground black pepper**
$1\frac{2}{3}$ cups	**chicken broth**
1 can (10 ounce)	**whole mild green chiles – drained and cut into thin strips**
1 to 3	**canned or fresh jalapeño peppers – seeds removed and minced ****

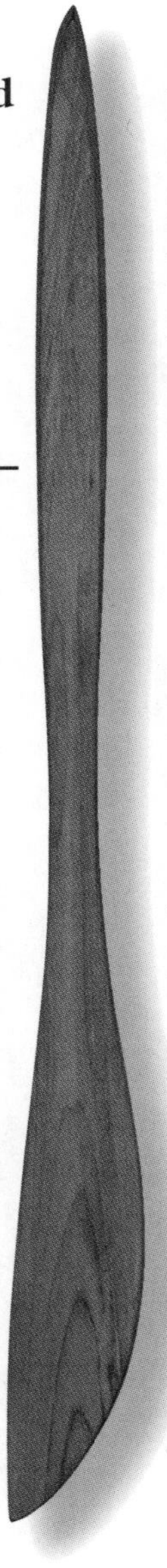

Put the *posole* and water in a large kettle and bring to a simmer. Cover and cook slowly until puffed and almost tender, about $3\frac{1}{2}$ hours. When the *posole* is almost done, heat 2 tablespoons oil in a skillet and sauté the onions and garlic until lightly browned, about 10 minutes. Drain on paper towels. Add another tablespoon of oil to the skillet and brown the pork cubes, a few at a time, adding more oil as needed. Drain.

Add the cooked onion, garlic, and pork to the *posole*, along with the spices and chicken broth. Mix well and simmer slowly for another 2 hours. Add the green chiles and jalapeños. Simmer, covered, for about 1 hour, until both pork and *posole* are tender. Taste for salt, and adjust as needed.

**Dried hominy is available in most specialty food shops.*

** *One jalapeño will make a mild stew, and three, a torrid one. A popular New Mexican variation is to add red chile powder, to taste, in place of the green chiles and jalapeños.*

Best Ever Cake

SERVES UP TO 24

This easy, delicious cake is even better if left overnight at room temperature.

INGREDIENTS

2 cups	**sugar ***
2 cups	**flour**
2 teaspoons	**baking soda**
2	**eggs**
1 can (16 or 20 ounce)	**crushed pineapple, undrained**
1 teaspoon	**vanilla extract**

Icing:

1 stick (4 ounces)	**butter – at room temperature**
1 package (8 ounce)	**cream cheese – at room temperature**
$1\frac{1}{2}$ cups	**powdered sugar**
1 teaspoon	**vanilla extract**
1 cup	**walnuts or pecans – chopped (garnish)**

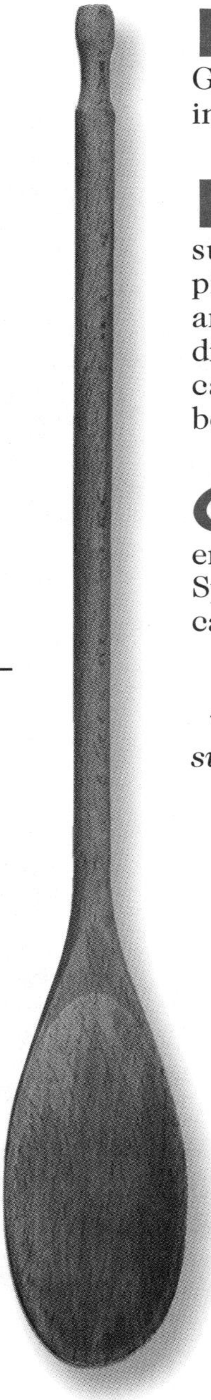

Preheat oven to 350 degrees. Grease and flour a 9 x 13-inch baking dish.

In a large mixing bowl, combine the sugar, flour, baking soda, eggs, pineapple, and vanilla. Mix well and pour into the prepared baking dish. Bake for 40 to 45 minutes. Let cake cool for 10 to 15 minutes before icing.

Combine all of the icing ingredients, except the nuts, and beat well. Spread evenly over the top of the cake. Sprinkle with chopped nuts.

**For 7000 feet and above, reduce sugar to $1\frac{1}{2}$ cups.*

Kringle Pastry

SERVES 30

A holiday favorite that is delectable any time of year.

INGREDIENTS

2 cups	**flour**
Pinch of	**salt**
2 sticks (8 ounces)	**butter – at room temperature**
5	**eggs**
1 tablespoon plus 1 cup	**water**

Icing:

$1/2$ cup	**powdered sugar**
1 to $1\,1/2$ tablespoons	**milk**
$1/2$ cup	**pecans, walnuts, or other nuts – chopped**

Preheat oven to 450 degrees.

Mix 1 cup of the flour with the salt and cut in $1/2$ cup of the butter, as if for pie crust. Mix 1 egg with 1 tablespoon water, and beat into the flour mixture. Pat into the bottom of a $15\,1/2$ x $10\,1/2$ x $3/4$-inch pan.

In a saucepan bring 1 cup water and the remaining $1/2$ cup butter to a boil. Add 1 cup flour, stirring until the mixture pulls away from the sides of the pan. Cool slightly, then add the remaining 4 eggs, one at a time, mixing well. Spread on top of the crust. Bake for 10 minutes, then reduce heat to 400 degrees and bake for 25 minutes longer. Remove from the oven and frost immediately.

For the icing, combine the powdered sugar and milk, mixing well. Drizzle over the hot pastry and sprinkle evenly with chopped nuts. Cut into squares while still hot.

"I Hate Fruit Cake" Fruit Cake

SERVES 32 TO 64, DEPENDING ON THICKNESS OF SLICES

The name of this recipe says it all. The recipe makes 4 loaf cakes, which may also be used for holiday gift giving.

INGREDIENTS

4 cups	**flour**
4 cups	**sugar**
2 teaspoons	**baking powder ***
2 teaspoons	**baking soda**
2 teaspoons	**cinnamon**
3 cups	**shredded coconut ****
3 cups	**dried cranberries ****
2 cups	**walnuts, pecans, or other nuts – diced**
2 cups	**oil**
1 cup	**liquor *or* fruit juice *****
3 tablespoons	**vanilla extract**
10	**eggs**

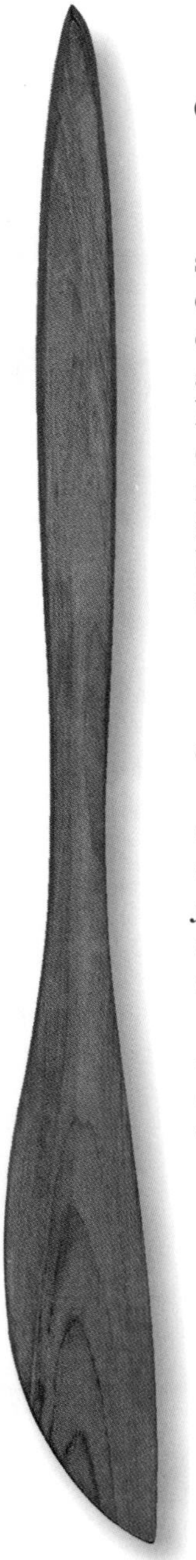

Preheat oven to 350 degrees. Grease and lightly flour 4 loaf pans.

In a large bowl, combine the flour, sugar, baking powder and soda, and cinnamon. Add the coconut, dried cranberries, and nuts, mixing well after each addition. Add the oil, liquor or fruit juice, vanilla, and eggs. Beat with mixer on low to medium speed, and mix well. Pour into the prepared loaf pans, and bake for 1 hour and 25 minutes on the center rack of the oven.

**For 7000 feet and above, use only $1^1/_2$ teaspoons baking powder.*

***In place of the coconut and dried cranberries, you may use any combination of chopped dried fruits, such as apricots, prunes, dates, apples, etcetera, as long as the combination totals 6 cups.*

****Use a sweet liquor, such as sweet vermouth, dark rum, or brandy. For a non-alcoholic cake, use any fruit juice.*

Chocolate Chile Truffles

MAKES 50 TRUFFLES

These piquant and decadently delicious candies were invented by one of our Kitchen Angels. For the holiday season, dust the truffles with red and green chile powders.

INGREDIENTS

12 ounces	**milk chocolate**
$1/2$ cup	**heavy cream**
$1/2$ stick (2 ounces)	**unsalted butter**
2 tablespoons	**Kahlua or coffee liqueur**
$1/2$ cup	**cinnamon**
$1/2$ cup	**Chimayo or medium-hot red chile powder**

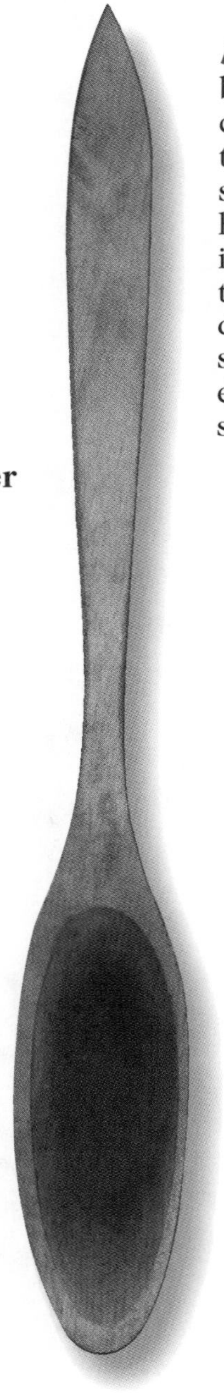

Melt the chocolate, cream, and butter in a heavy saucepan, stirring constantly. Stir in the liqueur. Pour the mixture into a bowl and chill for several hours, until the chocolate hardens. Roll into balls about $1/2$-inch in diameter. Dip each ball into the cinnamon, then the chile powder. Refrigerate the truffles until serving time. They will keep, refrigerated in an airtight container, for several days.

Thank you so much for the beautiful Christmas basket. It was an unexpected pleasure. Your caring help has lifted my spirits on many occasions. G.D.

Hot Mulled Cider

MAKES 4 CUPS

Perfect for a chilly evening, or after a hike on a cold day.

INGREDIENTS

1 quart	apple cider
10 whole	cloves
1 cup	maple syrup
1/4 to 3/4 cup	rum (optional)
4 sticks	cinnamon

Freshly grated nutmeg (garnish)

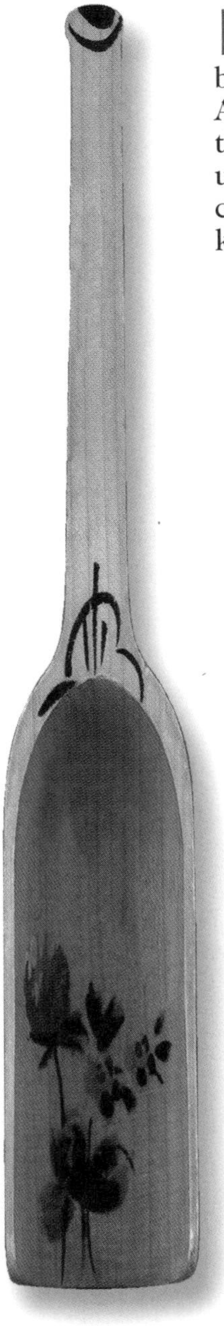

Bring the cider and cloves to just below a boil in an enamel saucepan. Add the maple syrup and stir until thoroughly mixed. Add the rum, if using. Pour into 4 mugs. Add a cinnamon stick to each, and sprinkle the top with nutmeg.

Hot Mulled Wine

MAKES 12 SERVINGS

Keeps the blood warm on a snowy night.

INGREDIENTS

2 cups	**water**
1 cup	**sugar**
$^{1}/_{4}$ cup	**whole cloves**
4 to 6 sticks	**cinnamon**
1	**lemon – seeds removed and thinly sliced**
1	**seedless orange – thinly sliced**
1 bottle (750 milliliters)	**red wine**
$^{1}/_{2}$ cup	**brandy (optional)**

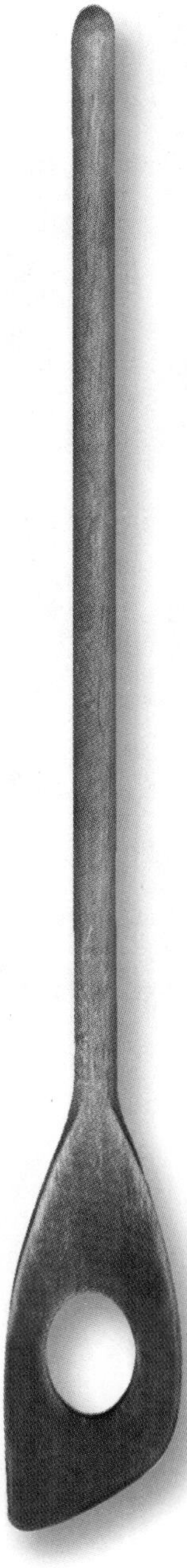

In a large saucepan, bring the water, sugar, cloves, and cinnamon to a boil. Reduce heat and simmer for 5 minutes. Remove from heat. Add the lemon and orange slices, and steep for 10 minutes. Return the pan to medium heat, and add the wine and brandy, if using. Heat, but do not boil. Serve immediately, or keep warm on the stove's lowest setting.

It was even better than a visit from angels every evening! It was a visit from Santa Claus with a surprise each time! Thank you so much for the delicious dinners. They came at a time when I needed help badly. S.O.

Photo by Jack Parsons

Afternoon Party on New Year's Day

Sponsored by:
Carolyn and Harry Hummer

Afternoon Party on New Year's Day

Many people think that New Year's Day is more fun than the evening before. There is a fresh year spread out ahead, 365 days to accomplish that list of resolutions vowed so sincerely on New Year's Eve – to leave a dull job for a more fulfilling one, or lose a few pounds, or take a long-dreamed-of vacation. New Year's Day makes you think of all the ways to enjoy life in the upcoming year. It can also be a day of reflection and preparation. But, as we all know, "Life happens while we are planning for the future."

One way to spend New Year's Day is to head for one of the Indian pueblos to watch the dances performed in conjunction with the ceremonial Transfer of Canes. This tradition honors the Spanish invaders' presentation of gold canes to each pueblo to signify its individual sovereignty as a nation. Nowadays, elaborately decorated canes are presented to new pueblo leaders, and many pueblos celebrate the day with eagle, turtle, cloud, basket, or other dances. Each pueblo decides on its own festivities, so check the schedule with the Eight Northern New Mexico Pueblos.

Or, perhaps you will want to continue celebrating the holiday festivities by throwing an informal daytime party, to toast the New Year and watch the gladiatorial football games on TV. Here is a suggested menu of wonderful dishes for a good-sized group of friends. (Tell them to postpone their diets for one more day.) Don't forget to make sure that each of your guests has at least one serving of black-eyed peas...they are said to bring a whole year's worth of good luck.

Menu

Bloody Mary Soup

Hungarian Cabbage Soup

Venison Goulash

Southwestern Quiche

Fruity Turkey Salad with Poppy Seed Dressing

New Mexican Spiced Beef

Baked Black-Eyed Peas with Rice and Cheese

Squash with Tempeh

Pauline's Pralines

Holiday Cranberry Clafouti

Wine, Soda, Beer, and Coffee

Bloody Mary Soup

SERVES 10 TO 12

The best-known hangover cure is *hair of the dog*, a term coined back in the 14th century, based on the belief that the burnt hair of a dog is an antidote to its bite. As a follow-up to New Year's Eve partying, this soup should certainly qualify. It may be served hot or cold.

INGREDIENTS

1 large can (46 ounce)	**tomato juice**
1 large can (46 ounce)	**vegetable juice**
3 tablespoons	**prepared horseradish**
2 tablespoons	**Worcestershire sauce**
1 teaspoon	**hot pepper sauce**
1 tablespoon	**fresh dill – minced, or 1 teaspoon dried dill**
1 tablespoon	**celery leaves *or* scallion – minced**
1	**lime – juiced and grated zest**
1 cup	**vodka**

Salt and freshly ground pepper, to taste

1 cup	**sour cream (garnish)**
$^1/_4$ cup	**fresh dill – minced (garnish)**
10 to 12	**celery sticks (garnish)**

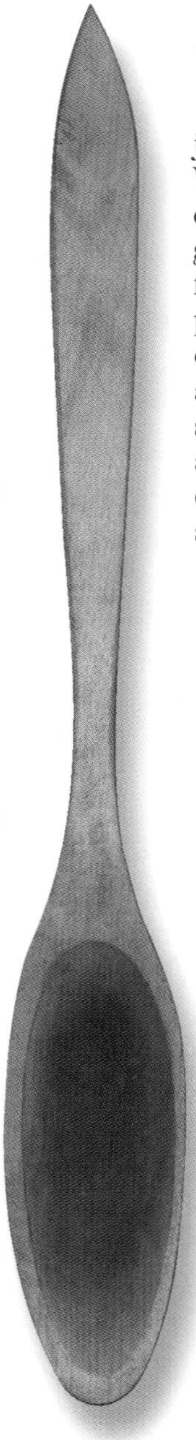

In a large saucepan, combine the juices with the horseradish, Worcestershire, hot pepper sauce, dill, celery leaves, lime juice, and grated zest. Bring to a boil. Remove from heat. Add the liquor, salt, and pepper. Adjust seasonings, if necessary. Pour the soup into mugs and garnish each with a dollop of sour cream, a sprinkling of dill, and a celery stick. May be served hot or cold, along with pita crisps or bread sticks.

Hungarian Cabbage Soup

SERVES 8 TO 10

A comforting, stick-to-your-ribs soup for a cold day or night.

INGREDIENTS

2 pounds	beef flanken or chuck steak – cut in cubes
1 large	cabbage – shredded
1 can (28 ounce)	whole tomatoes
1 can (28 ounce)	tomato purée
1 large	onion – sliced
1 teaspoon	salt, or to taste
1/4 cup	sugar, or to taste
3 tablespoons	lemon juice, or to taste

Water

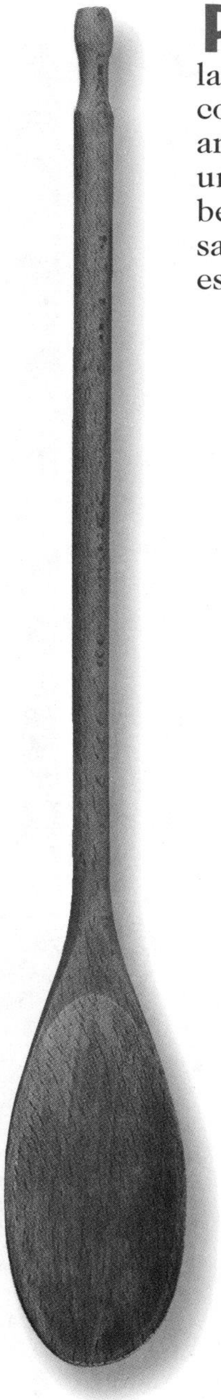

Place all of the ingredients in a large soup pot, and add water to cover. Bring to a boil. Reduce heat and simmer, covered, for 2 hours, until the meat is tender. Taste before serving, adding additional salt, sugar, and lemon juice, if necessary.

Venison Goulash

SERVES 8 TO 12

This is an elegant stew if you have access to venison. Please note that preparations must begin a day in advance.

INGREDIENTS

6 pounds	**venison (from round) – cut in $1^{1}/_{2}$-inch cubes**
$^{1}/_{2}$ cup	**bacon – cooked and crumbled**
2 cups	**red wine vinegar**
5 tablespoons	**oil**
$1^{1}/_{2}$ cups	**carrots – sliced**
$1^{1}/_{2}$ cups	**celery – diced**
2 large	**onions – chopped**
$^{1}/_{2}$ teaspoon	**thyme**
Salt and freshly ground pepper, to taste	
2 cups	**red wine**
2 cups	**beef bouillon**
$^{3}/_{4}$ pound	**mushrooms – wiped clean and sliced**
2 tablespoons	**chives – chopped**

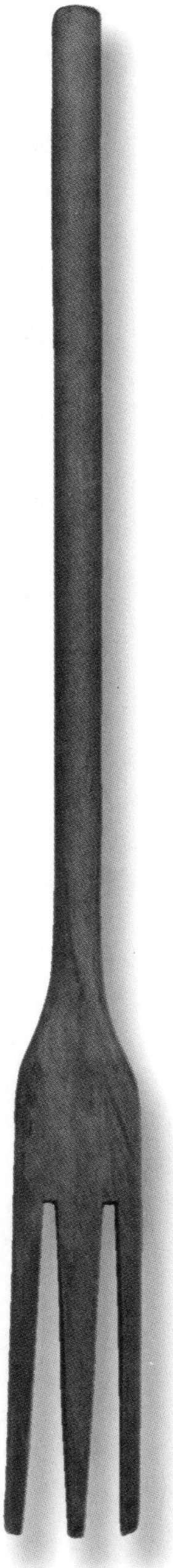

Mix together the venison, cooked bacon, and vinegar in a large bowl. Cover and refrigerate for 24 hours.

About $2^{1}/_{2}$ hours before serving, preheat oven to 325 degrees.

Drain the meat and pat it dry. Heat oil in a large skillet over medium-high heat. Brown the meat well, in batches, on all sides. Transfer to a large casserole, and add the carrots, celery, and onions. Season with thyme, salt, and pepper. Add the wine and bouillon. Cover and bake for $1^{1}/_{2}$ hours. Stir in the mushrooms and cook another $^{1}/_{2}$ hour. If sauce is too juicy, mix a tablespoon flour with $^{1}/_{4}$ cup water, and add to thicken. Just before serving, garnish with chopped chives.

Southwestern Quiche

SERVES 4 (MAIN DISH) OR 8 (APPETIZER)

A savory twist on an old favorite. Tasty as an appetizer or main course.

INGREDIENTS

$^1/_2$ package (11 ounce)	pie crust mix
1 teaspoon	red chile powder
2 tablespoons	cold water

Filling:

$^3/_4$ cup (3 ounces)	Cheddar cheese – grated
$^1/_2$ cup (2 ounces)	Monterey Jack cheese – grated
3 large	eggs – lightly beaten
1 teaspoon	salt
$^1/_4$ teaspoon	white pepper
$1^1/_2$ cups	half-and-half, or light cream
1 can (4 ounce)	diced green chiles
1 can (2.25 ounce)	sliced ripe olives, drained
2 tablespoons	scallions – diced

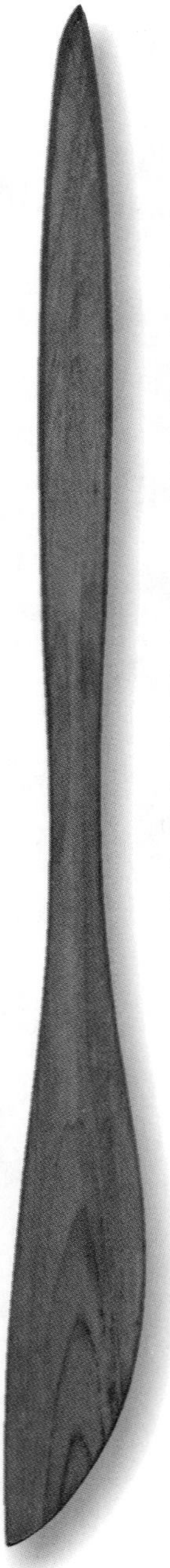

Preheat oven to 350 degrees.

In a medium bowl, blend the pie crust mix with the chile powder. Add water, and mix with a fork until the dough holds together. Form the dough into a smooth ball. Roll out on a floured surface until $1^1/_2$ inches larger than an inverted 9-inch pie plate. Ease the crust onto the pie plate and flute the edges.

Mix the cheeses together in another bowl, and spread evenly over the bottom of the pie crust. In the same bowl, mix the eggs with the remaining ingredients. Pour over the cheese-covered pastry. Bake for 40 to 45 minutes, or until a knife inserted in the center comes out clean. Serve immediately.

Fruity Turkey Salad with Poppy Seed Dressing

SERVES 6 TO 8

This salad is so delicious you may find yourself roasting a turkey solely for the leftovers.

INGREDIENTS

2/3 cup	**vegetable oil**
1/4 cup	**fresh lemon juice**
1/4 cup	**white wine vinegar**
2 tablespoons	**honey**
2 tablespoons	**Dijon mustard**
3 tablespoons	**red onion – minced**
3 tablespoons	**poppy seeds**
1	**orange – grated zest only**
1/2 cup	**dried apricots – slivered**
1/2 cup	**dried figs – slivered**
5 to 6 cups	**leftover roasted turkey – shredded**
1/3 pound	**sharp Cheddar cheese – cut into 1 1/2-inch matchsticks**
4	**celery ribs – chopped**
3/4 cup	**pecan halves – lightly toasted and coarsely chopped**

Salt, to taste

Assorted greens (garnish)

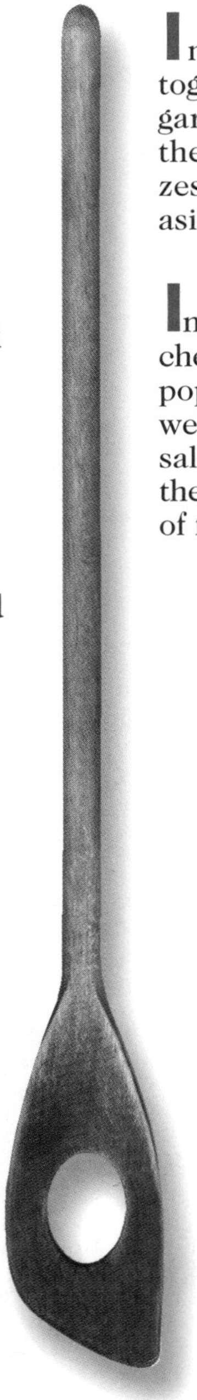

In a small mixing bowl, whisk together the oil, lemon juice, vinegar, honey, and mustard. Stir in the onion, poppy seeds, and orange zest. Add the apricots and figs. Set aside for 30 minutes.

In a large bowl, combine the turkey, cheese, celery, and pecans. Pour the poppy seed dressing over, and toss well. Add salt to taste. Chill the salad for several hours to mellow the flavors. Serve mounded on a bed of fresh, leafy greens.

NEW MEXICAN SPICED BEEF

SERVES 12 TO 20

Don't be shocked: the brisket must marinate in the refrigerator for 14 to 21 days before cooking. It is great for a buffet or cocktail party. Leftovers make wonderful sandwiches, except there never seems to be any left over.

INGREDIENTS

8 to 10	**cloves of garlic – peeled**
8 tablespoons	**pickling spices**
3 tablespoons	**meat tenderizer**
3 tablespoons	**sugar**
3 tablespoons	**salt**
1 tablespoon	**cinnamon**
1 tablespoon	**ground cumin**
3 tablespoons	**coriander seeds**
1 teaspoon	**medium to hot red chile powder**
1 whole (5 to 7 pound)	**boned beef brisket**

Waxed paper, brown paper, aluminum foil, plastic wrap, and masking or cellophane tape

Assorted mustards

Party rye or pumpernickel bread, or French bread slices

In a blender or food processor, purée the garlic, pickling spices, tenderizer, sugar, salt, cinnamon, cumin, coriander, and chile to a granular consistency. Trim as much fat from the brisket as possible and rub both sides with the garlic-spice mixture. Wrap the brisket thoroughly in the following way, so that no air can seep in while marinating: cover completely with waxed paper and secure with masking tape, then with brown paper (or a cut-up grocery bag) sealed with tape, then with a layer of foil. Now place in plastic bags or seal tightly with several layers of plastic wrap. Secure completely with more tape. Store on the bottom shelf of the refrigerator for 14 to 21 days.

On serving day, preheat oven to 300 degrees. Unwrap the brisket and place in a shallow baking pan with a small amount of water, not enough to cover the brisket. Cover the pan lightly with foil and cook for 2 or 3 hours – depending on thickness of brisket – until the meat is cooked through; it should not be rare.

Place the spiced beef on a serving platter. When cool, carve it into very thin slices. Serve the beef with a selection of mustards and breads.

Baked Black-eyed Peas with Rice and Cheese

SERVES 8 TO 10

Legend has it that black-eyed peas will bring a whole year's worth of luck when eaten on New Year's Day. This is a delicious way to get lucky.

INGREDIENTS

4 cups	**cooked brown rice (from $1\frac{1}{4}$ cups raw rice)**
$2\frac{1}{2}$ cups	**cooked black-eyed peas ***
3 tablespoons	**olive oil**
1 large	**onion – chopped**
2 or 3	**green chiles – seeded and chopped ****

Salt and freshly ground pepper, to taste

1 cup	**lowfat ricotta cheese**
$1\frac{1}{2}$ cups (6 ounces)	**Cheddar cheese – grated**

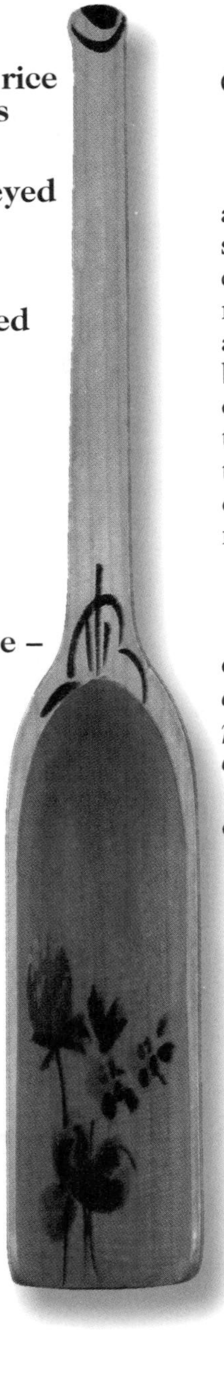

Preheat oven to 350 degrees. Grease a 9 x 13-inch baking dish.

In a large bowl combine the rice and black-eyed peas. Heat oil in a skillet and sauté the onion and green chile until softened. Toss into the rice mixture, and season with salt and pepper. In another bowl, combine the ricotta and Cheddar cheeses. Layer half of the rice mixture in the prepared baking dish, then half of the cheese. Repeat layers. Bake, uncovered, for 35 to 40 minutes.

** If desired, substitute 2 cans (15 ounce) black-eyed peas, drained and rinsed, for dried black-eyed peas that must be soaked overnight and cooked for several hours.*

*** Can substitute a can (4 ounce) of diced green chiles.*

Squash with Tempeh

SERVES 4

A lovely vegetarian main dish that takes advantage of the microwave to lessen cooking time. The recipe may be easily increased for a party.

INGREDIENTS

2 medium	**acorn or delicata squash**
1 cup	**water**
6 ounces	**tempeh – crumbled ***
1	**bay leaf**
1 teaspoon	**powdered vegetable bouillon**
1	**clove of garlic**
1 to 2 tablespoons	**olive oil**
1	**parsnip – peeled and diced**
1 medium	**onion – diced**
1/2 cup	**celery – diced**
1 tablespoon	**tamari or soy sauce**
1/2 teaspoon each:	**thyme, marjoram, and oregano**

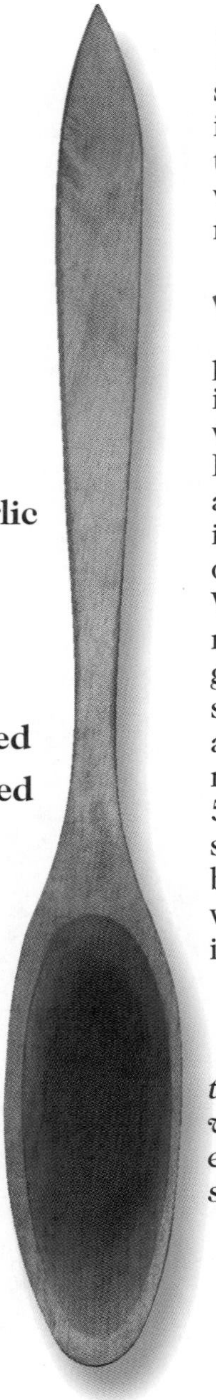

Split the squash in half. Scoop out seeds and place, flesh side down, in a microwave dish. Add 1/2 cup of the water, and cover with plastic wrap. Microwave until done, 9 to 14 minutes.

While the squash is cooking, place the tempeh, bay leaf, remaining 1/2 cup water, bouillon, and whole garlic clove in a saucepan. Bring to a boil, then reduce heat and simmer for 15 minutes. Heat oil in a skillet and sauté the parsnip, onion, and celery until softened. When the tempeh has finished simmering, remove the bay leaf and garlic clove. Add the tempeh to the skillet with the sautéed vegetables and season with the tamari, thyme, marjoram, and oregano. Cook for 5 to 10 minutes more, stirring occasionally, until the seasonings are blended. Stuff the cooked squash with the tempeh filling. Serve immediately.

**Tempeh is textured soybean protein "meat." It comes in many flavors, and can be found in the refrigerated compartments of health food stores.*

Pauline's Pralines

Makes 2 to 3 Dozen

A no-bake cookie that is a favorite of our Kitchen Angels clients.

Ingredients

1 cup	**sugar**
1 cup	**light corn syrup**
1$^3/_4$ cups	**peanut butter**
6 cups	**corn flakes or other cereal**

In a heavy saucepan, bring the sugar and corn syrup to a full rolling boil. Remove from heat and stir in the peanut butter. Add the cereal and mix well. Drop by spoonfuls onto waxed paper and allow to set until firm.

I was released from the hospital around 4 p.m. and by 5 p.m. a hot meal was delivered to my door. Kitchen Angels bent over backwards to see that I had a meal with only one hour's notice. [There is] so much caring, comfort, support, and love provided in every meal created and every client served. N.T.

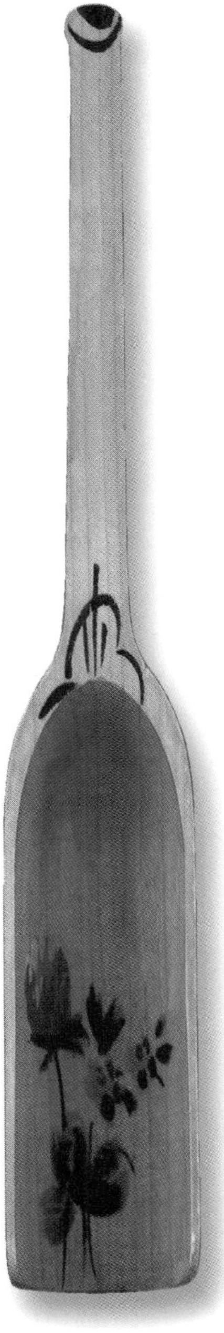

Holiday Cranberry Clafouti

SERVES 2 TO 4

Another inventive use for cranberries, and easy to increase for a crowd.

INGREDIENTS

6 ounces	cranberries *
1	lemon – grated zest only
6 tablespoons	sugar
$1/2$ cup	unbleached all-purpose flour
$1/4$ teaspoon	salt
2	eggs
1 cup	milk
1 tablespoon	unsalted butter
1 to 2 tablespoons	powdered sugar (garnish)
$1/2$ cup	sour cream (garnish)

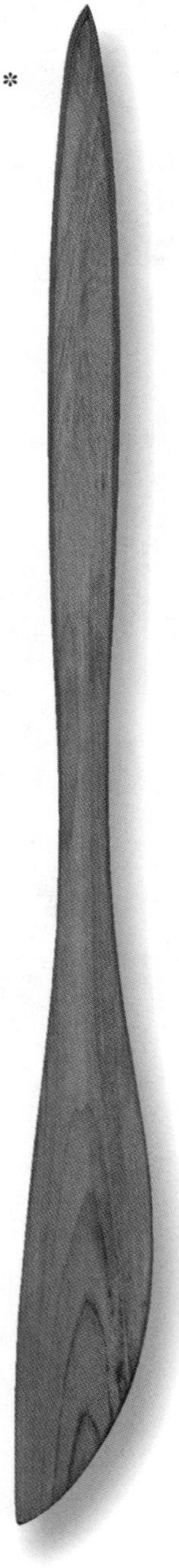

Preheat oven to 425 degrees.

Cut the cranberries in half. In a small bowl, combine the lemon zest and 2 tablespoons sugar; set aside. In a large bowl, sift together the flour and salt. In another bowl, beat the eggs gently and whisk in milk. Add to the flour, a little at a time, and blend until smooth. Stir in the lemon zest-sugar mixture. Let the batter rest.

In a 10-inch ovenproof skillet, melt butter over medium heat, allowing it to coat the bottom and halfway up the sides. When the butter is bubbling, add the cranberries. Stir until they are softened and coated with butter, 2 to 3 minutes. Sprinkle with the remaining 4 tablespoons sugar (if using another fruit, use only 2 tablespoons) and cook until the sugar has dissolved and become syrupy, about 2 minutes. Remove from heat. Stir the egg batter and pour it evenly over the fruit. Place the skillet in the oven and bake for 20 minutes, or until golden brown and puffed at the edges. Before serving, top each portion with a sprinkling of powdered sugar and a dollop of sour cream.

**In summer, substitute any fresh fruit.*

PHOTO BY TOM PARRISH

SNUGGLING UP ON A SNOWY EVENING

SPONSORED BY:
SANTA FE LAND AND HOMES

Snuggling up on a Snowy Evening

The day starts out with a clear blue sky, sun blazing on blinding white mountains, a perfect one for hitting the slopes or cross-country trails. But uh oh! By the time you are in your ski clothes, clouds have blown in and the first flakes have begun to float to the ground. In no time at all it is not just snowing...it's a blizzard. Such is the changeable nature of Santa Fe weather. Regardless of the season, there is no predicting. Take a look at today's forecast in the newspaper. Does it resemble anything that is going on outside?

You wonder, "Will the snow continue all day? Into the night? Tomorrow?" And next, "Do I have enough firewood? Is the propane tank full? Are there batteries for the radio? Candles? Pet food? Dinner?"

Thank goodness you are well prepared with a cupboard and freezer full of comfort foods. A significant other may be joining you for dinner or, if not, pick up the phone before the lines go down and invite over someone special. Or, perhaps you are hoping someone unexpected will show up, such as a downhill racer in a skin-tight ski suit, wanting to borrow a cup of cocoa.

Once you've worked through your fantasies, open up the bottle of vintage Château Margaux that you've been saving, and let it breathe. Tonight is going to be warm and cozy, and the following recipes for two will make for a delicious evening. Let it snow!

Menu

Curried Yam Soup
or
Chile-Chicken Corn Chowder

Shrimp Masala
or
Dijon Chicken
or
Eggplant Scallop

Romaine with Yogurt-Dill Dressing

Baked Fudge

Hot Tea and Wine

Curried Yam Soup

SERVES 4

This soup freezes well, and may be made in advance. The recipe provides enough for lunch the next day if the blizzard still rages.

INGREDIENTS

1 tablespoon	**olive oil**
1 large	**red onion – chopped**
2	**Granny Smith apples – peeled, cored, and chopped**
1 quart (32 ounces)	**unsalted chicken broth**
1 tablespoon	**mild or hot curry paste, *or* 1 teaspoon curry powder**
2 medium	**yams – baked, peeled, and chopped**
$^1/_2$	**lemon – juiced**
2	**cloves of garlic – crushed or minced**

Salt, to taste

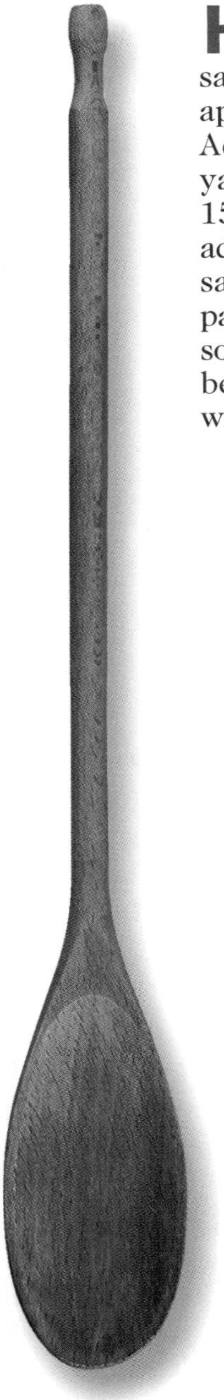

Heat oil in a heavy saucepan, and sauté the onions until soft. Add the apples and cook for 2 or 3 minutes. Add the broth, curry paste, and yams. Reduce heat and simmer for 15 minutes. Remove from heat and add the lemon juice and garlic. Add salt, and more lemon juice or curry paste, if desired, or more broth if the soup is too thick. The soup may also be puréed in a blender or mashed with a potato masher before serving.

Chile-Chicken Corn Chowder

SERVES 2 TO 4

Frozen peas can be added for a touch of color. For a vegetarian chowder, omit the chicken.

INGREDIENTS

1 large	potato – peeled and diced
1 tablespoon	olive oil
1 whole	chicken breast, skinless and boneless – cut into cubes
Salt and freshly ground pepper, to taste	
$^1/_2$ teaspoon	garlic powder
$^1/_2$ medium	onion – chopped
1 package (10 ounce)	frozen corn – thawed
2 medium	carrots – diced
1 to 2 tablespoons	diced green chiles from a 4-ounce can
$^1/_4$ teaspoon	oregano
$^1/_4$ teaspoon	thyme
1 can (14.5 ounce)	lowfat chicken broth
1 cup	milk
$^1/_2$ cup (2 ounces)	Cheddar cheese – grated

In a small saucepan, boil the diced potato in water to cover. When tender, remove from heat. Drain, reserving 2 tablespoons of potato water, and set aside.

Heat oil in a large soup pot. Dust the cubed chicken with salt, pepper, and garlic powder. Sauté until golden, about 10 minutes. Remove from pan and set aside. Add the onion to pan. Sauté for 2 minutes, then add the corn and cook, stirring, for 10 minutes.

Remove 1 cup of the corn and place in a blender or food processor with $^1/_2$ cup of the cooked diced potato and 2 tablespoons of the potato water. Liquify, and set aside.

To the remaining corn and onion mixture in the soup pot, add the carrots, green chile, oregano, and thyme. Cook over medium heat until the mixture is golden. Stir in the broth, milk, and liquified corn mixture. Add the remaining diced potato and the sautéed chicken. Reduce heat and simmer for 15 to 20 minutes. Serve in bowls with a sprinkle of grated cheese.

Shrimp Masala

Serves 2

A spicy dish to warm you up on a cold evening. Quick to put together, especially if you have cleaned shrimp in the freezer. Serve with basmati rice.

Ingredients

1/2 pound	**shrimp – peeled and deveined**
1/2 teaspoon	**tumeric powder**
1 tablespoon	**olive oil**
1 medium	**red onion – cut into strips**
1 or 2	**cloves of garlic – chopped**
1 medium	**tomato – cut into 8 wedges, *or* 1 can (15 ounce) diced tomatoes, drained**
1 tablespoon	**ginger- garlic paste (equal portions of mashed fresh ginger and garlic)**
1 or 2 teaspoons	**mild, medium, or hot red chile powder**
1/2 teaspoon	**garam masala ***
1/4 cup	**water**
1 tablespoon	**lemon juice**
1/4 cup	**fresh cilantro leaves (garnish)**

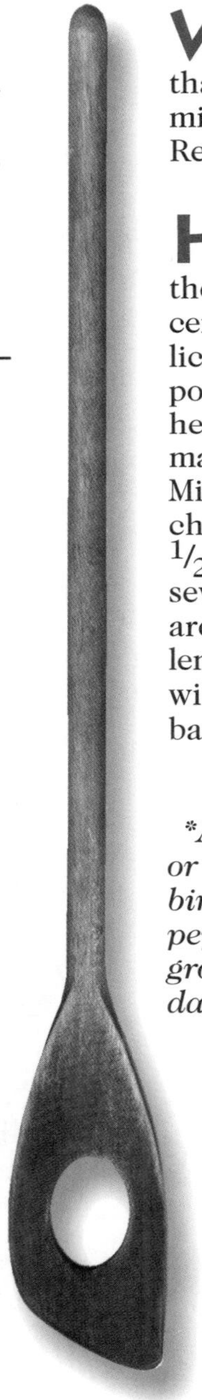

Wash and drain the shrimp, or thaw, if frozen. Put in a bowl and mix in 1/4 teaspoon tumeric powder. Refrigerate at least 30 minutes.

Heat oil in a large skillet. Sauté the onion and garlic until translucent. Add the tomatoes, ginger-garlic paste, and 1/4 teaspoon tumeric powder. Cover and cook over low heat. When the tomatoes are soft, mash them with the back of a spoon. Mix in the shrimp, along with the chile powder, garam masala, and 1/2 cup water. Simmer, covered, for several minutes, until the shrimp are done; do not overcook. Stir in lemon juice before serving. Garnish with cilantro leaves. Serve with basmati rice.

**Available at East Indian grocers or large grocery stores. It is a combination of ground cumin, black pepper, cinnamon, ground cloves, ground coriander, and ground cardamon.*

Dijon Chicken

SERVES 2

An easy dish for a cold evening.

INGREDIENTS

2 tablespoons	**butter or olive oil**
1 small	**whole chicken – cut into serving pieces ***
Salt and freshly ground pepper, to taste	
1	**onion – sliced**
1 cup	**chicken broth**
2 tablespoons	**Dijon mustard**
1/2 cup	**dry white wine**

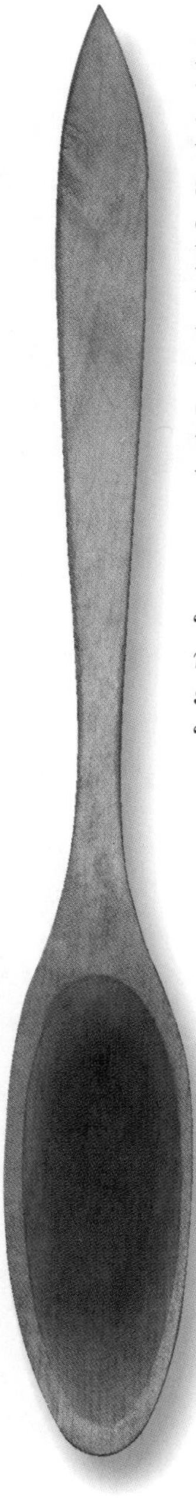

Melt butter or oil in a large skillet. Sprinkle the chicken with salt and pepper, and cook over medium-high heat until browned on both sides. Remove to a platter. Drain off any excess grease from the skillet and sauté the onion slices until translucent. Add the broth, mustard, and wine. Mix until combined, then return chicken to the pan. Simmer until the chicken is cooked through, about 30 minutes. Serve with rice, orzo, or couscous.

**This will serve either two people, with leftovers, or four. As an alternative, you can use 2 boneless and skinless chicken breast halves, which will cook faster.*

Eggplant Scallop

SERVES 2

A satisfying vegetarian entrée that is quick to put together on a snowy evening.

INGREDIENTS

1 medium	**eggplant – peeled and cut into $1^1/_2$-inch cubes**
Boiling salted water	
1 tablespoon	**butter or olive oil**
1 medium	**onion – sliced**
1	**clove of garlic – minced**
1 teaspoon	**basil**
1 can (10 $^3/_4$ ounce)	**condensed tomato soup**
$^1/_2$ cup	**water**
$^1/_4$ teaspoon	**salt**
$^1/_2$ cup	**seasoned bread crumbs, *or* herb-seasoned stuffing mix**
$^1/_4$ cup (1 ounce)	**Parmesan cheese – grated**

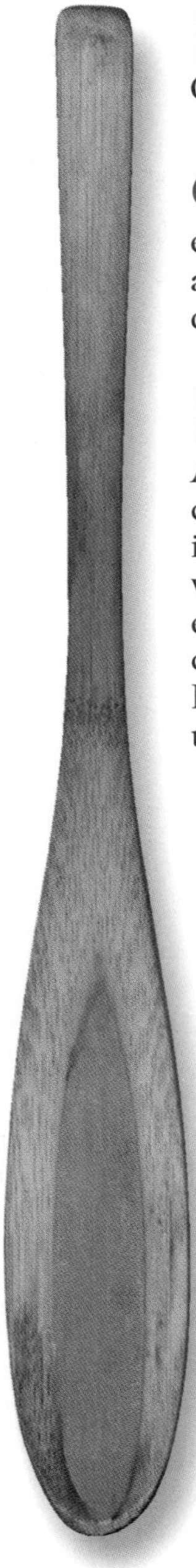

Preheat oven to 350 degrees. Grease a 10 x 16-inch baking dish.

Cook the eggplant in boiling salted water for 10 minutes. Drain, and place in the prepared baking dish.

Heat butter or oil in a saucepan. Add the onion, garlic, and basil, and cook until the onion is tender. Stir in the soup, water, and salt, mixing well. Pour this mixture over the eggplant. Sprinkle with breadcrumbs or stuffing mix, and grated Parmesan. Bake for 30 minutes, until bubbly.

Romaine with Yogurt-Dill Dressing

SERVES 2

The dressing can be made well ahead of time as it keeps for a week in the refrigerator.

INGREDIENTS

Yogurt-Dill Dressing:
(makes $1\frac{1}{4}$ cups):

1	lemon – juiced
1	clove of garlic – mashed or minced
$\frac{1}{2}$ teaspoon	salt
$\frac{1}{2}$ teaspoon	celery salt
1 tablespoon	fresh dill – minced, or 1 teaspoon dried
$\frac{1}{4}$ teaspoon	freshly ground pepper
1 cup	plain yogurt
1 medium head	romaine lettuce – washed and dried

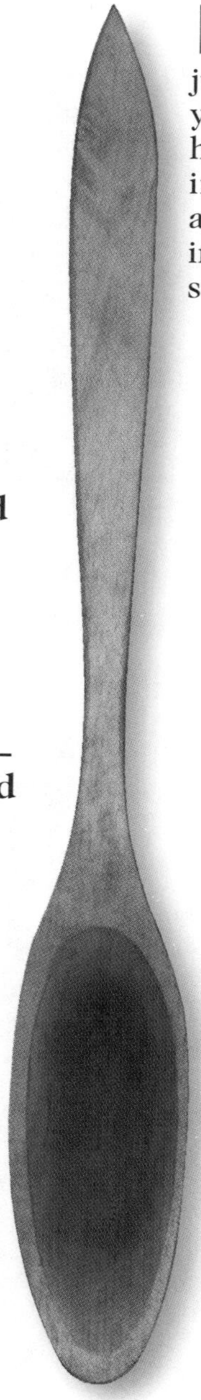

In a small bowl, blend the lemon juice, garlic, and spices. Add the yogurt and mix gently. Chill for an hour before using, or for 15 minutes in the freezer. At serving time, arrange whole romaine leaves on individual salad plates and drizzle some dressing over the top.

Baked Fudge

MAKES 9 TO 12

Very rich brownies – the perfect comfort food any time of year. No altitude adjustments are necessary.

INGREDIENTS

1/2 cup	**sifted flour**
1/2 cup	**cocoa powder**
2 cups	**sugar**
4	**eggs – well beaten**
1 cup (2 sticks)	**butter – melted**
1 cup	**pecans – chopped**
1 teaspoon	**vanilla extract**
1 cup	**heavy cream – whipped, *or* 1 pint vanilla ice cream (garnish)**

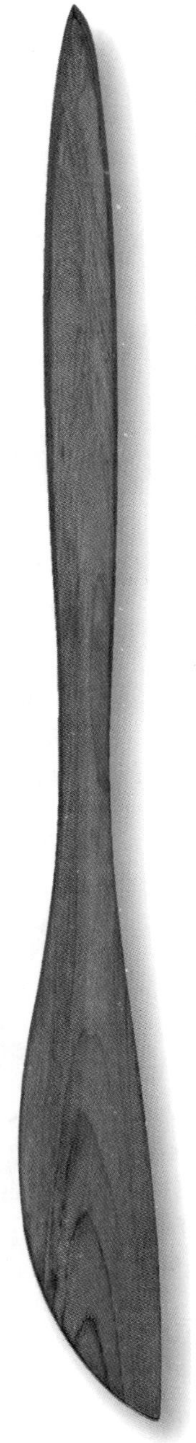

Preheat oven to 350 degrees. Grease an 8-inch square baking dish.

Mix the flour, cocoa, and sugar in a large bowl. Add the eggs, blending thoroughly. Stir in the melted butter, pecans, and vanilla. Beat well. Spread into the prepared baking dish. Set in a larger pan, and pour hot water 1/2- to 1-inch up sides of the pan. Bake for 55 minutes. Cut into squares. Serve with whipped cream or vanilla ice cream, if desired.

Courtesy of Ski Santa Fe, Photo by Jay Blackwood

Aprés-Ski Supper for Friends

Special Thanks to:
Las Campanas Santa Fe

Several ski pals phone to say that snow is coming in, and plans are made to meet on the slopes in the morning. Although you may not have heard the weather forecast, it is easy to keep your eye on the changing winter conditions: the Santa Fe Ski Basin can be viewed from all over town. Resting on top of the Sangre de Cristo Mountains that rise spectacularly behind our city, you can see when clouds are covering it and, after they've passed, whether there is fresh snow on the trees or not. Enthusiastic Santa Fe skiers have learned to distinguish the degrees of whiteness left behind.

Our local ski area – sixteen miles from the heart of town – is a jewel. The trails are challenging to all levels of ski afficionados, and the views from the top are magnificent. If you can get away on a weekday, you might even have the ski trails to yourself (well, almost).

The Ski Basin hosts several annual special events. The United Way Celebrity Ski Classic provides a weekend's worth of fun for teams of four, each including a film, television, music, or sports celebrity. Another event – the Jimmy Heuga Express MS Fundraiser – combines Marathon and Giant Slalom skiing, and the winner earns a free trip to Vail to race in the next level of competition.

Before you head off to enjoy the new powder, you remember that it's your turn to cook for your ski buddies. Anticipating how hungry you always are after a day on the slopes, you head off to the market. In the parking lot, you see the clouds coming in over the mountain. "I'm going to knock off their socks," you say. Did you mean with the snowboard you just bought, or were you thinking of our dinner for eight to ten? Best news of all, this menu may be prepared the night before.

Aprés-Ski Supper for Friends

Menu

Antipasto

Chili con Portabellini
or
White Chili with Chicken
or
Chili con Carne

Cauliflower and Broccoli Salad

Lemon Angel Pie

Beer or Wine and Hot Tea

ANTIPASTO

SERVES 8

Traditionally, antipasto goes before pasta, but it is great with chili, too. This quick-to-assemble recipe must be chilled for 24 hours before serving, and is perfect with big chunks of crusty bread.

INGREDIENTS

1 jar (16 ounce)	**giardiniera or marinated garden salad, drained ***
1 can (13.75 ounce)	**artichokes hearts, undrained – halved, or 1 jar (12 ounce) artichokes marinated in oil**
2 jars (4.5 ounce)	**whole mushrooms, drained, or 1 jar (8 ounce) pickled mushrooms**
1 can (6 ounce)	**medium pitted ripe olives, drained**
1 can (15 ounce)	**tomato sauce**
1 can (7.5 ounce)	**oil- or water-packed tuna, undrained**
8 large	**butter lettuce leaves – washed and dried**

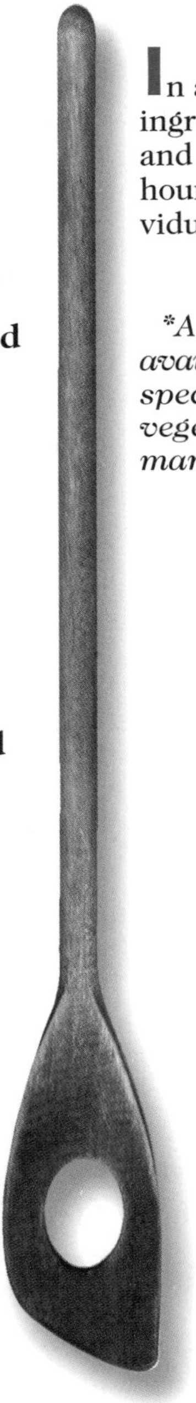

In a large bowl, combine all of the ingredients, except for the lettuce, and chill in the refrigerator for 24 hours. At serving time, mound individual portions on lettuce leaves.

**A marinated vegetable mixture available at Italian grocers or in the specialty, condiment, or canned vegetable section of large supermarkets.*

Chili con Portabellini

SERVES 4

Portabella mushrooms give this vegetarian chili its heartiness. An easy recipe to increase for a large group.

INGREDIENTS

2 tablespoons	olive oil
1 large	onion – chopped
2 large	cloves of garlic – minced
8 ounces	portabella mushrooms – cleaned and coarsely chopped
2 tablespoons	ground cumin
1 tablespoon	medium or hot red chile powder
1 can (28 or 35 ounce)	tomatoes, undrained – chopped coarsely
1 can (15 ounce)	kidney beans, drained
2 tablespoons	bacon-flavored bits

In a large skillet or saucepan, heat oil over medium-high heat. Add the onions and garlic and sauté until translucent. Add the mushrooms and cook until soft and the liquid has evaporated. Add the cumin, chile powder, tomatoes, beans, and bacon bits. Bring to a boil. Reduce heat and simmer for 1 hour. Serve immediately.

For me, this has been a year of trials, challenges – and blessings. You and the food you bring me are definitely a big blessing! Thank you for caring. A.G.

White Chili with Chicken

SERVES 8 TO 10

A delectable variation on traditional chili, this recipe uses white beans instead of kidney or black beans. Begin preparation the night before serving.

INGREDIENTS

5 cups	**water**
3 cans (14.5 ounce)	**chicken broth**
4 or 5 large	**chicken breast halves**
1 pound	**dried white or Great Northern beans – soaked overnight**
1 tablespoon	**olive oil**
2 large	**white onions – chopped**
3 or 4	**cloves of garlic – minced**
2 cans (4 ounce)	**diced green chiles**
1 1/2 teaspoons	**oregano**
2 tablespoons	**ground cumin**
1/4 teaspoon	**ground cloves**
1/4 teaspoon	**cayenne powder**

Salt and freshly ground pepper, to taste

1 cup	**sour cream (garnish)**
1 cup (4 ounces)	**Monterey Jack cheese – shredded (garnish)**
1 can (3 ounce)	**sliced ripe olives, drained (garnish)**
1 cup	**salsa (garnish)**
1/2 cup	**scallions – chopped (garnish)**
1/2 cup	**fresh cilantro leaves – chopped (garnish)**

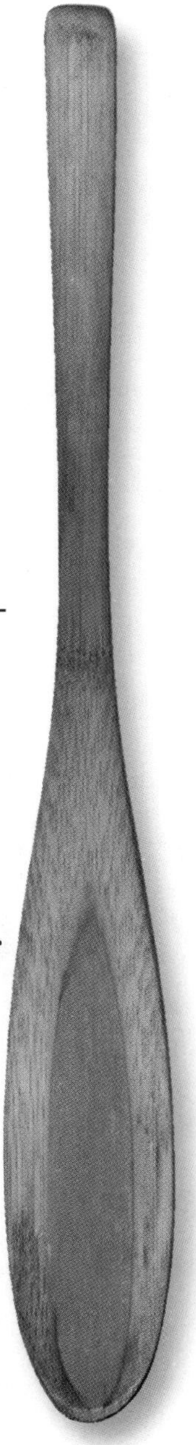

In a large pot, bring water and broth to a boil and add the chicken breasts. Reduce heat and poach for 20 minutes, or until done. Remove the chicken to a plate, and add the beans – pre-soaked and drained – to the pot. Bring to a boil. Reduce heat, and simmer for about 3 hours, or until the beans are soft. In the meantime, skin, bone, and shred the chicken meat, and set aside.

When the beans are tender, heat oil in a small skillet and sauté the onions and garlic until translucent. Add to the beans, along with the green chiles, oregano, cumin, cloves, and cayenne. Stir well. Add the shredded chicken, and more water, if necessary. Season to taste with salt and pepper. Simmer for 1 hour. Ladle into soup bowls, and serve with one or all of the garnishes.

Chili con Carne

SERVES 8 TO 10

The Traditional. This Kitchen Angel's recipe was featured in *Bon Appetit*. Begin preparation the night before serving.

INGREDIENTS

$1\frac{1}{2}$ pounds	**dried pinto beans – washed and soaked overnight**
5 large	**yellow onions – coarsely chopped**
5 large	**cloves of garlic – minced**
4 to 5 tablespoons	**olive oil**
4 pounds	**boned lean beef chuck – cut in $\frac{1}{2}$-inch cubes**
5 tablespoons	**mild to hot red chile powder, or to taste**
$1\frac{1}{2}$ teaspoons	**cinnamon**
$\frac{1}{2}$ teaspoon	**thyme – crumbled**
1 teaspoon	**salt, or to taste**
$\frac{1}{4}$ teaspoon	**pepper, or to taste**
$1\frac{1}{2}$ cups (or more)	**strong beef stock**

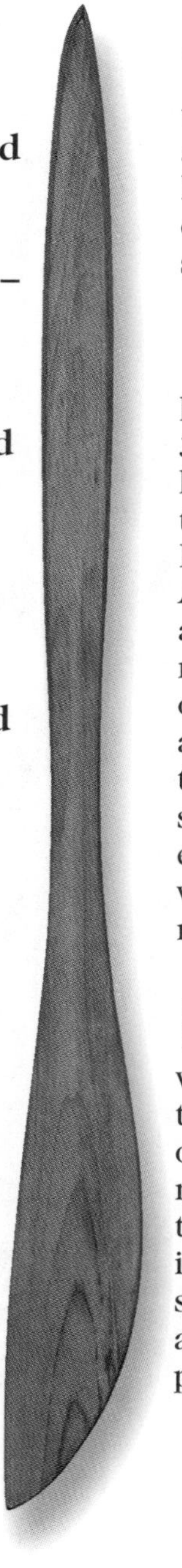

Set the beans and their soaking water in a large kettle over moderate heat, and bring to a boil. Reduce heat to a gentle simmer. Cover and cook $1\frac{1}{2}$ hours until the beans are softened but still *al dente*.

In the meantime, in a second large kettle, sauté the onions and garlic in 3 tablespoons oil over moderate heat for 8 to 10 minutes, or until translucent and lightly browned. Remove and drain on paper towels. Add 1 tablespoon oil to the kettle and brown the beef, in batches, over moderately high heat, adding more oil, if necessary. Return the onions and garlic to the kettle, along with the chile powder, cinnamon, thyme, salt, and pepper. Turn heat to lowest point and let flavors mellow while the beans are cooking the required $1\frac{1}{2}$ hours.

Pour the beans and their cooking water into the beef kettle, and add the beef stock. Cover and simmer over low heat for $2\frac{1}{2}$ or 3 hours more, until both beef and beans are tender, adding more stock or water if mixture seems too thick. Adjust seasonings before serving, adding additional salt, pepper, and chile powder, if needed.

Cauliflower and Broccoli Salad

SERVES 8 TO 10

A crunchy, healthy, and delicious winter salad.

INGREDIENTS

1 cup	**mayonnaise**
3 tablespoons	**yellow onion – diced**
$^{1}/_{3}$ cup	**sugar**
$^{1}/_{3}$ cup	**Romano or Parmesan cheese – grated**
2 strips	**bacon – cooked crisp, and crumbled**
1 small to medium	**cauliflower**
1 pound	**broccoli**
1 cup	**frozen peas – thawed and blanched (optional)**

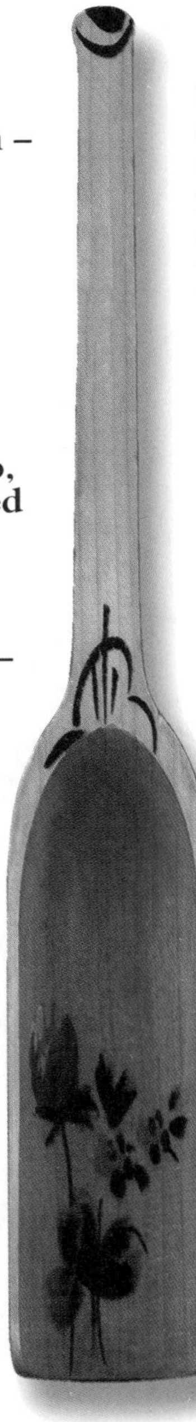

In a large salad bowl, combine the mayonnaise, onion, sugar, cheese, and bacon. Break the cauliflower into florets, and cut into bite-sized pieces. Cut the broccoli into florets, and peel and cut stalks into $^{1}/_{2}$-inch thick slices. Add the cauliflower, broccoli, and peas, if using, to the mayonnaise mixture. Toss well and serve immediately.

Lemon Angel Pie

SERVES 8 TO 10

No altitude adjustment is needed for this heavenly pie. Please note that it must be prepared at least 8 hours in advance.

INGREDIENTS

<u>Meringue Shell:</u>

4	**egg whites**
1 cup	**sugar**
$^1/_4$ teaspoon	**cream of tartar**
$^1/_3$ cup	**sliced almonds**

<u>Filling:</u>

4	**egg yolks**
$^1/_2$ cup	**sugar**
2	**lemons – juice and grated zest**
$^1/_8$ teaspoon	**salt**
2 cups	**heavy cream**
Sugar, to taste	

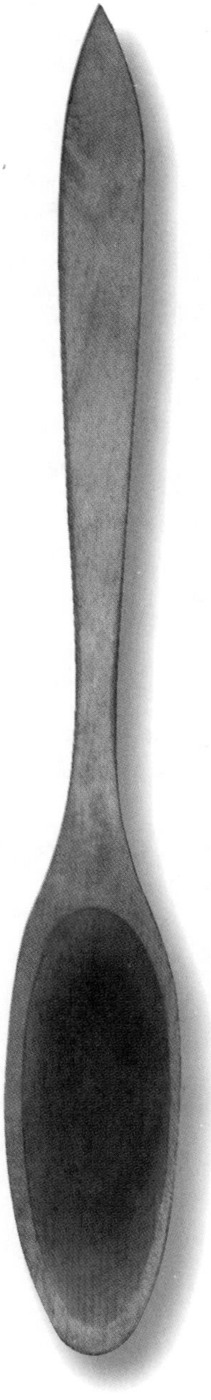

Preheat oven to 275 degrees. Grease a 10-inch pie plate.

Beat the egg whites until stiff, then beat in the sugar and cream of tartar. Spread the meringue into the prepared pie plate. Arrange sliced almonds around the rim. Bake for 2 hours. Cool before filling.

Beat the egg yolks in a small saucepan. Place over medium heat and whisk in $^1/_2$ cup sugar, lemon juice, and salt. Cook only until the sugar is dissolved, stirring constantly. Cool.

Whip the cream. Fold *half* of it, unsweetened, into the cooled egg mixture, and pour this into the cooled meringue shell. Add a bit of sugar, to taste, to the remaining whipped cream and spread it evenly over the pie. Sprinkle with grated lemon zest. Chill for 8 hours before serving.

Photo by Tom Parrish

A Winter Potluck

In Memory of:
Norma and Jack Green

No matter how much we love to ski or sled or make snow sculptures, there is a certain point in winter when we begin to long for warm weather and a social life. We have dieted and exercised according to our New Year's resolutions, but now our winter hibernation is beginning to give way to cabin fever. It is time to kick up our heels and party, but the cold weather makes us too sluggish to cook for a crowd.

This is exactly the time for which the Potluck Dinner was invented, so what are you waiting for? Invite your friends over and tell them not to come empty-handed. Have the non-cooks supply beverages, and all you have to do is set out plates and napkins.

Part of the fun is seeing what actually shows up. How many soups? How many chickens? Will there be a slant towards desserts? Too many beans? Is it possible there will be no starch? (Hardly!) And what fun, too, are all the different platters and casserole dishes the food comes prepared on or in. It is truly the luck of many pots that brings this amusing mélange to your table. There will be plenty for people to take home as well. Not just the dishes that they arrived with, but also those of others. Will there be one lonely dish no one wants to sample, a little devil of defiance on the table? No! Never! (But it might be fun to imagine, to actually prepare it, like an April Fool's joke. What might that be? Hmmmmmm. Are you feeling mischievous in mid-winter?)

Our potluck section features a potpourri of recipes that feed varying numbers of people – in the true spirit of potluck – since some people are comfortable cooking for four, and others (such as our Kitchen Angels chefs) for fifty.

A Winter Potluck

Menu

Green Chiles with Sun-dried Tomatoes and Goat Cheese

Newcomer's Green Chile Stew

Red Miso Kale Soup

Southwestern Pinto Bean Soup

Cranberry-Glazed Chicken

Sesame Honey Chicken

Beef and Broccoli Casserole

Husband's Delight Casserole

Goulash

Lamb or Veal Stew with Mint and Lemon

Linle's Stew (1969)

(Menu continued on next page)

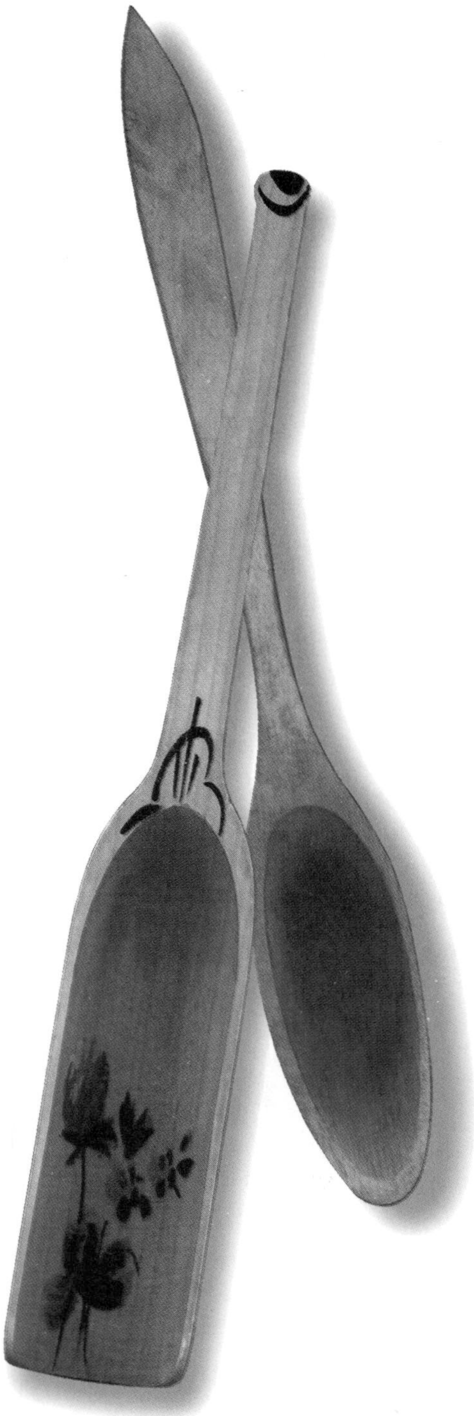

A Winter Potluck

Menu-continued

Pork Sparerib Jambalaya

Salmon Shepherd's Pie

Noodle Pudding

Pasta with Rapini

Roasted Potatoes and Vegetables

Swedish Red Cabbage

Asian Vegetable Salad with Sesame Sauce

Corn Salad with Tequila Dressing

Flour Tortillas

White Cornbread

Cream Cheese Cake

Date-Pecan Tea Cake

Linda's Outrageous Chocolate Chip Cookies

Pineapple Bread Pudding

Red Velvet Cake

Soda, Beer, Wine, and Coffee

Green Chiles with Sun-dried Tomatoes and Goat Cheese

SERVES 4 (MAIN DISH) OR 8 (APPETIZER)

Preparation for this elegant appetizer or vegetarian entrée must begin at least 3 hours ahead of time. The results are well worth it!

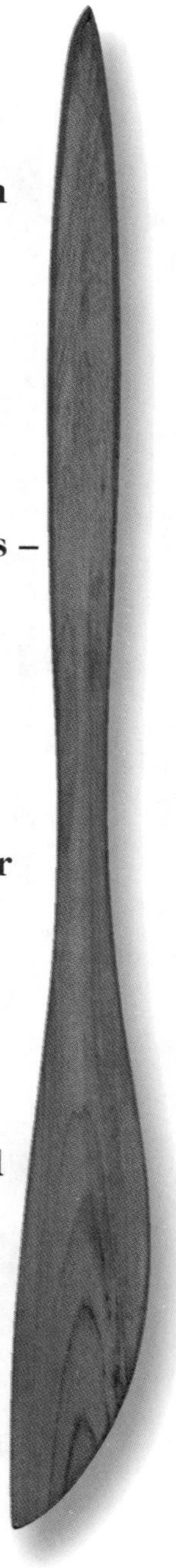

INGREDIENTS

8 whole	**fresh Anaheim or New Mexican green chiles – roasted**
12 ounces	**mild soft goat cheese**
1 package (3 ounce)	**cream cheese – at room temperature**
8	**red bell peppers – roasted**
$^1/_3$ cup plus	**extra virgin**
3 tablespoons	**olive oil**
$^1/_2$ teaspoon	**salt**
1 tablespoon	**sugar**
$2^1/_2$ tablespoons	**balsamic vinegar**
$^3/_4$ cup	**oil-packed sun-dried tomatoes – drained and diced**
4 cups	**mesclun salad greens – washed and dried**
$^1/_2$ cup	**piñon nuts – lightly toasted**

Peel the roasted chiles and slit each lengthwise. Remove all seeds, but leave the stems intact; set aside. In a food processor, purée the goat and cream cheeses until smooth. Remove to a small bowl and chill until firm. Peel and seed the roasted red peppers. Place in a food processor along with $^1/_3$ cup of the olive oil, the salt and sugar, and $1^1/_2$ tablespoons of the balsamic vinegar. Purée until smooth and remove to a bowl. Cover and refrigerate.

Lay the green chiles open and flat on a platter. Divide the chilled cheese filling among the chiles, and press each into a flattened log. Sprinkle each with about 1 tablespoon of the diced sun-dried tomatoes. Close and reshape chiles. Chill, covered, for at least 2 hours.

At serving time, toss the salad greens with the remaining 3 tablespoons olive oil and 1 remaining tablespoon balsamic vinegar. Divide the red pepper purée among 4 or 8 plates, depending upon serving size. On one side of each plate, place a mound of the greens and sprinkle with piñon nuts. Place one or two chiles over the red pepper purée. Serve immediately.

Newcomer's Green Chile Stew

SERVES 6 TO 8

If available, use fresh green chiles.

INGREDIENTS

2 tablespoons	olive oil
1 large	onion – cut in 1/2-inch cubes
3 cloves	garlic – peeled and coarsely chopped
2 whole	chicken breasts, skinless and boneless – cut into 1/2-inch cubes *
2 cans (14.5 ounce)	fat free chicken broth, *plus* 2 cans water
6 medium	red or white new potatoes – scrubbed and cut in 1/2-inch cubes
1 large	carrot – cut in 1/2-inch slices
1 or 2 cans (4 ounce)	mild to hot diced green chiles **
1/2 cup	canned diced tomatoes

Salt or soy sauce plus freshly ground pepper, to taste

1 teaspoon	basil (optional)
1 to 2 teaspoons	medium red chile powder (optional)
1/2 teaspoon	garlic powder (optional)
1/4 cup	fresh cilantro leaves (optional)

Heat oil in a heavy soup pot and sauté the onions, garlic, and cubed chicken until onions are transparent. Add the broth and water. Scrape the chicken particles from the bottom of the pot. Add the remaining ingredients, including optional seasonings, if using. Bring to a boil, then reduce heat and simmer for 1 to 2 hours, until the chicken (or meat) is tender. During cooking, add more broth or water, if needed. If desired, thicken the stew by whisking together 1 or 2 tablespoons flour with 1/2 cup of the broth, then stirring it back in the stew. Serve with flour tortillas or sourdough bread.

**You may substitute 3 or 4 pork chops, bones removed. Lamb or beef may also be used.*

***Depending upon how spicy you want the stew. You can substitute fresh chopped green chiles (see note at top).*

Red Miso Kale Soup

SERVES 50

Soup for a crowd! Substitute cabbage, if you wish, but use light yellow miso instead.

INGREDIENTS

4 sticks (1 pound)	**butter**
$^1/_4$ cup	**olive oil**
8 to 12	**onions – chopped**
1 to 2 bulbs	**garlic – peeled and chopped**
5 to 8 pounds	**kale or collard greens – washed and coarsely chopped**
20	**carrots – peeled and sliced**
1 bunch	**celery – sliced or chopped**
Water	
1 container (16 ounce)	**red miso**
10 to 12	**vegetable bouillon cubes**
4 tablespoons	**oregano**
4 tablespoons	**dill weed**

Soy sauce *or* liquid amino acids, to taste

Salt and freshly ground pepper, to taste

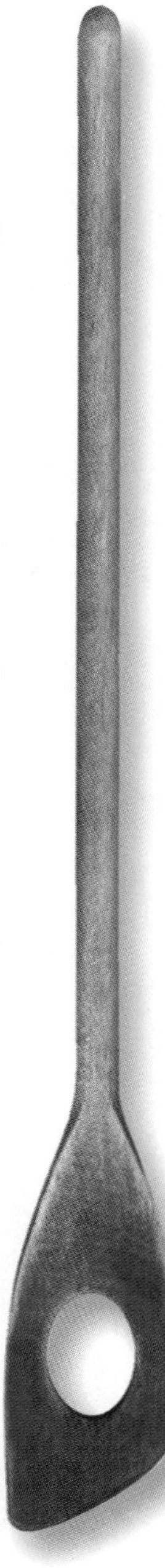

In a very large soup pot, melt butter with olive oil. Sauté all of the chopped vegetables until they are limp but not completely cooked, stirring frequently. Fill the pot with water and bring to a boil. Take 1 or 2 cups of the boiling soup water and place it in a medium bowl. Whisk in the miso and combine well. Pour the miso mixture back into the soup pot. Stir in the bouillon cubes, oregano, dill, soy sauce, salt, and pepper. Reduce heat and simmer, covered, for about 30 minutes, until the vegetables are soft.

Each meal means so much to me! The program makes my life so much better and easier. I love the security it gives me and the feeling of being valued. I love the exchanges with the delivery angels. R.D.

Southwestern Pinto Bean Soup

SERVES 8 TO 10

A hearty winter favorite. Begin preparations a day ahead because the beans must soak overnight.

INGREDIENTS

2 cups	**dried pinto beans**
1 pound	**cooked ham – cut into cubes**
1 quart	**water**
2 cans (13.5 ounce)	**tomato juice**
4 cups	**chicken stock**
1 medium	**onion – chopped**
3	**cloves of garlic – minced**
3 tablespoons	**fresh parsley leaves – chopped**
1/4 cup	**red bell pepper – chopped**
4 tablespoons	**brown sugar**
1 teaspoon	**crushed bay leaves**
1 teaspoon	**oregano**
1/2 teaspoon each:	**rosemary, marjoram, basil, ground thyme, and celery seed**
4 whole	**cloves**
1 tablespoon	**chili powder**
1 teaspoon	**salt**
1/2 teaspoon	**ground cumin**
1/2 teaspoon	**curry powder**
1 cup	**sherry**
1 cup	**crème fraîche *or* sour cream (garnish)**
8 to 10 sprigs	**fresh cilantro (garnish)**

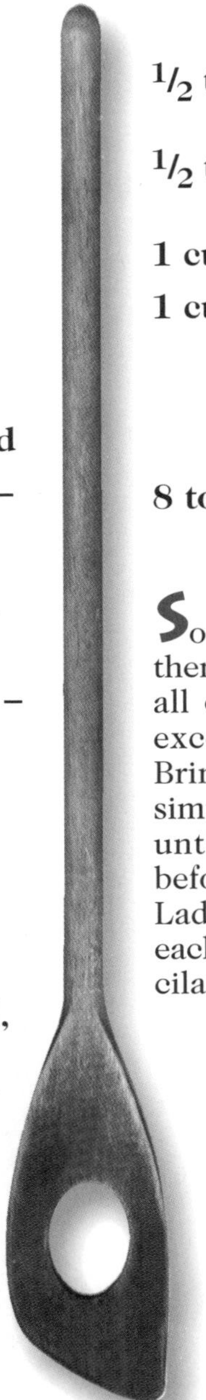

Soak the beans overnight. Drain them and place in a large kettle with all of the remaining ingredients, except the sherry and garnishes. Bring to a boil. Reduce heat and simmer, covered, for about 3 hours, until the beans are tender. Just before serving, stir in the sherry. Ladle soup into bowls and garnish each serving with crème fraîche and cilantro sprigs, if desired.

Cranberry-Glazed Chicken

SERVES 6

Wonderful – and easy – during the holidays or any time of year.

INGREDIENTS

6	chicken breast halves
Salt and freshly ground pepper, to taste	
1/4 cup	butter or margarine
1 can (8 ounce)	whole-berry cranberry sauce
2 tablespoons	soy sauce
1 1/2 tablespoons	lemon juice

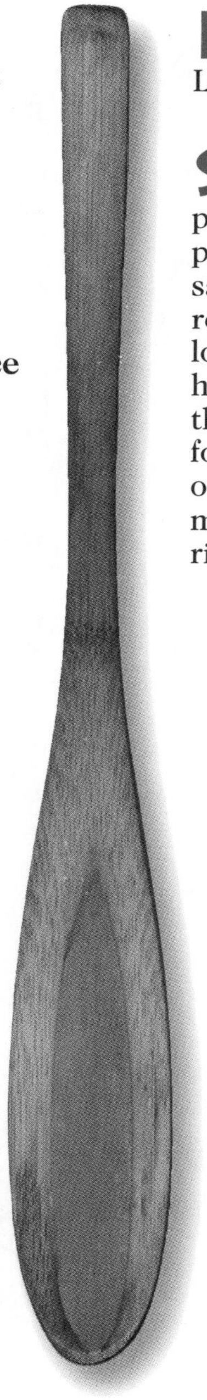

Preheat oven to 400 degrees. Lightly grease a baking dish.

Season the chicken with salt and pepper. Place, skin side down, in the prepared baking dish. In a saucepan, melt butter and add the remaining ingredients. Cook over low heat until the cranberry sauce has liquified. Pour the sauce over the chicken and bake, uncovered, for 30 minutes. Turn the chicken over and bake for 15 or 20 minutes more, or until done. Serve with rice.

Sesame Honey Chicken

SERVES 6

Fast, easy, and sublime.

INGREDIENTS

$^1/_2$ cup	butter or margerine – melted
$^1/_4$ cup	Dijon mustard
1 teaspoon	curry powder
1 tablespoon (heaping)	chutney
$^1/_2$ cup	honey
6	chicken breast halves, skinless and boneless
$^1/_4$ cup	toasted sesame seeds (garnish)

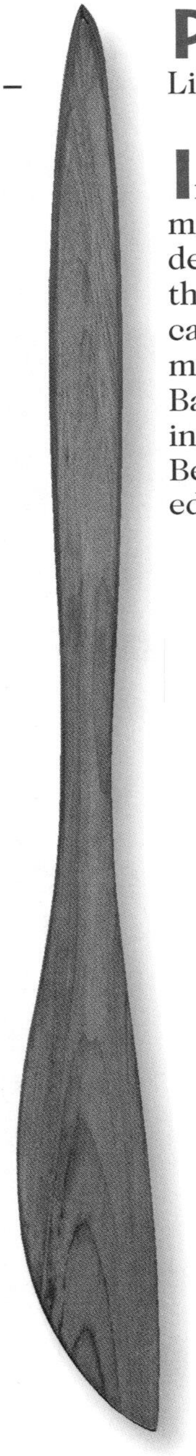

Preheat oven to 350 degrees. Lightly grease a baking dish.

In a small bowl, whisk together the melted butter, mustard, curry powder, chutney, and honey. Arrange the chicken breasts in the prepared casserole and pour the honey-spice mixture evenly over the chicken. Bake for 1 hour, or until done, basting every 20 minutes with the sauce. Before serving, sprinkle with toasted sesame seeds.

Beef and Broccoli Casserole

SERVES 4

Comfort food at its best.

INGREDIENTS

1 pound	**lean ground beef**
2 boxes (10 ounce)	**frozen chopped broccoli – thawed**
1/2 teaspoon	**salt, or to taste**
1/2 teaspoon	**garlic powder, or to taste**
1 small	**onion – chopped**
1 carton (8 ounce)	**sour cream, or to taste**

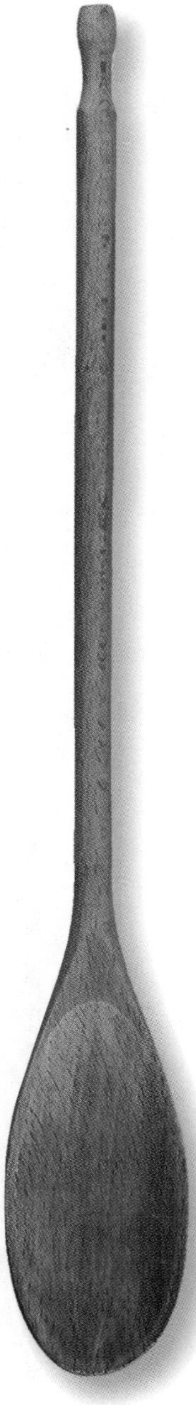

Brown the beef in a large skillet over medium-high heat, stirring often. Drain off the fat, then add the broccoli, salt, garlic powder, and onion. Cook over low heat, stirring occasionally, until the broccoli is hot but still *al dente.* Stir in the desired amount of sour cream, blending well. Serve immediately over rice or noodles.

Husband's Delight Casserole

SERVES 8

The name says it all. Best when assembled a day ahead of baking.

INGREDIENTS

1 pound	lean ground beef
2	cloves of garlic – crushed
1 teaspoon	salt
1 teaspoon	sugar
Freshly ground pepper, to taste	
2 cans (8 ounce)	tomato sauce
1 package (8 ounce)	small egg noodles
5	scallions – finely chopped
1 package (3 ounce)	cream cheese – at room temperature
1 carton (8 ounce)	sour cream
1/2 cup (2 ounces)	Cheddar cheese – grated

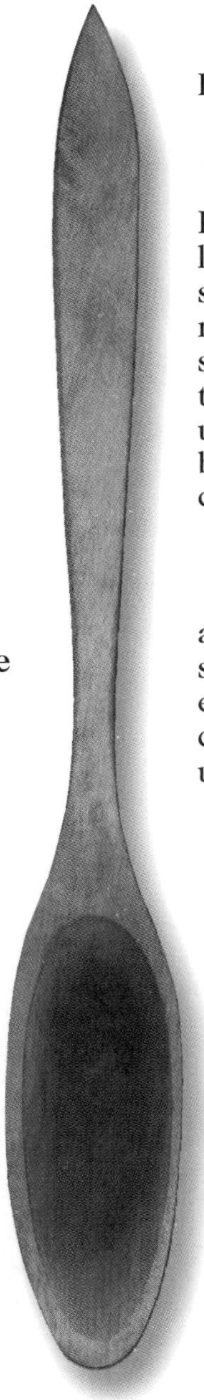

Preheat oven to 350 degrees. Lightly grease a baking dish.

Brown the beef in a large skillet. Drain off the fat, then add the garlic, salt, sugar, pepper, and tomato sauce. Cover and simmer for 15 minutes. While the beef mixture is simmering, bring a large pot of water to a boil. Add the noodles and cook until *al dente*, then drain. In a small bowl, combine the scallions, cream cheese, and sour cream, mixing well.

In the prepared baking dish, arrange layers of the noodles, meat sauce, sour cream mixture, and grated cheese, ending up with the cheese. Bake for 20 to 30 minutes, until heated through.

Goulash (Gulyas)

SERVES 6

A wonderful wintery beef stew.

INGREDIENTS

4 slices	**bacon**
2 medium	**onions – sliced**
1 to $1\frac{1}{2}$ tablespoons	**imported Hungarian paprika**
2 pounds	**beef stew meat – cut into 1-inch cubes**
1 tablespoon	**salt**
1 teaspoon	**caraway seeds**
1	**green bell pepper – seeded and sliced**
1 or 2	**tomatoes – sliced**
Water	
2	**cloves of garlic – minced**
4 small	**potatoes – peeled and quartered**

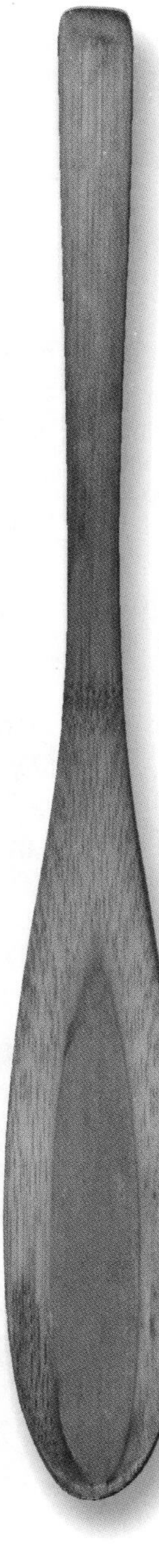

In a Dutch oven or heavy 3-quart pot with a tight-fitting lid, brown the bacon. Remove the bacon and crumble into pieces; set aside. In the same pan, brown the onions in the bacon drippings until transparent. Remove pot from heat and stir in the paprika. Add the beef, salt, caraway seeds, cooked bacon, green pepper, and tomatoes. Return to the stove and cover tightly. Simmer over low heat, stirring occasionally and adding small amounts of water as needed. Cook for $1\frac{1}{2}$ to 2 hours, until the beef is tender. Add the garlic and potatoes and enough water to completely cover the stew. Bring to a boil, then lower heat and simmer for 30 minutes. Serve with rice, if desired.

Lamb or Veal Stew with Mint and Lemon

SERVES 25 (MAIN DISH) TO 40 (AS PART OF BUFFET)

A savory dish for a crowd. Dried mint may be substituted, but fresh leaves are best.

INGREDIENTS

10 pounds	**lamb or veal stew meat – cut into $1^1/_2$ -inch cubes**
4 or more tablespoons	**olive oil**
3 tablespoons	**butter**
10 large	**cloves of garlic – minced**
10	**onions – each cut into 6 wedges**
6 tablespoons	**flour**
$^1/_2$ teaspoon	**cayenne pepper**
4 teaspoons	**salt, or to taste**
4 cups	**chicken broth**
$1^1/_2$ cups	**dry white wine**
3	**lemons – juice and grated zest**
3 cups	**cream – heated and reduced by half or more**
$^1/_2$ cup	**fresh mint leaves – chopped**
1 additional	**lemon – grated zest only (optional)**

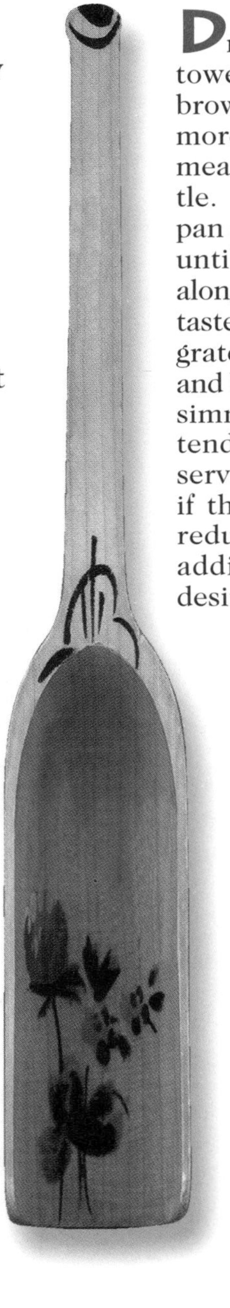

Dry the stew meat with paper towels. Heat oil in a skillet and brown the meat in batches, adding more oil if necessary. Transfer the meat to a Dutch oven or large kettle. Heat butter in a large frying pan and sauté the garlic and onions until softened. Add to the meat, along with the flour, cayenne, salt to taste, broth, wine, and the juice and grated zest of 3 lemons. Mix well and bring to a boil. Reduce heat and simmer, covered, until the meat is tender, about $1^1/_2$ hours. Before serving, remove some of the sauce if there is too much. Stir in the reduced cream, mint leaves, and additional grated lemon zest, if desired.

Linle's Stew (1969)

SERVES 4 TO 6

The stew is named for the author's daughter (pronounced Lin-lee) who, as a toddler, used to sit on the counter while her mother cooked. She would munch on vegetables, then throw them into the skillet. That's not the way we would prepare it at Kitchen Angels, but it is a foolproof recipe. You can add the ingredients in any order.

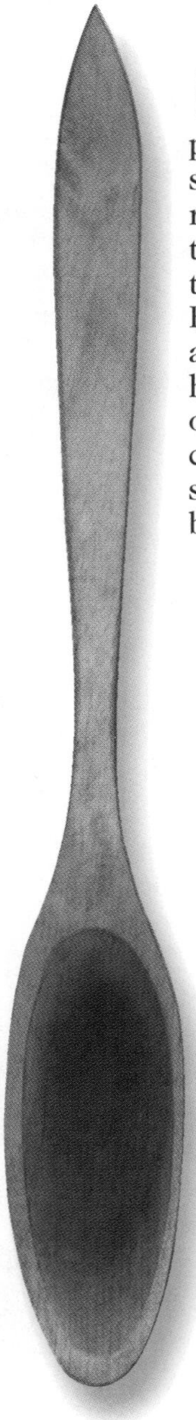

INGREDIENTS

1 tablespoon	**olive oil**
1 to $1^1/_2$	**pounds beef chuck – cut into cubes**
1 tablespoon	**Worcestershire sauce**
1 can (6 ounce)	**tomato paste**
2 cups	**water**
$^1/_2$ cup	**dry white wine**
$^1/_2$ cup	**ketchup**
$^1/_2$ teaspoon	**salt**
1 tablespoon	**basil**
2	**beef bouillon cubes, crumbled**
1	**celery rib – chopped**
1 medium	**onion – chopped**
1	**clove of garlic – chopped**
1	**green bell pepper – seeded and chopped**

Heat oil in a large skillet or heavy pot. Add the beef and Worcestershire, and brown. Add all of the remaining ingredients, blending in the tomato paste and stirring until the bouillon cubes are dissolved. Bring to a boil, then reduce heat and simmer, covered, for $1^1/_2$ or 2 hours, until the beef is tender. Serve over rice or noodles or with precooked vegetables of your choice, such as carrots, potatoes, or green beans.

Pork Sparerib Jambalaya

SERVES 4 TO 6

A tasty twist on this famous rice dish.

INGREDIENTS

1 to 2 tablespoons	peanut oil
1 large	onion – chopped
2	green bell peppers – seeded and chopped
3	cloves of garlic – minced
4	celery ribs – sliced
1 can (28 ounce)	tomatoes
3 1/2 cups	chicken stock
1 or 2	link sausages – sliced and browned
1 pound	pork spareribs – cut up and browned
1 cup	cooked ham – cut in cubes
3 teaspoons	thyme
2 teaspoons	hot pepper sauce
1/4 cup	Worcestershire sauce
2 cups	raw rice

Salt and freshly ground pepper, to taste

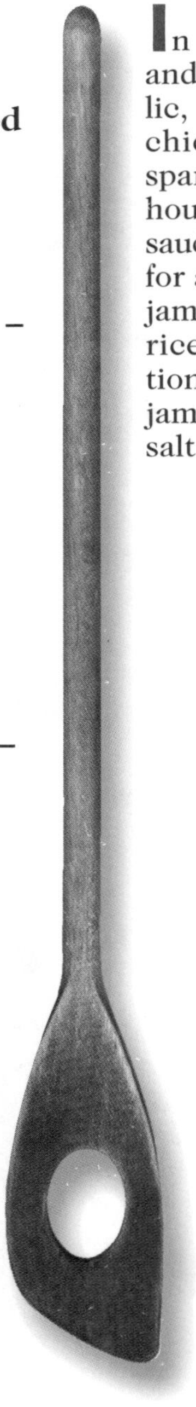

In a large heavy pot, heat the oil and sauté the onion, peppers, garlic, and celery. Add the tomatoes, chicken stock, sliced sausage, spareribs, and ham. Simmer for 1 hour. Add the thyme, hot pepper sauce, and Worcestershire. Simmer for another 20 minutes. While the jambalaya is simmering, cook the rice according to package directions. Mix the cooked rice into the jambalaya, and season to taste with salt and pepper.

Salmon Shepherd's Pie

SERVES 4 TO 6

A quick-and-easy main course, and a favorite of our Kitchen Angels clients.

INGREDIENTS

3 large	**potatoes – peeled and cubed**
1 tablespoon	**butter**
1/4 cup (or more)	**milk**
1 tablespoon	***wasabi* powder, or to taste (optional) ***
Salt and freshly ground pepper, to taste	
2 cans (14.75 ounce)	**salmon – drained, bones removed, and flaked**
1 pound	**Swiss cheese – grated**
1 tablespoon	**butter (optional)**

Preheat oven to 350 degrees. Grease an ovenproof casserole or gratin pan.

Bring a large pot of water to a boil. Add the potatoes and cook until soft. Drain the potatoes and mash them with butter and milk. Add the *wasabi*, if using, and salt and pepper to taste. In the prepared casserole, layer the mashed potatoes, flaked salmon, and cheese, in that order. Dot with butter, if desired, and bake for about 45 minutes. Let stand for 10 minutes before serving.

**Wasabi is powdered Japanese horseradish, found in the oriental section of most supermarkets.*

Noodle Pudding

SERVES 8 TO 10

An unusual, tasty main or side dish.

INGREDIENTS

1 package (16 ounce)	**wide egg noodles**
$1^1/_2$ cups	**milk**
$^1/_2$ cup	**sugar**
4	**eggs – lightly beaten**
$^1/_2$ teaspoon	**vanilla extract**
1 carton (8 ounce)	**cottage cheese**
1 carton (8 ounce)	**sour cream**
2 tablespoons	**butter – melted**
$^1/_2$ cup	**corn flakes – crushed**
1 to 2 tablespoons	**cinnamon**
1 to 2 teaspoons	**sugar**

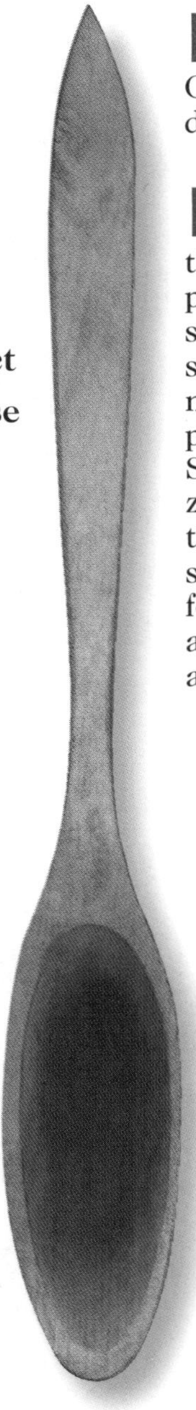

Preheat oven to 350 degrees. Grease a large ovenproof baking dish.

In a large pot of boiling water, cook the noodles until done. Drain and place in a large bowl. Add the milk, sugar, eggs, vanilla, cottage cheese, sour cream, and 1 tablespoon of the melted butter. Combine well, and pour into the prepared baking dish. Sprinkle with corn flakes and drizzle 1 tablespoon melted butter over the top. Dust with cinnamon and sugar, to taste. Bake, uncovered, for 45 minutes. Remove from oven and let stand for 5 minutes. Slice and serve.

Pasta with Rapini

SERVES 4

Rapini – also called broccoli rabe, *brocoletti di rape*, or Italian broccoli – is a sharp-flavored green of the cabbage family, and does not taste like broccoli. It looks like a poorly developed head of broccoli, with more leaves and stems than flowers, and all of it – leaves, stalks, and flowers – are eaten. If unavailable, turnip tops may be used.

INGREDIENTS

1 bunch	**rapini**
1 tablespoon	**olive oil**
2	**shallots – thinly sliced**
2	**cloves of garlic – minced**
Crushed red pepper flakes, to taste	
1 cup (or more)	**water**
1 package (12 ounce)	**spaghettini – broken into 2-inch lengths**
Pinch of	**salt**

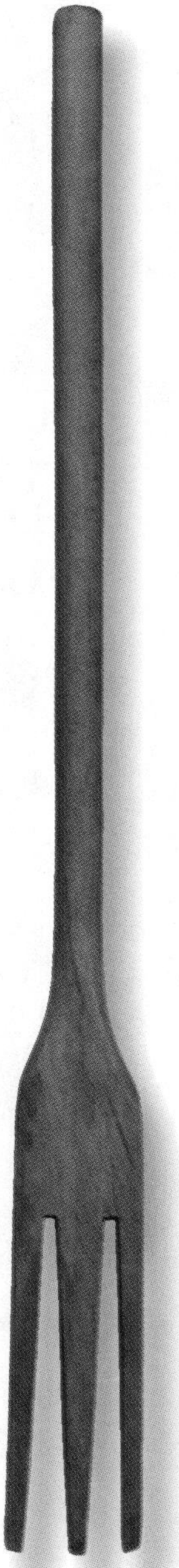

Trim off and discard the large, tough leaves of the rapini. Cut florets into 3-inch pieces. Cut the tender stems into 3-inch lengths and peel. Set aside.

Heat oil in a large skillet or heavy kettle. Sauté the shallots for 2 minutes, then add the garlic and red pepper flakes. Sauté for another minute, but do not let the garlic brown. Add 1 cup water and bring to a boil. Add the spaghettini and salt, stirring well. When the water returns to a boil, add the rapini and cook over low- to medium-heat, stirring often. Add more water, if needed, to keep the spaghettini from sticking. Cook for 10 to 15 minutes, until the pasta is done. At that point, the water will have become incorporated into the sauce. Serve immediately.

Roasted Potatoes and Vegetables

SERVES 6

A delicious accompaniment to chicken, fish, or chops.

INGREDIENTS

2 pounds	**red new potatoes – cut into eighths**
2 tablespoons	**olive oil**
1 cup	**fresh green beans – cut into $^1/_2$-inch pieces**
1 cup	**carrots – thinly sliced on the diagonal**
1 small	**red onion – cut into wedges**
2 teaspoons	**dried rosemary**
1 teaspoon	**dried sage**
$^1/_4$ teaspoon	**garlic powder, *or* 1 clove of garlic – minced**

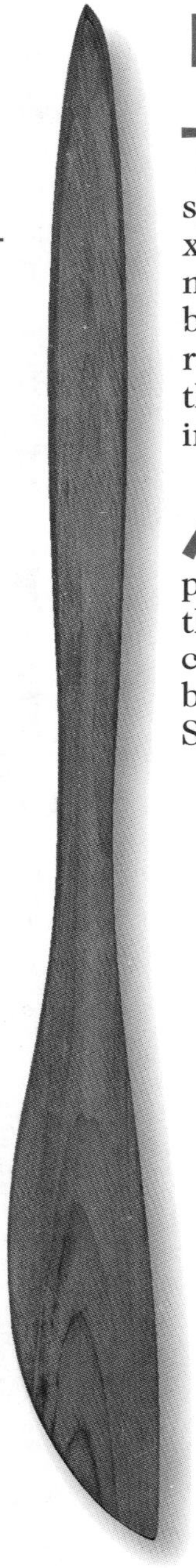

Preheat oven to 450 degrees.

Toss the potatoes with 1 tablespoon of the oil. Place in a 15 x 9 x 2-inch baking dish. Bake for 20 minutes. In a large bowl, mix the beans, carrots, and onion with the remaining 1 tablespoon of oil. Add the rosemary, sage, and garlic, tossing well.

After 20 minutes, remove the potatoes from the oven and stir in the vegetables. Return to oven and continue baking until the vegetables are tender, about 25 minutes. Serve warm.

Swedish Red Cabbage

SERVES 12

A savory side dish that is especially good in winter.

INGREDIENTS

2 tablespoons	**bacon drippings *or* butter**
1 large	**red cabbage – cored and shredded**
2 large	**apples – peeled, cored, and sliced**
1 medium	**yellow onion – chopped**
$^1/_2$ cup	**sugar**
1 cup	**vinegar**
$1^1/_2$ cups	**water**
1	**bay leaf**
$^1/_8$ teaspoon	**ground cloves**
$^1/_8$ teaspoon	**ground allspice**
$^1/_4$ teaspoon	**pepper**
1 teaspoon	**salt**
2 tablespoons	**cornstarch**
$^1/_4$ cup	**water**

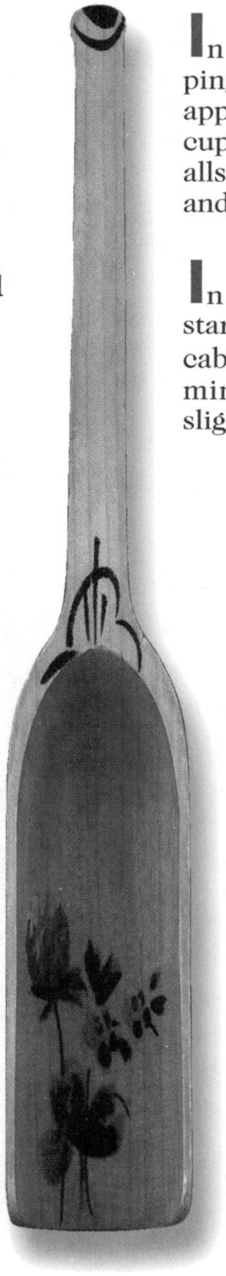

In a large pot, heat the bacon drippings or butter. Add the cabbage, apples, onion, sugar, vinegar, $1^1/_2$ cups water, bay leaf, ground cloves, allspice, pepper, and salt. Mix well and simmer, covered, for $1^1/_2$ hours.

In a small bowl, combine the cornstarch and $^1/_4$ cup water. Add to the cabbage slowly, stirring. Cook for 5 minutes longer until cabbage is slightly thickened.

Asian Vegetable Salad with Sesame Sauce

Serves 6 to 8

Ingredients

4 cups	cold water
$1\frac{1}{4}$ pounds	broccoli, about 1 medium head – cut into 1-inch florets
$1\frac{1}{2}$ pounds	napa cabbage – cut into $\frac{1}{8}$-inch slices
1 pound	carrots – peeled, cut thinly on the diagonal, and then into matchsticks
$\frac{1}{2}$ pound	sunflower sprouts

<u>Sesame Sauce:</u>

$\frac{1}{2}$ cup	sesame seeds – toasted
1 tablespoon	fresh lemon juice
2 teaspoons	soy sauce
1 tablespoon	sunflower oil
2 to 4 tablespoons	water
$\frac{1}{4}$ teaspoon	chile pequin or cayenne pepper (optional)
1	clove of garlic – crushed (optional)
1 teaspoon	black sesame seeds (garnish)

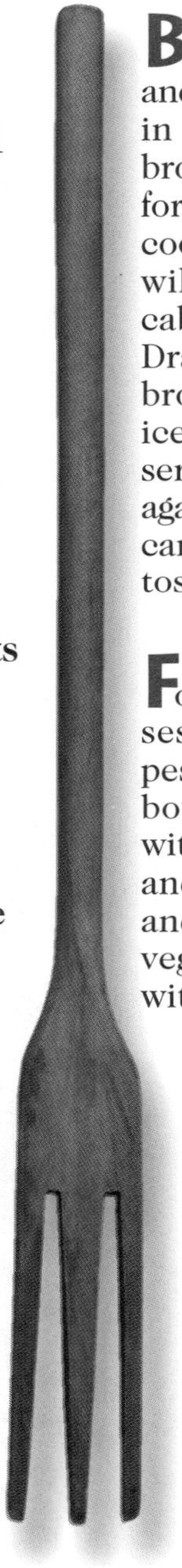

Boil water in a large saucepan, and blanch and shock the vegetables in the following manner: put the broccoli into boiling water and cook for 2 minutes. Add the cabbage and cook for 1 minute. (The broccoli will appear bright green and the cabbage will be hot but still crisp.) Drain, then immediately plunge the broccoli and cabbage into a bowl of ice water to "shock" them and preserve their color and texture. Drain again. Place in a large bowl. Add the carrot matchsticks and sprouts, and toss.

For the sauce, grind the toasted sesame seeds with a mortar and pestle or in a blender. In a small bowl, combine the ground seeds with the lemon juice, soy sauce, oil, and water. Add the chile powder and garlic, if using. Pour over the vegetables and toss well. Garnish with black sesame seeds.

Corn Salad with Tequila Dressing

SERVES 20

This tasty salad can be prepared a day ahead.

INGREDIENTS

5 packages (10 ounce)	**frozen corn – thawed, drained, and patted dry ***
2	**red bell peppers – seeded and diced**
3 medium	**zucchini – diced**
2 small	**red onions – diced**
1/2 bunch	**Italian parsley – leaves chopped**

Tequila Dressing:

1 teaspoon	**cumin seed – toasted and smashed**
4	**cloves of garlic – minced**
1 cup	**safflower oil**
1/2 cup	**red wine vinegar**
2 tablespoons	**sugar**
1 teaspoon	**salt**
2 tablespoons	**tequila**
1	**lime – juiced**

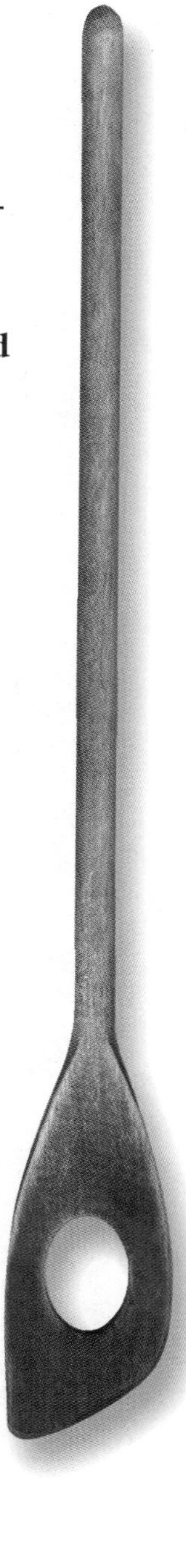

In a large bowl, combine the corn, red pepper, zucchini, onion, and parsley. In a small bowl, whisk together the dressing ingredients. Pour over the corn mixture and toss well. Refrigerate, covered, if not serving immediately.

**If available, select a mixture of white and yellow corn kernels.*

Flour Tortillas

MAKES 20 TO 24

Tortillas are the perfect accompaniment for New Mexican meals.

INGREDIENTS

3 cups	**all-purpose or unbleached flour**
1 teaspoon	**baking powder**
1 teaspoon	**salt**
$^1/_4$ cup	**lard or vegetable shortening**
1 cup	**warm water**

Sift the flour, baking powder, and salt into a large bowl. Cut in lard with a fork or pastry blender until mixture is the texture of coarse meal. Add the water, pouring as evenly as possible over the surface of the dry ingredients. Mix with a fork until the dough comes together in a ball. Let stand, uncovered, at room temperature for 15 minutes.

Shape the dough into $1^1/_2$-inch balls. Roll each into a circle on a lightly floured board, or use a tortilla press. The dough should be slightly thinner than pie crust. Cook the tortillas in a lightly greased skillet until nicely browned on both sides. Serve hot.

WHITE CORNBREAD

SERVES 6 TO 8

This easy, lowfat recipe needs no altitude adjustment.

INGREDIENTS

2 cups	white self-rising cornmeal
1	egg, or equivalent egg substitute
1/2 teaspoon	baking powder
1 1/2 cups	lowfat buttermilk
1/2 teaspoon	salt (optional)
1/2 teaspoon	ground cumin (optional)
1 can (4 ounce)	diced green chiles (optional)

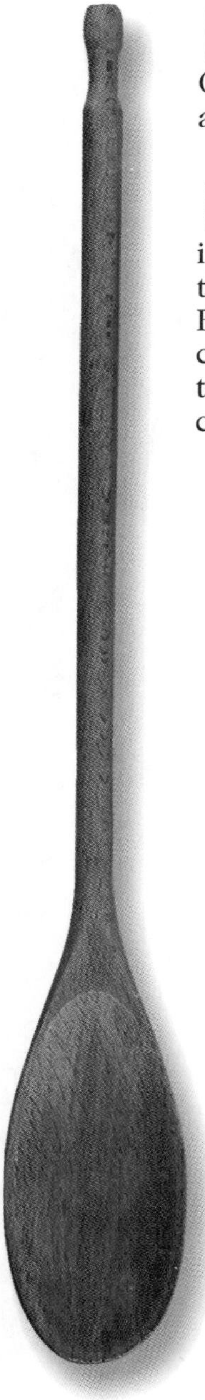

Preheat oven to 400 degrees. Grease a 2-quart cast iron skillet, and put in oven to heat.

In a bowl, mix together all of the ingredients until well blended. Pour the batter into the heated skillet. Bake for 20 minutes, or until the cornbread is golden brown and a toothpick inserted into the center comes out clean.

The entrees are a major delight, surprising me with their uniqueness each day. I save the bread and the wonderful soups for lunch, also the fruit. Thank you so much for letting me be visited by angels. K.N.

Cream Cheese Cake

SERVES 6

This needs no altitude adjustment. It does not need to be topped with fruit although berries, in season, add a festive touch. Best when made a day ahead.

INGREDIENTS

8 double	**graham crackers – crushed**
1/4 cup	**butter or margarine – melted**
1 package (8 ounce)	**cream cheese – at room temperature**
2	**eggs**
2 teaspoons	**vanilla extract**
1/2 cup plus 2 tablespoons	**sugar**
1/2	**lemon – juiced (optional)**
Dash of	**salt (optional)**
1 cup	**sour cream**

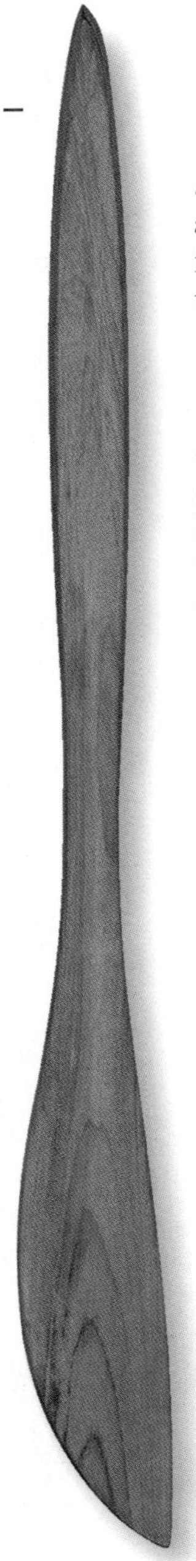

Preheat oven to 350 degrees.

Mix the graham cracker crumbs and melted butter. Pat into an 8-inch pie plate and bake for 5 minutes. Cool for at least 5 minutes.

In a bowl, mix the cream cheese, eggs, 1 teaspoon vanilla, and 1/2 cup sugar. Beat until smooth. Mix in the lemon juice and salt, if using. Pour the cream cheese mixture into the crust. Bake at 350 degrees for 15 minutes, or until set but not firm. Cool for 5 minutes, leaving the oven on.

Mix the sour cream with the remaining teaspoon vanilla, and the remaining 2 tablespoons sugar in a small bowl. Smooth gently across the top of the cream cheese mixture. Bake for another 5 minutes. Chill, preferably for 24 hours, before serving.

Date-Pecan Tea Cake

SERVES 12 OR MORE

This delectable, moist cake with caramel icing bears no resemblance to conventional fruit cake, despite the addition of chopped dates.

INGREDIENTS

1 cup	boiling water
1 cup	dates – pitted and chopped
$^{1}/_{2}$ teaspoon	baking soda *
1 cup	sugar
4 tablespoons ($^{1}/_{4}$ cup)	butter – at room temperature
1	egg – beaten
1 teaspoon	vanilla extract
$1^{1}/_{3}$ cups	flour – sifted
$^{1}/_{2}$ teaspoon	baking powder *
$^{1}/_{3}$ teaspoon	salt
$^{1}/_{3}$ cup	pecans – chopped

<u>Icing:</u>

5 tablespoons	brown sugar
5 tablespoons	heavy cream
2 tablespoons	butter
$^{1}/_{2}$ cup	pecans – chopped (garnish)

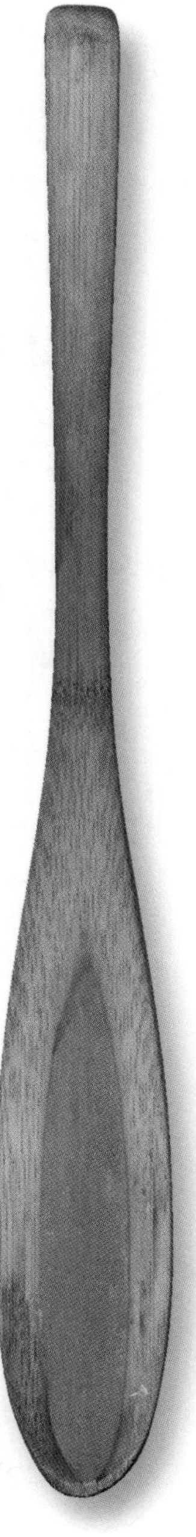

Preheat oven to 375 degrees. Lightly grease a small tube pan.

Pour boiling water over the dates and baking soda in a small bowl. Mix and set aside. In a large bowl, beat together the sugar and butter. Mix in the egg and vanilla. In a separate bowl, mix together the sifted flour, baking powder, and salt. Add to the egg mixture, and beat well. Stir in the chopped pecans. Add the date mixture and mix thoroughly. Pour into the prepared tube pan, and bake for 30 to 35 minutes, or until a toothpick inserted into the center comes out clean. Remove cake from the pan, and place on a serving platter. Pour icing over the cake while still warm.

For the icing, mix together the brown sugar, cream, and butter in a small saucepan. Bring to a boil and boil for 3 minutes, stirring. Drizzle over the cake, and sprinkle the top with chopped pecans.

**Adjusted for 7,000 feet and above. For lower altitudes, increase the baking soda and baking powder by $^{1}/_{2}$ teaspoon each, and bake at 350 degrees for 25 to 30 minutes.*

Linda's Outrageous Chocolate Chip Cookies

MAKES 6 DOZEN

These collected first prize in a cookie contest. For best results, begin preparations the night before.

INGREDIENTS

1 cup	**white sugar**
1 cup	**brown sugar**
1 stick (4 ounces)	**butter – at room temperature**
1 cup	**creamy peanut butter**
1 tablespoon	**vanilla extract**
2 tablespoons	**milk**
2 large	**eggs**
1 cup	**white flour**
1 cup	**whole wheat flour**
1 cup	**oats**
1 teaspoon	**baking soda ***
2 cups	**chocolate chips**

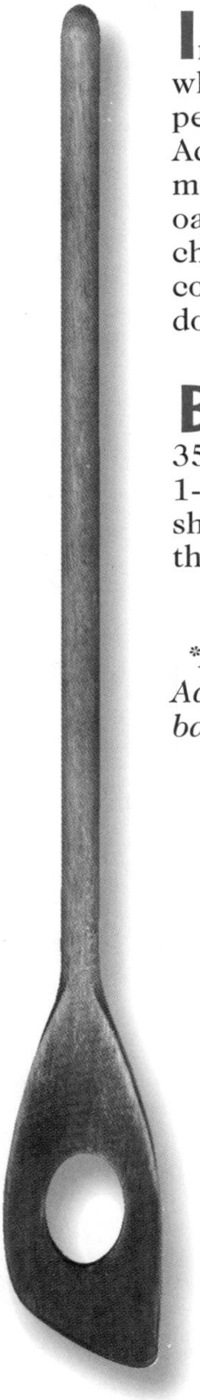

In a large bowl, cream together the white and brown sugars, butter, peanut butter, vanilla, and milk. Add the eggs and mix well. In a medium bowl, combine the flours, oats, baking soda, and chocolate chips. Slowly add to the egg batter, combining well. Chill the cookie dough overnight, covered.

Before baking, preheat oven to 350 degrees. Form the dough into 1-inch balls and place on cookie sheets. Bake on the center rack of the oven for 12 minutes.

**Adjusted for 7,000 feet and above. Add an additional 1/2 teaspoon baking soda for lower altitudes.*

Pineapple Bread Pudding

SERVES 6 TO 8

A great way to use stale bread. Delicious, also, as a side dish with baked ham.

INGREDIENTS

1 stick (4 ounces)	**butter – at room temperature**
$^3/_4$ cup	**sugar**
4	**eggs**
1 can (16 or 20 ounce)	**crushed pineapple, undrained**
5 or 6 slices	**white bread – crusts removed and cut into 1-inch cubes**

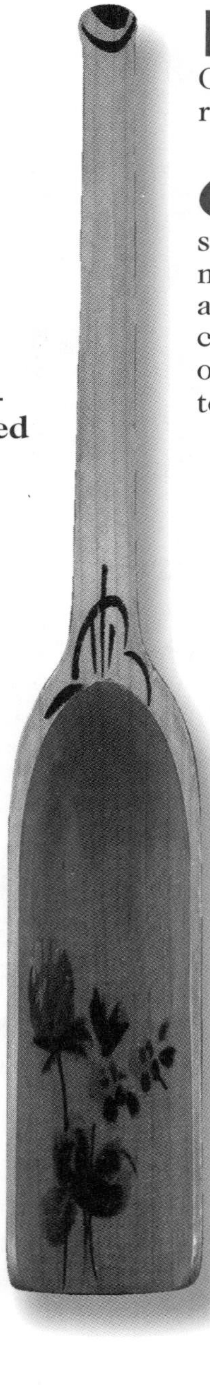

Preheat oven to 350 degrees. Grease a 2-quart ovenproof casserole.

Cream together the butter and sugar. Add the eggs, one at a time, mixing well. Stir in the pineapple and bread cubes. Pour into greased casserole and bake for 40 minutes, or until the pudding is set and the top is lightly browned.

Red Velvet Cake

SERVES 16

A spectacular cake for any season.

INGREDIENTS

$1\frac{2}{3}$ cups	sugar
5 tablespoons	vegetable shortening
1 large	egg white
1 large	egg
3 tablespoons	unsweetened cocoa powder
1 bottle (1 ounce)	red food coloring
$2\frac{1}{4}$ cups	all-purpose flour *
1 teaspoon	salt
1 cup	lowfat buttermilk
$1\frac{1}{4}$ teaspoons	vanilla extract
1 tablespoon	white vinegar
1 teaspoon	baking soda

Cream Cheese Frosting:

$\frac{1}{2}$ cup (2 ounces)	unsalted butter – at room temperature
1 package (8 ounce)	cream cheese – at room temperature
1 box (1 pound)	powdered sugar
$1\frac{1}{2}$ teaspoons	vanilla

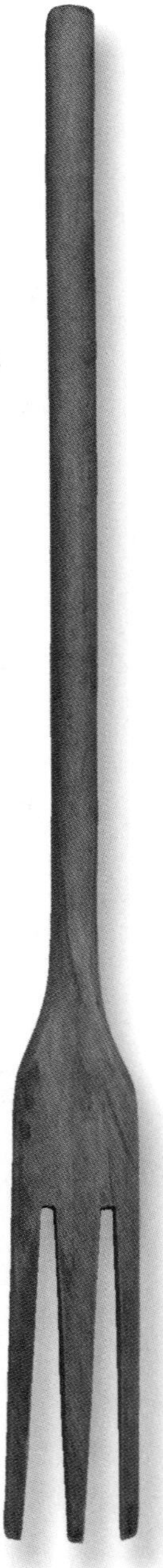

Preheat oven to 350 degrees. Grease and flour two 9-inch round cake pans.

Beat the sugar and shortening at medium speed in a mixing bowl until well blended, about 5 minutes. Add the egg white and whole egg. Beat well. In a small bowl, combine the cocoa and food coloring. Stir well and beat into the batter.

In another small bowl, combine the flour and salt. Beat into the batter alternately with the buttermilk, beginning and ending with the flour mixture. Mix in vanilla. In a small bowl, combine the vinegar and baking soda. Add to the batter, mixing well. Pour into the prepared cake pans. Bake for 30 minutes. Remove from oven and cool.

Combine the frosting ingredients in a bowl, and mix well. Spread between and on top of the cooled cake layers.

**For higher altitudes: add one additional tablespoon flour.*

Cookbook Angels and Sponsors

Cookbook Angels

Our thanks to the following individuals, businesses, and foundations who have provided financial and in-kind contributions to make this book possible. All are angels to whom we are truly grateful.

Season Sponsors

Ramona Brandt – Capital Ford
Louise M. Larkins, In Memoriam
Beth and Charles Miller, Sol y Sombra
Tom Parrish

Event Sponsors

Capitol City Title Services, Inc.
Caroline and Dick Carlson
Nancy Dickenson
Carolyn and Harry Hummer
Claudia Jessup and Jonathan Richards
Michael Mahaffey & Associates Architects
The MarketPlace Natural Grocery
Susan Munroe and Terry Smith
Jane O'Toole
Frances Richards
Santa Fe Land & Homes
The Santa Fe Opera
Marilyn Seckler and Ted Ore
Simons Cuddy & Friedman, LLP
John Tyson
Sarah and Mike Tyson
Michael Umphrey, Town & Ranch Inc.
Elisabeth Wagner Architect
Linda and Mike Waterman

Additional Thanks to

Carol Anthony
Anthony Cardinale
Julie Dean
Linda Durham
Deanna Einspahr
John Fincher
Barbara and Ted Flicker
Get Type & Graphics
Gregory S. Green
Timothy Hollis
Arlene LewAllen
Joan Logghe
Ali MacGraw
Deborah Madison
Chris O'Connell
Insty Prints, Vic Perry
Rob Sckalor
Ski Santa Fe
Scott Stephen
Manya Winsted

Photography:

Jay Blackwood
Jerry Harper
Charles Mann
Elliott McDowell
Gene Peach
Mark Nohl
Tom Parrish
Jack Parsons
Ken Robbins
Robert Shaw

Recipe Donor Angels

Liza Abeles
Laurie Archer
Mrs. Dale B. Baldwin
Liz Barnes
Dale Bohls
Elizabeth Bradley
Sucha Cardoza
Jane Carhart
Mary Cassidy
Sarah Leah Chase
Susan Clough
Barbara Cohen
Beverly Cohen
Charlotte Cooke
Nelson A. Danish
Betty T. Davis
Lucetta B. Drypolcher
Gay Dunlap
Linda Evans
Carol Feiring
Barbara Flicker
Diane Forsdale
Jeanne Frazier
Stephanie Gonzales
Adrien Gordon
Jeanne Gozigian
Mary Nelle Gunter
Harry Hamburg
Pauline Harper
Audrey Hays
Christine Hickman
Craig Hoopes
Linda Hughes
Carolyn Hummer
Linda Jenkins
Claudia Jessup
Stephanie E. Johnson
Hanna Kaiser
Pauline Kurth
Linda Lally
Rand Lee
Harriet Levine
Mitra Lujan
Tony McCarty
Betsy Blankett Milićević
Janie Miller
Susan Munroe
Alan Nebelthau
Patsy Ornelas
Gwynne Pardington
Eva Marie Parker
Susie Parrish
Tom Parrish
Martha Payne
Frances Richards
Jonathan Richards
Maria Robbins
Hilda Rush
Bette Sallee
Bob Samples
Dorothy Schoech
Suzanne A. Shaw-Chavez
Cliff Simon
Jane Stacey
Peter Stephenson
Karen Stevens
Gerry Stoesz
Margaret Strane
Gillian Sutton
Christiana Torricelli
Fred and Martha Vang
John Vollertsen
Lynn Walters
Andrea Denson Wechsler
Robin Young
Linda Zappe

Cookbook Committee

Editor-in-Chief: Claudia Jessup
Associate Editor: Tom Parrish

Editorial Committee:
Susan Duquid
Susan Munroe
India Richards

Copy Editors:
Jeanne Frazier
Linda Hughes
Frances Richards
Jonathan Richards

Recipe Committee:
Dale Bohls
Carol Feiring
Jeanne Frazier

Design:
Jerry Harper

Illustration:
William Rotsaert

Kitchen Angels, Inc.

Tony McCarty, Executive Director
Martha Payne, Administrative Assistant

Board of Directors
Michael Tyson, President
Carolyn Hummer, Vice President
Linda Hughes, Treasurer
Jill Markstein, Secretary
Tony Anaya, Jr.
Judy Costlow
Linda Dressman
Rona Kramer
Steve Michel
Ted Ore
Tom Parrish
Sarah Taylor

Index of Recipes

APPETIZERS AND HORS D'OEUVRES

BEVERAGES

BREADS AND MUFFINS

BREAKFAST AND BRUNCH

CHUTNEYS, CONDIMENTS, AND STUFFING

EGGS, CHEESE, PASTA, AND GRAINS

EGGS AND CHEESE

PASTA AND GRAINS

MEATS, FISH, AND FOWL

BEEF

CHICKEN AND TURKEY

FISH AND SEAFOOD

GAME

Notes

Notes

Cookbook Order Forms

Mail orders to: Kitchen Angels
500 N. Guadalupe – Suite G-505
Santa Fe, NM 87501

Phone orders: 505-471-7780
Fax orders: 505-471-9362

Books may also be ordered from our website: www.kitchenangels.org

---

Please send me______ copies of Seasons of Santa Fe! @ $19.95 each * __________

Postage and Handling in U.S. @ $ 4.00 each ** __________

Total enclosed $ __________

** Bulk purchase discounts available.*

*** 4th class book rate; express shipping is extra.*

Name ____

Street ____

City ______________________________ State ________ Zip________

Enclosed is my check or money order for________________.

(Please make checks payable to Kitchen Angels.)

___Visa ___MasterCard #______________________ Expiration date:_____

Signature: ____

The proceeds of this book will go to Kitchen Angels, a not-for-profit corporation.

Please send me______ copies of Seasons of Santa Fe! @ $19.95 each * __________

Postage and Handling in U.S. @ $ 4.00 each ** __________

Total enclosed $ __________

** Bulk purchase discounts available.*

*** 4th class book rate; express shipping is extra.*

Name ____

Street ____

City ______________________________ State ________ Zip________

Enclosed is my check or money order for________________.

(Please make checks payable to Kitchen Angels.)

___Visa ___MasterCard #______________________ Expiration date:_____

Signature: ____

The proceeds of this book will go to Kitchen Angels, a not-for-profit corporation.